DEREK WALCOTT'S POETRY

DEREK WALCOTT'S POETRY

AMERICAN MIMICRY

REI TERADA

NORTHEASTERN UNIVERSITY PRESS
Boston

Northeastern University Press

Library of Congress Cataloging-in-Publication Data

Terada, Rei, 1962–
Derek Walcott's poetry : American mimicry / Rei Terada.
p. cm.
Includes bibliographical references and index.
ISBN 1-55553-126-1
1. Walcott, Derek—Criticism and interpretation. 2. Postmodernism
(Literature)—West Indies. 3. Mimesis in literature. I. Title.
PR9272.9.W3Z84 1992
811—dc20 92-4027

Designed by Virginia Evans
Composed in Meridien by Coghill Composition Co., Richmond, Virginia.
Printed and bound by The Maple Press, York, Pennsylvania.
The paper is Sebago Antique, an acid-free sheet.

MANUFACTURED IN THE UNITED STATES OF AMERICA
96 95 94 93 92 5 4 3 2 1

CONTENTS

ACKNOWLEDGMENTS

THE GRADUATE SCHOOL of Arts and Sciences at Boston University provided scholarship support for part of this project. I thank the Department of English, Boston University, for helping me to obtain that support, and for their thoroughgoing, persistent collective kindness. I am also grateful to colleagues, students, and staff members at the Department of Afro-American Studies, Harvard University. In addition, I have had the chance to discuss portions of this project with dozens of people from various universities over the last few years. I learned from all our conversations. Members of the English Department at Wellesley College, in particular, will recognize their contributions to my reading of "The Light of the World." Eyal Amiran, Laurence Breiner, Paul Breslin, Emily Dalgarno, Gerald P. Fitzgerald, David Mikics, Robert Ryan, and David Wagenknecht all made valuable remarks of various shapes and sizes. My student Lisa Charles, of Castries, gave me photographs of St. Omer's work and information about St. Lucia. Bill Keeney shared his excellent notes from Walcott's poetry seminars at Boston University. Stephen Yenser managed to find several creative ways of helping me while I made late revisions, and I suspect that his help actually made my finishing possible. Ron Bloom and Jeanne Dubino lent me very necessary personal support. Patrick Keppel untangled syntax and soul.

I am grateful most of all to Bonnie Costello, who did so much work and pretended it was little, who saw my manuscript with startling clarity and treated it with equanimity, and whose influence I hope will grow more visible. She always helped me to have the courage of my peculiarities.

The following excerpts from the works of Derek Walcott are reprinted by permission of Farrar, Straus & Giroux, Inc.

From *Another Life*, copyright © 1972, 1973 by Derek Walcott

From *The Arkansas Testament*, copyright © 1987 by Derek Walcott

From *Collected Poems 1948–1984*, copyright © 1986 by Derek Walcott

From *The Fortunate Traveller*, copyright © 1980, 1981 by Derek Walcott

From *The Gulf and Other Poems*, copyright © 1970 by Derek Walcott

From *In a Green Night: Poems, 1948–1960*, copyright © 1962 by Derek Walcott

From *Midsummer*, copyright © 1984 by Derek Walcott

From *Omeros*, copyright © 1990 by Derek Walcott

From *Sea Grapes*, copyright © 1976 by Derek Walcott

From *Selected Poems*, copyright © 1964 by Derek Walcott

From *The Star-Apple Kingdom*, copyright © 1979 by Derek Walcott

Excerpts from *The Castaway and Other Poems* reprinted by permission of Jonathan Cape. Copyright © 1965 by Derek Walcott.

Quotations from Derek Walcott's classroom remarks reprinted by permission of Derek Walcott and William Keeney.

Excerpts from Richmond Lattimore's translation of *The Iliad* reprinted by permission of The University of Chicago Press. Copyright © 1951 by The University of Chicago.

Excerpts from Osip Mandelstam's *Selected Poems*, trans. Clarence Brown and W. S. Merwin, reprinted by permission of Atheneum Publishers, an imprint of Macmillan Publishing Company. Copyright © 1973 by Clarence Brown and W. S. Merwin.

Excerpts from Ezra Pound's *The Cantos* reprinted by permission of New Directions Publishing Corporation. Copyright © 1972 by the Estate of Ezra Pound.

Excerpt from Wallace Stevens's *Collected Poems* reprinted by permission of Random House, Inc. Copyright © 1954 by Wallace Stevens.

A version of the Epilogue appeared in *Postmodern Culture* 2, no. 1 (Sept. 1991).

LIST OF ABBREVIATIONS

AL	*Another Life*
AT	*The Arkansas Testament*
C	*The Castaway and Other Poems*
"CD"	"Crocodile Dandy" (review of Les Murray's *The Daylight Moon* and *The Vernacular Republic*)
"CM"	"The Caribbean: Culture or Mimicry?"
CP	*Collected Poems 1948–1984*
DMM	*Dream on Monkey Mountain and Other Plays*
EY	*Epitaph for the Young*
FT	*The Fortunate Traveller*
G	*The Gulf and Other Poems*
IGN	*In a Green Night: Poems, 1948–1960*
JS/OB	*The Joker of Seville* and *O! Babylon*
M	*Midsummer*
"MH"	"The Muse of History"
"MI"	"Magic Industry" (review of Joseph Brodsky's *To Urania*)
O	*Omeros*
"ORL"	"On Robert Lowell"
SAK	*The Star-Apple Kingdom*
SG	*Sea Grapes*
SP	*Selected Poems*
"WTS"	"What The Twilight Says: An Overture"

There was no line in the sea which said, this is new, this is the frontier, the boundary of endeavor, and henceforth everything can only be mimicry. But there was such a moment for every individual American, and that moment was both surrender and claim, both possession and dispossession. The issue is the claim.

—Derek Walcott,
"The Caribbean: Culture or Mimicry?"

🌿　🌿　🌿

INTRODUCTION

AMERICAN MIMICRY

*Once the meridian of European civilization has been
crossed, according to the theory, we have entered a mirror where
there can only be simulations of self-discovery.*

—"The Caribbean: Culture or Mimicry?"

ALTHOUGH I WILL call Walcott's poetic art "American mimicry," I intend neither "American" nor "mimicry" to retain the
meanings they often hold.[1] "America" here refers not to the United
States, nor to North America, but as Walcott puts it, to the land "from
Greenland right down to Tierra del Fuego."[2] "Mimicry," in turn, usually bears pejorative, if contradictory, connotations of imitation, servil-
ity, and mockery. It is a term Walcott uses frequently, but defines only
by example. There is an iridescence in Walcott's usage, as a result,
which I cannot wish away. To generalize, however, I take "mimesis" to
mean the representation of reality, and "mimicry" the representation
of a representation, a repetition of something itself repetitious. Further,
while Baudrillard's simulation, "the truth which conceals that there is
none,"[3] disguises the nonexistence of its original, mimicry tips the
hand of its nonoriginality *and* implies the nonoriginality of that which
it mimics. Mimicry can be conscious or unconscious, and requires no
particular tone or function; it can be critical, celebratory, or both. Mere
use of the idea of mimicry luckily does not halt discussion of the merit
or the meaning of any poem, any more than does the use of "mime-

sis." Even in Walcott's logic mimicry does not completely shed its negative associations. Nevertheless, for Walcott mimicry, with all its ambivalent freight, replaces mimesis as the ground of representation and culture.

Of course, Walcott has not invented these redefinitions; his is a poetry that knows there are no first times. Both redefinitions occupy prominent places in Postmodern poetry and poststructuralist literary theory, which have also interrogated the idea of a cultural or geographic center and the idea of originality. They are also postcolonial redefinitions, in that postcolonial cultures must remain especially aware of the dangerous uses to which notions of centrality and originality can be put. Although Walcott has arrived at his own version of American mimicry through his experience as a St. Lucian, he is interested as well in his own internationalism. The ambivalence that inheres in his particular situation has fostered a comparative frame of mind, one that searches out connections wherever it can. In a similar spirit, I want to consider the ways in which Walcott's St. Lucian art speaks to Americans from Greenland to Tierra del Fuego of American poetry's attitude toward Old World cultures, of the American present's attitude toward the past, and of American languages' positions in relation to other languages and the object world. On each of these fronts Walcott's poems challenge their readers to rethink Modernist genealogical, generic, and linguistic categories. My emphasis on a larger "America" need not deny that in many ways Walcott's poetry speaks distinctly to a Caribbean audience. In the course of discussion I will also have to expand my frame of reference beyond America, to Africa and Europe. Still, I want to attend to Walcott's provocative hypothesis—most explicitly set forth in his 1974 essay, "The Caribbean: Culture or Mimicry?"—that there is such a thing as a collective America, and that it has a characteristic art of mimicry. This is an examination of that hypothesis and its implications for American poetry.

"But let me tell you how this business begin."[4]

IN HIS REVIEW of Walcott's *Collected Poems 1948–1984*, James Dickey describes, by means of antitheses, "the force field in the middle of which Derek Walcott lives and creates": "Here he is, a 20th-century man, living in the West Indies and in Boston, poised between the blue sea and its real fish . . . and the rockets and warheads, between a lapsed colonial culture and the industrial North, between Africa and the West, between slavery and intellectualism, between the native Caribbean tongue and English learned from books, between the black and white in his own body, between the sound of the home ocean and the lure of European culture."[5] Although one might question some of Dickey's pairings ("slavery and intellectualism"?), his list gathers together the categories by which most readers consider Walcott and shows how those categories are usually organized. Dickey positions Walcott "between" versions of some of the most timeworn oppositions in Western civilization: nature and culture ("home ocean" and "European culture"), south and north ("the West Indies" and "Boston"), orality and literacy ("native Caribbean tongue" and "English learned from books"). I would add that Walcott also addresses the opposition between mimicry and originality, the central conflict of Western aesthetics. The mimicry/originality dichotomy can be expressed on an individual scale (in the relation between poet and precursor), on a cultural scale (American mimicry vs. Old World originality), or, most broadly, as the relation between representation and the object world, culture and nature. In Walcott's poetry particular historic or geographic contrasts do tend to expand, approaching exactly such large-scale, mythic ones. The internal logic of my chapters, and this book's progression from chapter to chapter, usually follows the wake of that expansion.

First, however, we need to see how Walcott draws his map of the world. Walcott unfolds what looks like a Renaissance map, openly subjective and etched with eccentric notations and supernatural creatures, "Like parchment charts at whose corners four winged heads spout / jets of curled, favouring gusts, their cheeks like cornets / till the sails belly as the hull goes hard about // through seas as scrolled as dragons in ornate knots."[6] Walcott's favorite birds (the sea swift, frigate bird, and the seagull upon whose hingelike screech the hemispheres hang), the letter X signifying ocean crossings, and, most of all, the fictive divisions of the equator and meridian, appear as prominently on Walcott's map as the continents of America, Africa, and Europe. We need a legend to translate these figures. Chapter 1 will begin to compile such a legend of images and to explicate Walcott's geographic imagination as he explains it in "Culture or Mimicry?" and demonstrates it in *Omeros*. Only then can we see where Walcott's America is placed and how it pertains to mimicry.

Chapter 2 particularizes Walcott's mimicry in practice. Reviewers and critics frequently point out that Walcott seems unusually open to influence and mingles his own voice with his precursors' to a surprising extent. For American and especially Caribbean poets, influence is a political problem. Reviewers and critics who wish to protect the British tradition sometimes treat Walcott's poetic appropriations as though they were thefts of property, and those who align themselves against that tradition sometimes treat them as treason. I agree with descriptions of Walcott's intertextuality, but disagree with the assumption that openness to influence, for whatever reason, debilitates a poet's work. Not all of Walcott's poems succeed, but those that fail do not fail because they expose their sources. Walcott's engagements with canonical precursors reveal at once resemblance to and difference from the British and French traditions—as language cannot help doing, since it can achieve neither originality nor repetition. Walcott also explores the awareness of mimicry he shares with other American poets like Lowell and exiles like Brodsky, and rejects the idea of literature as property in favor of that of an international community of poets who are all borrowers and thieves. By examining his openness to other texts, we can better understand how Walcott perceives himself and his tradition(s). More important, we understand that poetry is always a mimicry of the poetry of the past.

The relation of a postcolonial American poet to his academically accepted precursors parallels the relation of dialects and creoles[7] to officially authorized languages (the subject of Chapter 3). Those who strongly identify with a canonical language, as it were, may feel that a dialect or creole related to it has a secondary, derivative status, and even that the less sanctioned language is a debased imitation of the sanctioned one. Dialect and creole speakers, meanwhile, encourage native poets to help legitimate their local languages by composing in them. Thus, Walcott's poetic uses of St. Lucian languages and academic English have met with criticism from both Caribbean and non-Caribbean critics and reviewers. Although Walcott has always used traces of dialects and creoles, he intermingles languages and idiolects more freely and effectively as his career develops. From *Another Life* onward, especially, Walcott shows that languages do not possess strict borders and that every language owes something to others. As each author's poetry must be mimicry, each language, too, must finally be viewed as a creole—each American language, but also European ones, for creolization is the very model of language formation. Creoles serve as meeting places for many disparate linguistic strands; creoles, like poetic language, can therefore be seen as language building as though toward a lost unity—piecing together the Tower of Babel—instead of as language degenerating. Poems like "The Schooner *Flight*" emphasize, however, that this construction can never be other than incomplete.

Walcott is an accomplished watercolorist as well as a poet, playwright, and essayist. His interest in visual art may be related to his situation among many languages. In her study of bilingual Russian writers Elizabeth Klosty Beaujour speculates that "there may be some correlation between being bilingual and being artistically polymath."[8] Walcott certainly exhibits "perceptual polyglotism" (Beaujour, 104), writing poems that require the reader to think both visually and spatially, and at the same time to follow language literally and figuratively. He frequently examines the relations between visual art and poetry— searching the visual for clues about the verbal, pondering ways of combining the two, and wondering whether the arts are in fact two, one, or internally multiple. *Another Life* and *Midsummer* show that Walcott rejects an absolute boundary between visual and verbal art, for both arts, wrenched by the inadequacies of mediation, strive to introject and to reject each other, and neither can do either.

Relations between various means of representation and the object world (the focus of Chapter 4) form a subset of the relation between culture and nature (the focus of Chapter 5). The nature/culture relation fills Walcott with anxiety, since the Old World tends to see America and especially the Caribbean as uncultured. By describing nature in terms of culture and vice versa Walcott reduces the tragic sense of disconnection between nature and culture, object world and representation, without asserting that language leads straight to its referent. In addition, Walcott leaves open the possibility that language may be motivated at its root, although we may not be able to perceive it: "The word 'beetle' must have some metaphorical root, but who knows what it is now?"[9] Walcott believes, eccentrically enough, that Creole languages, as newer products of a newer world, have buried this root less deeply than older, academicized languages: "The metaphors that one heard from peasants describing a tree, a flower, an insect, anything, were not like the Latin names for those things" (Hirsch 1986, 287). Poetic language, which welcomes creolization, also works as though toward a lost nexus between language and the object world. That nexus or origin itself, however, exists only as a fictive goal that Walcott knows he will not reach.

Chapters 2 through 5, then, stand in parallel relation to each other. The angle of perception, however, widens from the relation between individual poet and precursor to the relation between representation and object world as a whole. Chapter 6 summarizes and updates these issues by way of *Omeros*. *Omeros* does not close out Walcott's career— he is even now at work on yet another "very, very long poem"[10]—but does revisit and revise Walcott's idea of mimicry. Since *Omeros* is, like Homer's *Odyssey*, a story about the genealogy of fathers and sons, it is also a parable of poetic influence. As a story about ocean crossings, it is Walcott's most developed fable of the meridian. And as a poem about writing poetry, it clarifies Walcott's notions of representation.

Although Walcott's significance as a contemporary poet is not in doubt, he is rarely discussed as a Postmodern poet. Rather, critical consideration of Walcott's poetry has focused upon the problematic relation of his formal traditionalism to his postcolonial themes. Although Walcott's postmodernity has not been acknowledged, the difficult relation of rhetoric to principle in Walcott's work points up limitations in definitions of Postmodernism which themselves conflate rhetoric with principle. Indeed, Walcott feels no need to emphasize or estrange rhetoric as some other Postmodern poets do, but only because rhetorical estrangement can be taken for granted in all language. In the epilogue I would like to consider Walcott's postmodernity through a reading of the late lyric "The Light of the World." In this poem Walcott explores the consequences and the boundaries of poetic "transport," in the senses both of lyric rapture and of metaphor. Here Walcott seeks the relation of poetic figuration to ordinary speech and finds that the former persistently inhabits the latter. We should see Walcott's style not as an example of rhetorical conventionality, but as an outgrowth of this quite Postmodern discovery.

It is probably obvious from the outline above that this book is not in the usual sense an introduction to Walcott's poetry. It does not provide much biographical or contextual information. It does not cover every major poem or even every volume, nor does it completely define a canon of best poems. *Sea Grapes*, *Another Life*, and *Midsummer*, for instance, receive less attention here only because other volumes more easily allowed me to discuss the specialized topics that interested me.[11] I have focused throughout upon tensions, conflicts, and cruces; the result is a kind of compendium of problems for readers of Walcott to consider. If it's not a problem, I don't mention it (though that doesn't mean that if it is a problem, I do mention it). I both fear and hope that its very specialization, its emphasis on poetic problems, makes this book broader than a close reading of Walcott's poetry might otherwise be. The more one reads Walcott's poems, the clearer it becomes that Walcott considers himself the type of the American poet, and, as if this were not enough, that the American poet is for him the type of *the* poet. The sense of displacement Walcott explores in self-examination may ultimately be characteristic of language itself. As one reads Walcott's poems the particular continually produces the universal, like an everlasting handkerchief from a magician's sleeve.[12] Clearly, I have found it difficult to write about Walcott without biting off more than I could chew. Perhaps, if we hold our breath, following books on Walcott will lay the groundwork for this one. Until then, a moment or two out of sequence never hurt anybody.

WALCOTT'S POETRY OFTEN represents the process of its own expansion. In one of Walcott's favorite metaphors language forms a tree, its system of underground roots and skyward branchings enlivened by the "sap of memory."[13] If we imagined the oppositions with which Walcott works forming a tree of dualisms, we might begin by separating "representation" from "object world." On the "object world" side of the fork, we would separate "south" from "north," and so on. But as this ordering progressed, the parallels would fall out of exact alignment, and their swervings reveal biases. In each pairing there is a hierarchy, a primary and a secondary term. If we stopped attending to the branchings and looked down either the "secondary" or the "primary" side of the tree, we would find that further parallels, impossible ones, had formed. It is untenable that "black" is to "white" what nature is to culture, or that south is to north as orality is to literacy—although these are the assumptions of much Eurocentric thought.

Many critics and reviewers, like Dickey, suggest that Walcott situates himself "between" the various oppositions; Helen Vendler's well-known review of *The Fortunate Traveller*, entitled "Poet of Two Worlds,"[14] takes such a stance. Walcott also uses the word "between" a great deal, and the idea of betweenness informs his choices of metaphor and structure. His often-anthologized early poem "A Far Cry from Africa" (1962),[15] for example, places the poet "Between this Africa and the English tongue I love." Even in this poem, however, betweenness is not a solution, but an arduous problem. Even here, betweenness cannot adequately conceptualize the poet's position, since betweenness doesn't necessarily question the authenticity of the oppositions supposedly surrounding the poet.

For twenty-one lines Walcott obliquely describes the Mau-Mau rebellion as "A wind . . . ruffling the tawny pelt/Of Africa" (*CP*, 17). Walcott depicts the war with characteristic political skepticism as a weakly rationalized, "Delirious" outbreak of predatory violence: "Statistics justify and scholars seize / The salients of colonial policy"; "The violence of beast on beast is read / As natural law, but upright man / Seeks his divinity by inflicting pain." Judging the war by its destructiveness rather than by its rationale(s), the poet can find no right side; the war sacrifices both "the white child" and "savages, expendable as Jews" (17).

Having cursed both houses, however, the poet finds nowhere to stand when he turns, in the third stanza,[16] to self-reflection:

> I who am poisoned with the blood of both,
> Where shall I turn, divided to the vein?
> I who have cursed
> The drunken officer of British rule, how choose
> Between this Africa and the English tongue I love?
> Betray them both, or give back what they give?
> How can I face such slaughter and be cool?
> How can I turn from Africa and live? (18)

The inexorability of Walcott's position is sometimes thought to suspend agency. Yet in practice Walcott's poetry rarely seems complacent. The poems tend not to lead one to believe that a problem's insolubility vanquishes the problem, for the inevitability of the poet's position does not make it any less agonizing. Although the poet asks how he can choose "between" untenable alternatives, he also incorporates both sides "in his own body" (as Dickey puts it). Standing "between" the conflict to choose sides, he simultaneously *contains* the conflict as a difference within his own identity. We should see Walcott's betweenness as neither a synthesis nor a separation, but a state of being that incorporates difference within itself.

The instability of Walcott's betweenness becomes obvious the moment we ask what it would mean to live "between"—to take one example—oral and written language. It could mean that Walcott's poetry emerges from an unbridgeable "gulf" between oral literature and writing; or it could mean that the two infinitely divide the distance between them, and that Walcott's poetry stands in place of that nonexistent, ultimate bisection. At times Walcott shows interest in both these possibilities, as though they could remain separate; at other times, his "gulf" figure suggests that *all* existence resides in that gulf. As the poet in "A Far Cry from Africa" stands between sides of a conflict, but also contains the conflict, the "gulf" figure itself vacillates to and from the logic of separation.[17] This vacillation, above all, remains a constant inconstancy throughout Walcott's work.

Since I don't discuss Walcott's poems chronologically, it might be worth indicating how I view his development. Walcott is a good (if rhetorically harsh) judge of his own poems,[18] and it is difficult to quarrel with his selection for *Collected Poems 1948–1984* (1986). With some exceptions, I follow Walcott's implicit appraisal here. I also agree with the critical consensus that Walcott begins to write his best poems with *The Star-Apple Kingdom* (1979). I only suggest that this isn't because he vanquishes his influences here (the language of the title poem, for example, bears a striking resemblance to Márquez's in *The Autumn of the Patriarch*). Rather, as Hirsch suggests and Walcott does not deny (1986, 212), Walcott's mimicry grows more fully "American" with the years, expanding its possibilities of reference. In his later poems Walcott calls more freely upon African-Caribbean language and folklore, fashioning a poetry more consistent with its own yearning after international community. In addition, Walcott makes advances in technique. He enlarges his poetic lexicon, and his rhetoric and imagery grow more daring. Drawing upon his theatrical experience, he ventures more frequently and fully into dramatic monologue (or as Brodsky calls it, "lyrical monologue"[19]). Walcott's passage toward a bold, inclusive style takes a large stride forward with *Another Life* (1973). The process of writing this long autobiographical poem encourages him, in effect, to fully creolize his poetry, to encompass a profusion of idiolects and descriptive systems. Although he has written beautiful brief lyrics like "Sea Grapes" and "Love after Love," Walcott usually requires a poem of at least medium length in order to develop his networks of metaphoric detail and his complex personae. On the other hand, *Another Life* and *Midsummer* (1984) suffer a little from a relative shapelessness. In the tightly focused yet multifaceted poems in *The Star-Apple Kingdom, The Fortunate Traveller* (1981), and *The Arkansas Testament* (1987), Walcott writes at the top of his powers. *Omeros* (1990), in spite of its scope, is similarly focused, segmenting Walcott's "epic streak" (Brodsky, 173) into flexibly formal cantos. In short, Walcott is on the whole a more colorful and rewarding poet in the second half of his career. Still, poetic "development" is a paradoxical matter. Few poets grow from acorns into oaks without shrinking, suspending growth, or metamorphosing into lindens along the way.

Walcott stresses that being American means being postcolonial. As a postcolonial poet Walcott has as his immediate Third World precursors Césaire, Neruda, and Guillén; as a Postmodern poet, he grew up reading Yeats, Eliot, and Crane. Of course, these are not really "two" strains, but two ways of focusing. Postmodernism is an international phenomenon, as was Modernism itself. Linda Hutcheon notes that "On the level of representation . . . postmodern questioning overlaps with similarly pointed challenges by those working in, for example, postcolonial and feminist contexts."[20] Postcolonial thought, that is, has influenced Postmodern literature worldwide, and postcolonial writers have found Postmodern methods and motifs congenial to their purposes.[21] This "overlap" of the American, the postcolonial, and the Postmodern delimits the field of Walcott's enterprise.

Walcott makes an effort to combine conceptual and linguistic flexibility with a strong sense of shape and music. His awareness of poetry as writing never disturbs his evocations of rhythm. In this as in so many other areas, Walcott's refusal to choose between preconceived alternatives produces poetry that raises more than the usual amount of difficulties, but also bubbles over with enchanting phenomena. Close readers will find themselves rewarded (if perhaps overwhelmed) by his ability to integrate meaningful details into a poem's texture. Imaginative and rhetorical abundance is typical of Walcott's poetry. Even though he remains alert to its perplexities, he never fears language. Metaphor remains something to which he looks forward:

> What sort of moon will float up through the almonds
> like a bobbing marker in the surf of trees?
> A quarter-moon, like an Iranian dagger?
> A capitol with wide spheres of influence?
> One with a birthmark like Gorbachev's head?
> A local moon, full of its own importance,
> a watchman's flashlight with fresh batteries,

startling the trickle from a kitchen drain,
pinning a crab to the hotel's wire fence,
changing its mind like a cat burglar,
probing locked harbours, rattling the foam's chain.

("Oceano Nox," *AT*, 52)

In this description of the moon, Romantic and Modern symbol of imagination, Walcott revels in a multitude of possibilities. Walcott makes a point of stressing, elsewhere, that we always see the moon through the colored lenses of culture and sensibility. Holland is illuminated by "A florin moon," Istanbul by "the curved scimitar/of a crescent moon" (*O*, 79, 204). In "Oceano Nox" Walcott suggests some of the qualities he would avoid: his moon does not associate with any of the authoritarian regimes lines 3–5 evoke, with their attendant inflexibility and violence. It is, in contrast, "a local moon." Calling it "full of its own importance," Walcott mocks himself, but we can also take the statement literally: local moons *are* important moons. He also suggests the qualities we may find in his own intelligence. Some of these characteristics battle each other, as his moon is both "watchman" and "cat burglar," and this change of mind is itself characteristic. Even more revealingly, in "The Lighthouse" (*AT*, 3–8) the poet glances up at a moon as intractable as he is: "A coin, tossed once overhead, / that stuck there, not heads or tails" (4). Walcott's poetry is indeed written under the sign of such a moon, or the moons he lists in "Oceano Nox." When it answers its own description, we value it for its proud provinciality, vigilance, freshness, surprise, trenchancy, contradiction, curiosity, and capacity to liberate.

A REVERSIBLE WORLD

The world is a circle, Corporal. Remember that.

—Dream on Monkey Mountain

POSTCOLONIAL POETS, aware that mapmaking connotes command, have long been annotating and redrawing the
maps of their regions. Susan Willis points out that Césaire, to take an
illustrious example, "imagines the map made for his own use . . . 'not
painted the arbitrary colours of scientists, but with the geometry of
[his] shed blood.' "¹ Walcott, too, remaps his world to reclaim it. Walcott begins with what he calls in *Midsummer* "the primal fault / of the
first map of the world, its boundaries and powers" (VII), then particularizes and reorganizes that map. Walcott vivifies conventional cartographical abstractions such as the vertical and horizontal dividing
lines of meridian and equator by using them as symbols in his own
idiosyncratic narrative of American discovery and settlement. This odd
mixture of cartographical markings and arcane imagery is the primary
vehicle for Walcott's interpretation of America.

Walcott suggests that the New and Old Worlds exist in mutually constitutive relation. America is formed by its knowledge of Europe (and,
increasingly in Walcott's middle and later poetry, of Africa), Europe by
its knowledge of America. Walcott explores the American position by

trying to imagine himself out of it. The meridian, the vertical line separating America from Europe, therefore dominates his cartography. The American sense of secondariness suggests that crossing the meridian into America means crossing a mirror into the territory of mimicry. De Man notes that "chiasmus" is "the crossing that reverses the attributes of words and of things"[2]; Walcott literalizes chiasmus in his imaginary journeys to "older" worlds, crossing in search of originals, of things themselves. Walcott is hardly the first to wonder whether American cultures are fated to mimic others; North Americans such as Crane, Eliot, James, and Poe,[3] as well as Caribbean and Latin American authors such as Carpentier and Fuentes, have explored this theme. It is Walcott's position that although we may seem to pass through the meridian, we never truly get beyond it. The meridian is actually a sort of "equator," for "the New // World" is "made exactly like the Old" (*O*, 319). This is in part simply because the globe is circular—"in its travelling all that the sea-swift does / it does in a circular pattern" (*O*, 188)—and on a sphere, designations like "horizontal" and "vertical" are shown to be arbitrary. As the history books of childhood would have it, it is Columbus who first fully experiences what Whitman calls "the rondure of the world,"[4] which folds all journeys back upon themselves (and yet is not so predictable that Columbus lands where he intends). In American legend, then, the disorienting experience of rondure occurs at the same time as the founding of modern America. For Walcott this disorientation *is* the American experience. Yet "the American experience" also extends beyond America, for this is a "reversible world" (*O*, 207) that doubles itself as though upon a hinge. When Walcott considers Europe in "Ruins of a Great House" or "Watteau," he finds that mimicry occurs on both sides of the map, "depending on what side of the mirror you are favoring" ("CM," 8). Walcott's map of a mutually constitutive America and Europe is, as John T. Irwin observes of all mutually constitutive oppositions, "like a Möbius strip in which a two-sided surface is turned into a one-sided surface but is still experienced as if it had two sides."[5]

For Walcott the reversible map of the globe is also the map of his poetic *oeuvre*. In *Omeros*'s penultimate chapter Walcott reviews the poem behind him, and likens his authorial progress from start to finish to the reversible geographic journeys the book describes:

> I followed a sea-swift to both sides of this text;
> her hyphen stitched its seam, like the interlocking
> basins of a globe in which one half fits the next
>
> into an equator, both shores neatly clicking
> into a globe; except that its meridian
> was not North and South but East and West. One, the New
>
> World, made exactly like the Old, halves of one brain,
> or the beat of both hands rowing that bear the two
> vessels of the heart with balance, weight, and design. (319)

In *Omeros* Achille and the persona of the poet follow swifts from America to Africa and to Europe and back; now the swift is revealed as the poet's muse as well, whom he has followed "to both sides of this text." *Omeros*'s front and back covers fold over each other as "East and West" (the globe, however, can be taken apart in two ways, north to south *and* east to west). The book, like the globe, has a vertical axis (its "seam") and a horizontal one (its sequence of pages). Halfway through this passage the image of the book fades and that of the globe brightens, inspiring more metaphors. The New and the Old Worlds recall two halves of a brain "made exactly like," or "the two / vessels of the heart." Blood "vessels" in turn recall sailing vessels, which likewise depend upon a periodic rhythm (of rowing). And the image of "vessels" finally joins the end of Walcott's chain of figures to its beginning, comparing the progress of a journey once again to the process of writing poetry: both depend upon a "beat" and upon "balance, weight, and design." This passage from *Omeros* not only reflects in miniature the structure and the principal images of Walcott's global map, but shows how far Walcott identifies that map with his poetry.

The swift, hyphen, equator, and meridian that appear here all gather conspicuous significance in Walcott's American mythology. First, to draw a copy of Walcott's map we would have to plot axes[6] along the compass points, north to south and east to west. For Walcott the vertical axis is the "meridian of Greenwich," which according to *Omeros* "decrees a great epoch" (196). Walcott calls the horizontal axis the "equator," "hyphen," or "horizon." The two axes superimposed form a plus sign or cross, and the cross ideographically represents the swift's shape with wings extended. It is also, of course, identical with the Christian sign of the cross, so that when Achille spots the swift "he ma[kes] / a swift sign of the cross" (6). When rotated on its side the cross becomes an X, which for Walcott stands for the "crossing" of the Middle Passage and for the dispersal which followed the Middle Passage, when Africans scattered over America toward each compass point as toward the endpoints of an X. In this context the X (or chiasmus) can indeed, as Derrida remarks, "be considered a quick thematic diagram of dissemination."[7]

The sea swift (less often, a frigate bird or gull), the "dart of the meridian" (*O*, 130), presides over the globe's axes. Walcott's swift, like Odysseus, Telemachos, or the displaced African-Caribbean Achille, is a vulnerable wanderer. The swift enters *Omeros* when Achille, having chopped down a tree for his canoe, "looked up at the hole the laurel had left" and "saw the swift // crossing the cloud-surf, a small thing, far from its home" (6). The swift arises in absence and appears only because the fishermen have dealt the woods an earth-shuddering "wound" (5). Yet as wanderer it is a figure of both fragility and power. In Homer, men, ships, and arrows are all "swift," and Athene "[leads] the way swiftly."[8] In *The Odyssey* Athene turns into "a bird soaring high in the air," and in that form inspires Telemachos (Lattimore, 35). Walcott's swift similarly guides Achille, "sho[oting] across // the blue ridges of the waves, to a god's orders" (131), and tows Achille's pirogue to his ancestral village in his dream of Africa (XXIV–XXV).

The swift repeats this combination of vulnerability and power in its main function, which is to "[sew] the Atlantic rift with a needle's line" (319).[9] Texts must be woven, and books have seams and semes. Walcott's swift, a poetic semestress, cross-stitches beginning to end, holding together "both sides of this text" (319), but also showing that the text, like the world, *needs* holding together.[10] The swift's hyphenating function is finally the faculty of poetic language itself, seaming disparate textual features. Poetic language too is an "equator": it compares,

DEREK WALCOTT'S POETRY

links, organizes systems of affinities. Derrida has observed precisely this capacity in the hyphen:

> If I say that the hyphen is not only *an* emblem, *a* motto, *a* coat of arms or *an* armorial crest but *the* symbol, this is so as to recall that *any* symbol is, *stricto sensu*, a hyphen, bringing together, according to the *symballein*, the two pieces of a body divided in contract, pact, or alliance.[11]

Since the hyphen functions as an equator, running east to west, it also recalls the horizon. Walcott not only perceives that the hyphen is horizontal, he proposes that the horizon is a hyphen. In "Marina Tsvetaeva," Tsvetaeva's "grace affects" "the horizon's hyphen" (*AT*, 47), and in Chapter XXXVII of *Omeros* "A bronze horseman halts at a wharf," "his wedged visor / shading the sockets' hyphenating horizons" (192). By comparing the tiny hyphen to the equator and horizon, Walcott stretches the hyphen over the circumference of human knowledge. Hyphens occupy the space between words, or so we believe. But if the horizon, the limit of human perception, is nothing but hyphen—a hyphen that hyphenates no pair of terms—then "betweenness" is all we can see. And if poetic language equates like and like (or unlike), we cannot see our way beyond its hyphenating horizon to "nonpoetic" language, either.

Equator and meridian, latitude and longitude, form the horizontals and verticals by means of which experience is ordered in time as well as space. According to Irwin, we find "in the era of Western European voyages of discovery and scientific exploration . . . the assumption that journeys to distant lands are journeys into the past, that the natives of these lands are men in an earlier state of cultural development than the Europeans who visit them" (174). Yet in the moment that Europeans discovered what seemed the "earlier" world of America, the European world began to be called "the Old World." From the American perspective, American settlement must refer to voyages from Europe and Africa. Thus, in Walcott, as in much other American literature, *Old* World(s) are associated with the past. Journeying through the meridian to either Europe or Africa involves reversing time and revisiting the past. Finally, in aesthetic terms Walcott's traveller through the meridian resembles anyone who tries to comprehend the "original" presence of the object world by examining its representations—or the contemporary poet, reading backward through the poetry of the past.

American poets are liable to possess a heightened consciousness that their art is mimicry, because America has more recently experienced the oppression of a centralized and yet distant authority. However, American mimicry is even more particularly Caribbean. The Caribbean region experiences North American as well as European domination, living "in the shadow of an America [the U.S.] that is economically benign yet politically malevolent" ("CM," 3). Still, Caribbean mimicry needs to point out mimicry in North America, and American mimicry needs to point out mimicry in Europe, since in this way Caribbean and American poets question the originality and prestige of other cultures. The concentric structures and infinite regressions that recur in Walcott's poems arise from this paradox, in which the American knowledge of difference presses the American poet to expose resemblance.

The geography beneath Walcott's poetry is already in place in "Origins," when "caravels [stitch] two worlds,"[12] and in *Another Life*, when a "harbour / open[s] on a seagull's rusty hinge" (iv. "The Pact," 21–22), "sandlerings rustily [wheel] / the world on its ancient, / invisible axis" (8.ii.27–29), "night pivots on a sea-gull's rusted winch" (11.v.20), and "Day pivot[s] on a sea-gull's screeching hinge" (17.iv.9). It is still there in *Midsummer*, where "the snake . . . link[s] two hemispheres, / since in the world's bitter half of churches and domes / another new epoch groan[s], opening on its hinge" (XXIV), and it persists through *The Arkansas Testament*, where Walcott "sp[ins] the globe's meridian, / show[s] its sealed hemispheres" (23). As we will see, *Omeros* also stages the two-way mirroring of "antipodal whar[ves]" (191). However, Walcott's essay, "The Caribbean: Culture or Mimicry?" (1973; published 1974), explains American mimicry most directly.

"CULTURE OR MIMICRY?," having first been composed for a conference on U.S.–Caribbean affairs, is the only piece of Walcott's

DEREK WALCOTT'S POETRY

prose that presents itself as a sociopolitical reflection, yet Walcott spends most of the essay following mimicry's poetic ramifications. The essay begins as a response to V. S. Naipaul and others who have lamented postcolonial mimicry of the West. In *An Area of Darkness*, for example, Naipaul gives the following illustration of mimicry:

> The Indian army officer is at first meeting a complete English army officer. He even manages to look English; his gait and bearing are English; his mannerisms, his tastes in drink are English; his slang is English. In the Indian setting this Indian English mimicry is like fantasy. It is an undiminishing absurdity; and it is only slowly that one formulates what was sensed from the first day: this is a mimicry not of England, a real country, but of the fairytale land of Anglo-India, of clubs and sahibs and syces and bearers. It is as if an entire society has fallen for a casual confidence trickster.[13]

Walcott's response builds upon the already double imitation Naipaul penetrates—an imitation "not of . . . a real country," but of a "fairytale land." But while Naipaul reels from the vertigo of this doubleness, seeing in it a twofold debasement, Walcott catches in it a breath of the commonplace. It is already clear in Naipaul that the *English* in India were not really English. In the Indian context their mannerisms were already absurd; Anglo-India even when it existed was a "fairytale land." Shouldn't we take the next step of wondering whether the Indian context merely underscored an absurdity that existed in England itself? Weren't "real" English clubs, for example, largely mimicking prior English clubs, a distant subculture of mythic grace? The overall movement of "Culture or Mimicry?" traces such a widening spiral of mimicry. The essay begins, following Naipaul, by considering its two terms as alternatives, but by its end Walcott has exchanged his title's "or" for an "*is*."

"Culture or Mimicry?" is rhetorically notable for its dexterous manipulations of light and shade, inside and outside, and for the *savoir-faire* with which it handles fluctuating Americas. Walcott begins with the ambiguous sentence "We live in the shadow of an America that is economically benign yet politically malevolent" (3). The second article ("*an* America") of this sentence implies the multiple Americas that immediately follow it. For although Caribbeans "live in the shadow of an America," Caribbeans also "were American even while we were British," and now "ask ourselves if, in the spiritual or cultural sense, we must become American" (3). For Walcott as for Whitman, being American apparently means containing multitudes.

In the essay's opening metaphor, empires are planetary bodies. "America" is the moon, casting a "shadow" upon the Caribbean and "threaten[ing] an eclipse of identity." "[T]he shadow of the British Empire has passed through and over . . . the Caribbean" (3), too, though presumably its moon has waned. Yet the "shadow" of the U.S. "is less malevolent than it appears" precisely because it is darker than it seems, because the U.S. is "black" in "so much of its labor, its speech, its music, its very style of living" (4). Further, optically, black *is* black precisely because it absorbs light; although Walcott agrees that as a predominantly "black" region, the Caribbean is good at "absorb[ing]" things, he maintains that it absorbs not light but darkness. It absorbs America's shadow, "can absorb it because we know that America is black" (4). In a trope common to the literature of the African diaspora, Walcott inverts Western connotations of light and dark. Lightning and illumination are conventional symbols of inspiration; Walcott notes that "We in the Americas are taught" Columbus's, Cortéz's, and other explorers' discoveries "as a succession of illuminations, lightning moments that must crystallize and irradiate memory if we are to believe in a chain of such illuminations known as history" (8). But for Walcott "these illuminations are literary and not in the experience of American man": "they are worthless" (8).

The word *absorb* splices the logic of light and dark to that of inside and outside, and so to the digestive metaphor of assimilation: "Remember our experience of different empires. Those experiences have been absorbed" (4). As Walcott paraphrases Naipaul, "Perhaps powerlessness leaves the Third World, the ex-colonial world, no alternative but to imitate those systems offered to or forced on it by the major powers" (5). "[M]ost [Third World] politicians are trapped in the concept of a world proposed by those who rule it," as Walcott sees it, "and these politicians see progress as inevitability" (5). Postcolonial politicians who accept the "major powers"' models of progress do bear out Naipaul in that "their mimicry of power defrauds their own people" (5). But while Naipaul believes that postcolonial culture goes awry because of its process of mimicry, Walcott admits that the content of its mimicry is at times ill-chosen, yet leaves open the possibility that mimicry, always normative, can be productive.

Walcott sees two "spiritual alternatives" to the "mimicry of power," both attached to the same digestive metaphor: "total rejection through revolution, for example," and "open assimilation of what is considered . . . most useful" (5). As Thomas C. Greene and others have shown,[14] the digestive metaphor for influence pervades classical Western literature. Now where influence has been "forced on" an entire culture, the digestive metaphor becomes emetic: "the tired slave vomits his past" (*AL* 22.i.18). Immediately after Walcott proposes "total rejection" and "open assimilation" as distinct alternatives, however, he maintains that "whichever method is applied, it is obvious that the metamorphosis is beginning" (5). Indeed, isn't "total rejection" already a contradiction in terms, insofar as *re*jection implies a previous introjection? Rejection cannot vaporize what precedes it; rather, it produces ruins in which a previous existence remains visible. The "surface" of the Caribbean "may be littered" with these ruins, "the despairs of broken systems and of failed experiments" (6). As for "open assimilation," that is also a contradiction in terms, insofar as openness implies the clearly perceptible, and assimilation, the discreetly identical. Beyond these supposed alternatives, then, "there is something else going on" (6).

In the next paragraph Walcott executes one of his most startling turns, and it is *the* turn from traditional metaphors of imitation, assimilation, and rejection to mimicry. He suggests that "the degradations have already been endured; they have been endured to the point of irrelevancy" (6). We can sense some of this irrelevance in the Naipaul passage above. Yet for Walcott, out of the ensuing "loss of history," out of an absence at the origin, "imagination as necessity, as invention" appears (6). Walcott surveys the situation and wonders, with Naipaul, how "life, if we can call it that in the archipelago" (6), can go on. Yet his wonderment dissolves into sheer admiration that life does manage to go on. Under such circumstances mimicry is not only normative but, as Walcott's suddenly generative language shows, aligned with the capacity to live: "Mr. Naipaul's epitaph on all West Indian endeavor has not *aborted* the *passion* with which West Indian culture continues to *procreate* this mimicry, because life, if we can call it that in the archipelago, defiantly continues" (6; italics mine). Only slightly later Walcott likens cultural mimicry to that gradual process of repetition, error, and difference we read of in Darwin. Biological difference asserts itself through mutation, producing "act[s] of imagination" and "endemic cunning" (10). Mutation, in turn, tends not toward originality but toward mimicry of other forms, as in "camouflage" (10). As Lacan remarks, "the facts of mimicry are similar, at the animal level, to what, in the human being is manifested as art."[15] By associating mimicry with procreation Walcott hints that language, like biology, survives by repeating itself and changes itself through error.[16]

In the next few pages Walcott explains American mimicry by means of a skeletal version of the narrative he repeats, sixteen years later, in *Omeros*. He begins his narrative with the crossing of the meridian, then steps behind its starting point to claim that American mimicry extends Old World mimicries:

> To mimic, one needs a mirror, and, if I understand Mr. Naipaul correctly, our pantomime is conducted before a projection of ourselves which in its smallest gestures is based on metropolitan references. No gesture, according to this philosophy, is authentic, every sentence is a quotation, every movement either ambitious or pathetic, and because it is mimicry, uncreative. The indictment is crippling, but, like all insults, it contains an astonishing truth. It is not, to my mind, only the West Indies which is being insulted by Naipaul, but all endeavor in this half of the world, in broader definition: the American endeavor. . . . Once the meridian of European civilization has been crossed, according to the theory, we have entered a mirror where there can only be simulations of self-discovery. . . . Somehow, the cord is cut by that meridian. Yet a return is also impossible, for we cannot return to what we have never been. . . . When language itself is condemned as mimicry, then the condition is hopeless and men are no more than jackdaws, parrots, myna birds, apes. (6–7)

DEREK WALCOTT'S POETRY

Even though "there is no such moment" as this crossing, still "there was such a moment for every individual American, and that moment was . . . both possession and dispossession" (8). We live in an "after," that is, even though it completes no "before." (Derrida writes, similarly, of Mallarmé's "mimicry" as a "double that doubles no simple."[17]) Although Walcott initially places mimicry on the American side of the meridian, when he imagines Europe in his poems he finds that the world always looks more original on the other side of the mirror. Originality and mimicry, Europe and America—each term occasionally plays the other's role, as Jackson Phillip (the black servant) and Harry Trewe (his white employer) each play both Friday and Crusoe in *Pantomime*.

Walcott no sooner writes that when language itself is mimicry "then the condition is hopeless" and "men are no more than . . . apes" than, in another reversal, he welcomes this "hopeless" situation: "The idea of the American as ape is heartening, however" (7). Indeed, Walcott enjoys depicting the poet as an ape. Naipaul believes it is a matter for despair that "The moment . . . a writer in the Caribbean, an American man, puts down a word . . . he is a mimic, a mirror man, he is the ape beholding himself" (8). But the narrator of "North and South" concludes, "[W]ell, yes, *je suis un singe*" (*FT*, 16), and in "Forest of Europe," Walcott and Brodsky "grunt like primates" over a poem by Mandelstam (*SAK*, 41).[18] The image of the poet as ape is actually "heartening" because it implies that language is irresistibly human in spite or because of the divisions it reveals, and because the capacity to mimic has helped the ape to survive.[19] This "anthropological idea of mimicry" associates mimicry with human evolution, dating it from "the self-naming grunt" of "the first ape" (7). Mimicry thus constitutes "the beginning of the human ego and our history" (7).

Walcott next compares the anthropological beginning of mimicry he has just imagined to Pope Alexander VI's division of the New World, for Alexander too was a "primate" who inaugurated a version of mimicry: "Alexander's meridian // gave half a gourd to Lisbon . . . / and half to Imperial Spain" (*O*, 193) in 1493. From "the first self-naming grunt" we need only "Advance some thousand years," as Walcott laconically suggests,

to the crossing of the mirror and the meridian of Alexander VI. . . .
[W]hat was the moment when the old ape of the Old World saw
himself anew and became another, or, was paralyzed with the
knowledge that henceforth, everything he did in the New World, on
the other side of the mirror, could only be a parody of the past?
(7–8)

This is a startling juxtaposition, made across more than just "some
thousand years," actually, and more than time. Yet one immediately
sees the basis for it. The self-naming scene takes place, for Walcott,
before a mirror ("Did the first ape look at his reflection in the mirror
of a pond in astonishment or in terror?" [7]). If Lacan sees in the mirror stage "the effect . . . of an organic insufficiency,"[20] Walcott declares
that "self-recognition or self-disgust . . . are the same" (7). The discovery of a "New" World that had after all always been there implied an
"insufficiency" in the basic competence of the "Old," and the discovery of the American future thus tainted the European past. In Lacanian
terms Europe suffered a "fragmented body-image," then assumed "the
armour of an alienating identity, which [has] mark[ed] with its rigid
structure the subject's entire mental development" (*Écrits*, 4), and Europe continues to struggle toward full "identification with the *imago*"
(*Écrits*, 5) of its American counterpart.

Finally, "Culture or Mimicry?" considers the implications of mimicry for American art by the examples of Carnival, calypso, and the
steel band. Carnival "emerged from the sanctions imposed on it," calypso "from a sense of mimicry, of patterning its form both on satire
and self-satire"; "[t]he banning of African drumming [at Carnival] led
to the discovery of the garbage can cover as a potential musical instrument" (9). These forms thus reflect the process by which the "original"
shows itself to be at the same time derivative, innovative, and influ-
ential: "Here are three forms, *originating from* the mass, which *are original* and temporarily as inimitable as what they first attempted to copy"
(9; italics mine). There is no distinction now between the derivative,
which has "originat[ed] from" something, and the "original," from
which subsequent forms derive. The "inimitable" has both "attempted
to copy" something and will, since it is only "temporarily" inimitable,

in its turn be copied. And "best of all," Carnival discards linear time, since the fiction of linear time braces the concept of originality: "on one stage, at any moment, the simultaneity of historical legends, epochs, characters, without historical sequence or propriety is accepted" (10).[21] If American art at large is to learn from these native genres, it will need likewise to acknowledge its mimicry and the temporal limits of its seeming inimitability—as "the [C]arnival mentality seriously, solemnly dedicates itself to the concept of waste, of ephemera, of built-in obsolescence . . . not the built-in obsolescence of manufacture but of art" (9).

"Culture or Mimicry?" stands at the center of Walcott's poetic in spite of its slenderness and its purportedly oblique relation to art. Its logic, which tracks the derivative back to originality and rediscovers it there in its domesticated form, characterizes Walcott's work; its idea of a self-consciously transitory art is elaborated and made concrete in *Another Life, Midsummer,* and elsewhere. The modifications of aesthetics we find in "Culture or Mimicry?" generate the intertextuality, the willingness to mix languages and genres, and the ephemerality of Walcott's best poetry. All of Walcott's poetry after 1974 builds upon its conclusions, and Walcott never lets go of the "reversible" map of the world he defines there.

O M E R O S' S L O O S E L Y C O M P L E M E N T A R Y voyages to Africa and to Europe (Chapters XXV–XXVIII and XXXVII) cast the crossing of the meridian into narrative form. In Chapter XXV, section I, a divine swift bears Achille to Africa. In section II Achille meets his ancestor, Afolabe. Their dialogue in section III compares African language to contemporary Caribbean language by means of a discussion of Achille's name. Chapter XXVI develops Achille's alienation from his ancestral society, which he suffers partly because he knows its future grief and partly because he feels perversely homesick ("as if [his] proper place / lay in unsettlement" [140]). Chapter XXVII recounts the first slave raid on Achille's village and Achille's solitary, failed attempt to defend his people as Homer's Achilles did. Finally, Chapter XXVIII reflects on the subsequent African diaspora and its linguistic consequences. Chapter XXXVII, meanwhile, considers the European-American experience of settlement, traveling to present-day Lisbon, the site of the inception of colonization (Portugal began what would become the modern European slave trade in 1441).

In these voyages the African-Caribbean Achille and the African-European-Caribbean poet alike find that by definition one cannot encompass one's own origin. In 1990 as in 1974, Walcott associates mimicry with survival. While "Culture or Mimicry?" argues for mimicry's ordinariness, it also demonstrates that recognizing this ordinariness begins rather than ends useful thought about mimicry (Walcott distinguishes, for example, the mimicry of folk musical forms from the mimicry of political mores). Walcott's comparison between *Omeros's* two journeys shows that he continues to bear such necessity of distinction in mind. Since journeys from either Africa or Europe culminate in Walcott, he stands at the X of their intersection; still, his chiastic self is asymmetrically divided in its loyalties. Achille's voyage and Walcott's are generally, not perfectly, matched. Descendants of the Middle Passage such as Achille have been severed from their ancestral communities in the most violent way, and those communities no longer exist to be recovered. Achille's trip is involuntary as Walcott's is not, and Achille's Africa is therefore distinctly imaginary as Walcott's Portugal is not. Achille encounters an ideal world untroubled by linguistic crises, while Walcott encounters quotidian mimicry in Portugal. Both journeys, however, are more significant for what they question than for what they recover; the comparison between them is not significant because it resolves the tension between Walcott's African, American, and European selves (it does not), but because Walcott uses the comparison of voyages to examine his impulse to make such comparisons.

Walcott shows more empathy with Africa, the "other" Old World, as his career develops. He increasingly details African influences on American (especially Caribbean) culture and acknowledges his own use of these resources. In Walcott's later poetry we often find motifs and attitudes he mocked five to fifteen years before. For example, in "The Muse of History" (1974) Walcott assails "The epic-minded poet" who "celebrates what little [ruin] there is, the rusted slave wheel of the

DEREK WALCOTT'S POETRY

sugar factory," claiming that "Morbidity is the inevitable result" (8–9); but Walcott himself does exactly this in "Roseau Valley" (1987).[22] Walcott claims in some early articles (1963–66) that Carnival is too undisciplined a model for theater, and that "The artist works in isolation from the crude, popular forms."[23] In "What The Twilight Says" (1970), he also draws a distinction between "calypsos" and "poems."[24] In other words, although Walcott respected Carnival and calypso in their own right, he didn't want to identify his own art with these folk forms.[25] By "Culture or Mimicry?," however, Carnival exemplifies theatrical imagination, and in "The Spoiler's Return" (1981), Walcott merges his voice with an actual calypso singer's.

Similarly, *Dream on Monkey Mountain* (1970) implies that Makak's African aspirations are little more than chimeras that distract him from his daily tasks. Walcott's tone at this point is rather like that of Achille's incredulous mate: " '[T]his morning I could use a hand. // Where your mind was whole night?' / 'Africa.' / 'Oh? You walk?'" (157). In *O Babylon!* (1976; revised and published 1978) Walcott begins to treat such yearnings more sympathetically. While the principals' Africanist ideals don't come to fruition in *O Babylon!*, Walcott makes an effort to allow them "hope for a future Zion and the will to make the best of their own world in the present."[26] Twelve years later, *Omeros* completes this process by rewriting the back-to-Africa theme Walcott satirizes in *Dream on Monkey Mountain*. Of course, *Omeros*'s strategies indicate that Walcott has not forgotten his criticisms of other treatments of the back-to-Africa theme. Walcott takes care not to imagine the journey to Africa "as an escape" (Hirsch 1979, 285), not "skipping the part about slavery, and going straight back to a kind of Eden-like grandeur" (Hirsch 1986, 222). Achille passes through a symbolic version of slavery in order to get to Africa ("A skeletal warrior / stood straight up in the stern and . . . / clamped his neck in cold iron" [133]), and again in order to leave. Still, although Achille's African experience is acutely uncomfortable throughout, Walcott's attitude toward Africa seems to be a case of delayed mourning. *Omeros*'s emphasis is elegiac—the more so since Walcott considers the loss of Africa to be "inconsolable" (*O*, 151).

As Walcott imagines it, each African craftsman suffers most from the loss of his particular craft:

> This one, who was a hunter,
>
> wept for a sapling lance whose absent haft sang
> in his palm's hollow. One, a fisherman, for an ochre
> river encircling his calves; one a weaver, for the straw
>
> fishpot he had meant to repair, wilting in water.
> They cried for the little thing after the big thing.
> They cried for a broken gourd. (151)

Since Walcott's own craft is poetry, the lost belief that the forms of language bear a necessary relation to the world is for him the most grievous casualty of the African diaspora.[27] *Omeros* therefore measures the centuries between Afolabe and Achille principally by the drift of language.

When Achille meets Afolabe, "Time st[ands] between them. The only interpreter" (136). On the one hand, this *deus ex machina* of time allows Achille to understand Afolabe directly. Walcott stresses the immediacy of their exchange by rendering it in dramatic form. Yet "Time st[ands] between them" in another sense as well, obstructing the communication it enables. What they understand most clearly is that they cannot understand each other, because Achille's language shows no connection to its referents; the name "Achille" is itself the poem's principal example of such disconnection. As Achille and Afolabe argue and play out their linguistic differences, we become conscious of the nearly incomprehensible sequence of events by which Achille came to be a St. Lucian fisherman named, of all things, Achille:

AFOLABE

Achille. What does the name mean? I have forgotten the one
that I gave you. But it was, it seems, many years ago.
What does it mean?

ACHILLE

Well, I too have forgotten.
Everything was forgotten. You also. I do not know.

The deaf sea has changed around every name that you gave
us; trees, men, we yearn for a sound that is missing.

AFOLABE

A name means something. The qualities desired in a son,
and even a girl-child; so even the shadows who called
you expected one virtue, since every name is a blessing,

since I am remembering the hope I had for you as a child.
Unless the sound means nothing. Then you would be nothing.
Did they think you were nothing in that other kingdom?

ACHILLE

I do not know what the name means. It means something,
maybe. What's the difference? In the world I come from
we accept the sounds we were given. Men, trees, water. (137)

Achille's name dramatizes the arbitrariness of language because, like
the names of many descendants of the African diaspora, it originates
from a different cultural tradition than his body. He would thus seem
to be a walking example of the gap between signifier and signified. As
Kimberly Benston explains, descendants of slaves may want to
"un[name] the immediate past" and to "stage" the newly liberated self
by their own acts of naming.[28] Achille's name, however, although it is
twice exotic (Francophone, or French Creole, from Greek), does not
refer to an "immediate past" Achille might like to shed, but to a mythical one so remote he seems not to have heard of it. Something of this
operates in slave names such as "Pompey"; the immediate past is
couched in mimicry of a distant one. There is no reason to believe that
Achille's name is so ironically intended (it is not, in the end, ironic per
se).[29] Still, Achille does not know why he carries it and, what's worse
(for Afolabe), does not care. Achille's sense of the arbitrary begins with
his own name and extends beyond proper names to all nouns: "Men,
trees, water." He accepts the modern assumption that we should not
look for reason in the particular forms of language, and feels that he
should no more be expected to explain his own name than to explain
why we call "trees" and "water" what we do. Afolabe, meanwhile,
finds the idea of arbitrary language unbearable:

And therefore, Achille, if I pointed and I said, There
is the name of that man, that tree, and this father,
would every sound be a shadow that crossed your ear,

without the shape of a man or a tree? What would it be? (138)

Afolabe's belief that he can "point" to a name, and that "every sound"
should disclose "the shape of a man or a tree," shows that he does not
distinguish names from their referents. To understand the meaning of
one's own existence, one understands one's name: "you, / if you're
content with not knowing what our names mean, // then I am not
Afolabe, your father. . . . I am not here" (138). For Afolabe a name
should not just be, but mean. Achille, in contrast, can assert only that
he was blessed with the sign of the cross—the one ideographic letter
he does know—and with "this sound whose meaning I still do not care
to know" (138).

The reader faced with this well-defined debate naturally wants to
ask who is right, Afolabe or Achille. Walcott seems sympathetic to both
positions. Achille (unlike the persona of the poet in *Omeros*) does not
have a systematic imagination, but is not without imagination; he does
not need things to be significant in order to appreciate them. There is
freshness and freedom in Achille's perspective, as in this passage in
which he ponders the stars:

Achille was

studying a heaven whose cosmology had been erased
by the crossing. He was trying to trace the armature
of studs and rivets where the constellations are placed,

but for him they were beads on an abacus, no more.
From night-fishing he knew the necessary ones,
the one that sparkled at dusk, and at dawn, the other.

All in a night's work he saw them simply as twins.
He knew others but would not call them by their given
names, forcing a silvery web to link their designs. (113–14)

As Whitman turns away from the "learn'd astronomer," Achille
turns from the mythographer and cosmologist. The irony is that for

such an unliterary sensibility, opposed to mythmaking, seeing stars "simply" means seeing them "as twins"; there is no need to double the stars by naming them, but only because they are already double. Further, the unliterary Achille himself bears a name that carries powerful literary connotations. The existence of these connotations Achille "do[es] not care to know" bears out Afolabe's insistence, in one of Walcott's more Dantesque phrasings, that "No man loses his shadow except it is in the night, / and even then his shadow is hidden, not lost. At the glow / of sunrise, he stands on his own name in that light" (138).

On the other hand, the Achille-Achilles correspondence is hardly one-to-one. It is true that during the raid on his village, "He hid and felt the same / mania that, in the arrows of drizzle, he felt for Hector" (147). Unlike Achilles, however (and to his credit), Achille is not a ferocious fighter. At first "He st[ands] in their centre, with useless arms" (144), and later, after killing an archer who must remind him of Philoctete, "sob[s] with grief / at the death of a brother" (148). Finally, just as Achille begins to develop heroic pretensions ("I can deliver / all of them . . . then I could / change their whole future, even the course of the river"), "a cord / of thorned vine looped his tendon, encircling the heel / . . . He fell hard" (148). It is difficult to resolve Walcott's ambivalence about linguistic significance into an intelligible statement here. In "Cul de Sac Valley" (*AT*, 9–15) a sphinx-shaped hill asks the poet a riddle about language. We might at this juncture ask an equally riddling question: "In the very moment that Achille, growing ambitious, most resembles Achilles, he falls from that resemblance, yet in the manner of his falling, resembles Achilles once more. Does Achille's name bind him to Achilles or not?"

When he looks at the stars Achille feels no desire to enmesh them in a "silvery web" of significance. Yet he himself is caught in just such a web. Achille is "raking the way clear of the net / of vines" as he falls, "unroping / himself from their thorns" (148). This "net / of vines," naturally composed of signs for the crossings that recur so obsessively in the poem and spell his fate, soon enslaves him "with its own piercing chain" (148). But what is that "net / of vines" besides a net of lines, the textual web in which the Nabokovian spider-author, Walcott, sets his characters? The implication is that although the belief in motivated language may have disappeared, it returns (or in Afolabe's terms, is illuminated) in fictions and in dreams—although its restoration doesn't necessitate its prior existence. Everything does fit into a plan (Walcott's), even Achille, who remains unconscious of it, and who thinks it makes no difference whether sounds have meaning. However, this coherence holds only so long as we remain within the province of the text itself. It may be that only this appearance of coherence within texts leads us to believe that it has disappeared elsewhere. We therefore confront such poetic significance with the same aggrieved question Afolabe asks of Achille: "Why did I never miss you until you returned?" (139). "There [is] no answer to this, as in life" (139).

Walcott describes the African diaspora as a four-way division, recalling the four compass points or endpoints of an X: "there went the Ashanti one way, the Mandingo another, / the Ibo another, the Guinea. Now each man was a nation / in himself, without mother, father, brother" (150). Since communities must agree on linguistic meanings, African languages splintered, too: "they made the signs for their fading names on the wood, / and their former shapes returned absently; each carried / the nameless freight of himself to the other world" (150). Yet as Pope Alexander's decree seams the globe in the act of dividing it, the survivors are knitted together by their dispersal: "they felt the seawind tying them into one nation / . . . in the one pain / that is inconsolable, the loss of one's shore" (151). Walcott's tale of division is therefore studded with X's of multiplication. Out of division the survivors bring multiplication, for "they crossed, they survived. There is the epical splendour" (149). They not only cross by surviving, they survive by crossing—by allowing their paths, bodies, and languages to cross one another's. Although some of the multiplications involved in the crossing are demonic, such as "the silver coins multiplying on the sold horizon" (149), God's advice to Adam and Eve, "Be fruitful and multiply," echoes through the end of Chapter XVIII. This movement of division-that-multiplies constitutes African-American and African-Caribbean culture:

> Their whole world was moving,
> or a large part of the world, and what began dissolving
>
> was the fading sound of their tribal name for the rain,
> the bright sound for the sun, a hissing noun for the river,
> and always the word "never," and never the word "again." (152)

The X-shaped reasoning of Walcott's last line, which points two phrases at each other (*always never/never again*), each of which again breaks into chiastic halves (*always/never, never/again*), is at first clearer than the terms within that reasoning. Although the grammatical referents don't want to be caught, one has to get out the net and try. "[W]hat began dissolving" is particularly fluid, for Walcott substitutes this kinetic circumlocution for a noun. "What" is, apparently, the mimetic, onomatopoeic language of "tribal name[s]." If we run past Walcott's quotation marks, and take "always" and "never" not as frozen examples of words but as functioning words within the sentence, we can paraphrase the passage: "[This kind of language] was always never and never again." If it was "always never," it never was; yet, despite its never having been, it now exists no more, since it "never again" will. Walcott's "after" follows no "before," much as Achille is for Afolabe "the smoke from a fire that never burned" (139). Notice as well that although the language Walcott describes "beg[ins] dissolving," it does not necessarily stop dissolving. It may to some degree "always," to some degree "never" dissolve. This is still the situation of American language, and if it is unstable, it is at least "moving."

Like Achille's trip to Africa, the poet's trip to Portugal in Chapter XXXVII chronicles a loss of perceived wholeness or glory. After the creation of a European empire in America directly caused African "unsettlement," that empire was prone to decay and dispersal. If Achille in Africa is "smoke from a fire that never burned," modern-day Lisbon's "castle in the olives" "is the ghost of itself" (192), "its own headstone" (193). Walcott takes an ironic refuge in such remembrances of mortality: "when a wave rhymes with one's grave, / a canoe with a coffin . . . that parallel / . . . cancels the line of master and slave" (*O*, 159). Walcott suggests that precisely the European pursuit of permanence rigidifies Europe and ensures its collapse. The European impulse to immortalize itself literally ends in ruins, making the collapse of Europe a public spectacle—which tourists from America now pay to see.

Since this journey from America to Europe works against American chronology, Walcott shows us time running backward:

> I crossed my meridian. Rust terraces, olive trees,
> the grey horns of a port. Then, from a cobbled corner
> of this mud-caked settlement founded by Ulysses—
>
> swifts, launched from the nesting sills of Ulissibona,
> their cries modulated to "Lisbon" as the Mediterranean
> aged into the white Atlantic, their flight, in reverse,
>
> repeating the X of an hourglass, every twitter an aeon
> from which a horizon climbed in the upturned vase.
> A church clock spun back its helm. Turtleback alleys
>
> crawled from the sea, not toward it, to resettle
> in the courtyard under the olives, and a breeze
> turned over the leaves to show their silvery metal. (189)

Walcott associates the meridian with a host of analogous figures: a mirror,[30] a fishline,[31] a capital I, a Roman numeral one.[32] A few of these come into play immediately here. The chapter begins with the usual Roman section number I, the word "I," and the sentence "I crossed my meridian," which crossing Walcott promptly represents with an X. The familiar meridian, X, and horizon form a grid over which to plot other images. The swifts act as divine messengers and guides, as they do throughout *Omeros*; their hourglass-shaped flight illustrates crossing and in the same motion gives it a temporal dimension. Since the "church clock [spins] back," we know that time is running backward for Walcott as he tracks the Portuguese path against its chronologic grain. While turtles and ships set off into the sea to found settlements, Walcott's "turtleback alleys" "[crawl] from the sea . . . to resettle / in the courtyard." The passage therefore sets up "antipodal" (191) perspectives, as Walcott terms them, evoking the chronology of American colonization by describing it in reverse. The two chronologies, the historical one and its belated mirror image, meet here at the hypothetical center of Walcott's X.

DEREK WALCOTT'S POETRY

In this mirror-world pronoun references and antonymic prepositions such as "here" and "there" become entangled. "Here" it is Sunday in Lisbon; "There," "no longer Lisbon but Port of Spain" (190). Even in Port of Spain, however, "Sunday" is apparently in exile. Sunday is "an old Portugee leathery as Portugal, via Madeira, / with a stalled watch for a compass,"[33] "in a cream suit, with a gray horned moustache" (189),[34] whose function is to regulate time—to "[slip] the sun's / pendulum back into its fob" or "re[wind] its hand" (190). Indeed, Sunday occupies a peculiar position in our conception of the week, as the last Biblical day and the first calendar day; time comes full circle there, where it overlaps itself, at once ending and beginning. The first section ends when "Sunday stops / to hear schooners thudding on overlapping wharves," so that the movement of Walcott's meditation on Sunday itself replaces an oppositional arrangement ("Here" vs. "There") with one that "overlap[s]" like an X.

A wharf, as the pivot point of a journey, is a place of insight, a good place at which to make comparisons. Its etymology reveals that a wharf is a place "to turn oneself"; in the second section of the chapter, Walcott, from his wharf, "tr[ies] seeing the other side"—meaning Lisbon, the side that had, from America, seemed other:

Across the meridian, I try seeing the other side,
past rusty containers, waves like welts from the lash
in a light as clear as oil from the olive seed.

Once the world's green gourd was split like a calabash
by Pope Alexander's decree. Spices, vanilla
sweetened this wharf; the grain of swifts would scatter

in their unchanging pattern, their cries no shriller
then they are now over the past, or ours, for that matter,
if our roles were reversed, and the sand in one half

replicated the sand in the other. Now I had come
to a place I felt I had known, an antipodal wharf
where my forked shadow swayed to the same brass pendulum.
                                                              (191)

Although the light is clear, Walcott can perceive the "other side" only by looking "past" the "rusty containers" of history and "waves like welts from the lash." In emotional terms imagining the "other side" means imagining "roles . . . reversed." This role-reversal in turn reaches its pivot point when Walcott evokes and revises Eliot's "Little Gidding"[35]: "Now I had come / to a place I felt I had known,"

> Yes, but not as one of those pilgrims whose veneration carried
> the salt of their eyes up the grooves of a column
> to the blue where forked swifts navigated. Far from it; instead,

> I saw how my shadow detached itself from them
> when it disembarked on the wharf through a golden haze
> of corn from another coast. My throat was scarred

> from a horizon that linked me to others, when our eyes
> lowered to the cobbles that climbed to the castle yard,
> when the coins of the olives showed us their sovereign's face. (191)

The two-way mirroring of "antipodal whar[ves]" reaches its limit here, near the center of this 33-tercet chapter, at the end of the seventeenth stanza. The eighteenth stanza, the center of the chapter's second section, changes course: "Yes, *but not* as one of those pilgrims." The chapter as a whole thus takes a chiastic shape, its three sections corresponding to the top, center, and bottom of an hourglass, and to America, meridian, and Europe. (This symmetry also follows that of "the sun's / pendulum" [190] and a "brass pendulum" [191] in the same chapter.) Like the world, an hourglass is reversible. At the beginning of the chapter's first section, "a horizon climbed in the upturned vase" (189); at the end of that section, the "market in slaves / and sugar decline[s] below the horizon" (190). Thereafter Walcott focuses on the difference between the hemispheres, following the "shadow" that "detache[s] itself" from the pilgrims. Whereas in the first section Lisbon's cream Sunday seemed to mirror Walcott, his "shadow" now takes over. The first and second sections of the chapter thus personify first his "white" then "black" lines of ancestry, although these do not carry equal weight. The shadow represents not only Walcott's African ancestry, but also—since it is a "forked shadow" like Lear's "forked animal"—his whole split self. The African side of his ancestry seems to determine consciousness, since it was the ancestor on that side who suffered, who felt the split that constitutes his current self.

The "horizon" of this African shadow's experience serves, like a hyphen, to link people together. But now the link is a demonic parody of human connection; the horizon becomes a link in slavery's chain, like the "gold-manacled vendors" (190) in the first section. And as the first section's "breeze / turned over the leaves [of Lisbon's history book?] to show their silvery metal" or mettle (189), Walcott reiterates that in slave days profit determined the whole "nature" of Lisbon: "the coins of the olives showed us their sovereign's face" (191). Today "A bronze horseman" represents Portugal, "his wedged visor / shading the sockets' hyphenating horizons" and "his stare fixed like a helm" (192).[36] Where Walcott comes from "We had no such erections / above our colonial wharves"; "We think of the past // as better forgotten than fixed with stony regret" (192). Instead of seeing "the past" as "an infinite Sunday," Lisbon possesses a crippling consciousness that its impotent present of "limp sails on washing lines" (193) seems absurd in comparison to its imperial seafaring past. Lisbon thus engages in a mimicry of its own past, its "sword . . . pointed to recapture the port of Genoa"; its "castle in the olives" "is the ghost of itself" (192) or "its own headstone" (193).

It is clear that the reader is meant to compare these two journeys from *Omeros*, but less clear how they finally measure up to each other. Walcott's treatment of the two journeys is asymmetrical. The desolation of Africa is certainly more thorough and more distressing. In terms of the historic and moral causes of these two deliquescences, there is, as we say, no comparison. The image of Africa is more easily idealized, for the same reasons, by literal and metaphoric dreaming. Still, Walcott has shown impatience, particularly in "The Muse of History," with the notion that there is ever literally "no comparison" between any two things or states. The tirelessly figurative surface of his poetry plainly expresses that impatience. The poet's challenge, for Walcott as for Donne, is precisely to equate things whose obvious and tenacious difference is assumed. It is impossible to say whether Walcott is led to link disparate worlds by his dependence on metaphor, or led to that dependence by his need to link worlds.[37] Yet in either case the experience of crossing the vertical "equator" of the meridian becomes an opportunity to explore equation.

In *Omeros* Walcott contemplates other means of constructing equivalences, only to find them as imperfect as metaphor. Poets often envy the exact sciences, but Walcott's cartographical latitudes and longitudes appeal as much for their fictitiousness as for their symmetry, and provide bases for comparison as arbitrary as they are dependable. Weights and measures, like poetic "measures," equate items along a single standard, and the result is tremulous. In a set of scales in Castries market, "each brass basin / balanced on a horizon, but never equal, / like the old world and new, as just as things might seem" (38). In Chapter XL books on a "barber's shelf" in Castries evoke the basin of a European fountain, the fountain of European self-forgiveness for what it has done to the Caribbean basin (205; Walcott's combination of the cheap and grand here also echoes Cervantes' barber's basin— the one that becomes Don Quixote's gold helmet). Later, Ma Kilman bathes Philoctete in an "old sugar-mill" basin (246), with "a rag / sogged in a basin of ice," "leaves leech[ing] to his wet / knuckled spine like islands that cling to the basin / of the rusted Caribbean" (247). As Philoctete's body expands to the size of his archipelago (like that of Blake's Albion), the set of scales in Castries market grows *in* scale to become the scales of an ironically imperfect and obdurate "justice." Walcott perceives that the instrument of measurement produces as much as exposes similitude. He balances Achille's voyage against his own only by virtue of the rhetorical instrument of comparison itself, as "the Antilles' / history" and "Rome's . . . / [are] only made level // by the iron tear of the weight" (38). Walcott focuses on the medium of comparison—the drop of iron by means of which the balance of objects becomes perceptible—as much as the objects compared. The drop of iron is tearlike because the poet makes comparisons out of a compassion that strives to forgive discord, but perhaps also because comparison itself is not only pitying but piteous (although no less valuable for that).

The poet's mental scales, like the fruit vendor's, find things "never equal," especially since he must take account of differences-within as well as differences-between. His irrepressible impulse to weigh perceptions despite the impossibility of achieving balance can therefore seem an irritable reaching after fact and reason. Walcott periodically vents this irritation: "When would the sails drop / from my eyes . . . ?" (271). On the very last pages of *Omeros*, Achille weighs a day's catch—"The copper scales, swaying, / were balanced by one iron tear; then there was peace" (324)—and goes home, "scrap[ing] dry scales off his hands" (325). Obviously, however, Achille will get new scales on his hands tomorrow, and Walcott new scales on his eyes. If scales on the eyes mean sin, let he who is without metaphor cast the first stone. Equation is involuntary; Walcott cannot argue away his impulse toward it by pointing out that there is always a difference or remainder. Rather, difference severs and binds the hemispheres along their meridian, as the distance between them also joins them in a "monumental groaning and soldering of two great worlds, like the halves of a fruit seamed by its own bitter juice" ("MH," 27).

FOR WALCOTT the meridian functions as a constitutive boundary between American and "Old" Worlds; but his choice of this figure to represent that boundary communicates his suspicion of boundaries, for the meridian is as amorphous as it is definite. The lexical life of the term "meridian" is various indeed. It means "apex," and although this connotation is growing archaic, it has not fallen entirely out of use (witness *Imperial Meridian*, a recent book on the British Empire by the historian C. A. Bayly[38]). Falling empires show that an apex can be as much a midpoint as a hinge. The Greenwich meridian, as pure a spatial boundary as one could imagine, governs the measurement of time as well. "Meridian" also means "noon," and noons occur with predictable frequency in Walcott's work, often as moments of suspension that serve as transitions. For example, before Achille dreams of Africa, he "look[s] up at the sun . . . vertical / as an anchor-rope" (128), and this touch of sunstroke's "stasis" apparently triggers his ensuing vision. At other times noon is a pastoral parenthesis, since "the banks [close] for an hour, the entire town / [goes] home for lunch" (*O*, 121; "meridian" means "siesta," too, or did at one time). Visual representations of noon are also interesting. At twelve-thirty or six o'clock the minute and hour hands of a clock are spread apart, but at noon, they overlap, appearing to fold over each other as though upon a hinge. At noon (or midnight, or, less dramatically, at six-thirty) a clock is relatively empty of visual information. For that minute it emulates the moon, "Calm as a kitchen clock without the hands" (*AT*, 52; *Omeros*'s blind Seven Seas reinforces Walcott's association between meridional clock and moon, for he "move[s] by a sixth sense, / like the moon without an hour or second hand" [12]). Or perhaps the nearly vacant noon clock resembles a sundial (another "meridian"), which traces time more gently and passively than a clock.

This same multiplicity to the point of formlessness typifies the spatial character of the meridian. "Simplicity" seems hardly a strong enough word to describe the plainness of a straight line. But by virtue of its plainness, the meridian becomes protean. Bent in half, it is a hinge (Derrida similarly writes of *la brisure*, the hinge, the "single word for designating difference and articulation" [*Of Grammatology*, 65]). Multiplied, the meridian divides the globe into latitudes and longitudes. Doubled and crossed, it is a chiasmus. Turned on its side, it is an equator, horizon, or hyphen; knotted, an ampersand. Absented, it is still a caesura. Set at a slant, it is the slash mark between horizontals and verticals like "time/space," or other oppositions like "black/white." In that the poet's self seams black to white "the human skin" is meridional, "the indeterminate boundary, the ambiguous limit, between inner and outer, subject and object, self and other" (Irwin, 154). It would seem, as Borges notes, that a straight line is the most artful of labyrinths.[39]

Whether regulating time or space, the meridian determines the intangible, but only by virtue of its own indeterminacy. Of what, really, is it the measure? Something too boundless, ironically, even to name. In "Guyana" Walcott ridicules "The surveyor" for attempting to control such boundlessness:

> The vault that balances on a grass blade,
> the nerve-cracked ground too close for the word "measureless,"

for the lost concept, "man,"
revolve too slowly for the fob-watch of his world,
for the tidal markings of the five-year plan. (*G*, 71)

Like all attempts to order experience, the meridian buckles under pressure when faced with this measurelessness. For the figure that constitutes his America and Europe, Walcott chooses a term that designates either a boundary as abstract as it is pure or an instrument of measurement as inexact as it is concrete. The meridian becomes, all told, an arrow pointing toward the absurd and the sublime. Rilke's "L'Ange du Méridien" celebrates a similar function of the meridian as sundial. Here, the sundial is a mechanism not of calculation, but of surrender. A stone angel on the cathedral of Chartres, holding the sundial, smiles—possibly because on its dial "the day's whole sum at once . . . stands in deep balance, as if all hours were ripe and rich." In his concluding question to the angel Rilke pushes the meridian's abstraction to its ecstatic edge:

> Was weißt du, Steinerner, von unserm Sein?
> und hältst du mit noch seligerm Gesichte
> vielleicht die Tafel in die Nacht hinein?

> [What do you know, stone creature, of our life?
> and is your face perhaps even more blissful
> when you hold your slate into the night?][40]

RILKE'S SUNDIAL, a late Romantic instrument like the Aeolian harp, represents the poetic longing for transparency of being. Where Rilke's meridian is passive and *full*, Walcott's actively constitutes what it measures. Still, Walcott's emphasis on the ambiguous meridian indicates that his poetic resources, like Rilke's, communicate as much by the extent and manner of their imprecision as by their accuracy. We can see, looking back over its assortment of associations, that the pliability of Walcott's "meridian," as founding figure, also marks its limitation. As the "rondure of the world" limits the extent to which one can travel, the meridian brings the meaningful full circle into the meaningless. Walcott's meridian is not only a boundary that separates America from Europe, mimicry from originality, for contrast and comparison, but a figure that demonstrates its own internal limit and the boundaries *of* those separations.

CHAINS OF LANGUAGE, CHAINS OF COMMAND: WALCOTT AND POETIC INFLUENCE

There is no beginning but no end. The new poet enters a flux and withdraws, as the weaver continues the pattern, hand to hand and mouth to mouth, as the rock-pile convict passes the sledge.

—"The Muse of History"

The English language is nobody's special property. It is the property of the imagination: it is the property of the language itself.

—Interview with Edward Hirsch (1986)

POSTCOLONIAL AND WESTERN critics alike have often focused their discussions of Walcott on the question of influence. What knottier case of influence could there be than a highly allusive, multilingual, "racially" mixed postcolonial poet? Whatever choices he makes, Walcott risks offending a part of his audience. Other international poets perhaps understand him best. In his review of *The Star-Apple Kingdom*, Seamus Heaney argues that Walcott could have modeled his work on Larkin or Neruda—an uncommon range of influences, to be sure. But Heaney concludes, "He did neither, but made a theme of the choice and the impossibility of choosing."[1] Walcott is, in his own phrase, "the mulatto of style" ("WTS," 9).

If Walcott did not exist, theorists of influence would have had to invent him. Reading Walcott's poetry beside criticism and reviews of it can't help revealing the limitations of popular assumptions about influence. Despite various poststructuralist critiques of originality, practical critics and especially poetry reviewers still write as though we can intuitively distinguish originality. Walcott's poetry and critical prose, however, do not aim to discover originality, for "the great poets have no wish to be different, no time to be original" ("MH," 25). Instead, Walcott highlights his own influences, especially sources that themselves highlight earlier sources. Even so, the opposition between originality and mimicry often haunts the language in which Walcott resists it. In at least three ways, then, Walcott's work throws into relief the simultaneous inadequacy and resilience of the idea of "originality": by provoking critical discussions of it; by the strength with which it presses against it; and by its tendency nevertheless to fall back upon it. Although I am more concerned with Walcott's work than its reception, a glimpse of that reception shows how Walcott's work typically raises issues of influence.

Postcolonial critics sometimes charge that Walcott's openness to the British canon is the linguistic equivalent of colonial nostalgia and cultural assimilation.[2] Meanwhile, Western critics (who have reviewed more than studied Walcott) tend to feel that he has not "assimilated" the Western tradition fully *enough*. Vendler asserts in 1982 that Walcott is "still, even as a fully developed writer, peculiarly at the mercy of influence," since "Hart Crane, Dylan Thomas, Pound, Eliot, and Auden [follow] Yeats in Walcott's ventriloquism" (23). For Vendler, Walcott's lyric grace, in "The Season of Phantasmal Peace," for example, best escapes the ill effects of poor assimilation—which we can recognize by its theatrical, melodramatic phrasing (23), "overpreciseness," and "labored effects of unnatural diction" (26). Calvin Bedient, also reviewing *The Fortunate Traveller*, similarly believes that Walcott's "mimicry of some of our poets . . . [does] not turn the trick" (31). He, too, notes that the flawed poems seem "excessively written" (33), "soft" in their imitation of Lowell and Bishop (32), and/or "precious" (40). These pejoratives harmonize with Vendler's description of Walcott's sometime artificiality and melodrama. But although Bedient's criticisms are comparable to Vendler's, he chooses divergent examples. He prefers the narratives to the lyrics, calling "The Season of Phantasmal Peace" ("the best poem in the new collection" for Vendler) "sentimental," "confuse[d]," "idle," and "counter-political, distracting the reader from actual conditions" (40). This aesthetic disagreement also marks a divergence of opinion about politics, or at least political tactics. Bedient assails Walcott's taste for abstraction as antihistorical, while Vendler favors the poem *because* it "says nothing explicit about Empire and the oppression of colonies," arguing that its political point gains strength from this tact. More to my point, however, reading the reviews side by side highlights the impressionism of both discussions of influence. Vendler sees some of Walcott's poetry as "ventriloquism," yet she also describes her favorite poem, "The Season of Phantasmal Peace," as "unashamed in its debt to Shakespeare, Keats and the Bible." The successful poem, too, owes a "debt"; the difference is that it has "assimilated" its creditors "into its own fabric" (27). It is difficult to define assimilation, though, by the only characteristic Vendler mentions, by its being "unashamed." How should we read for signs of poetic shame, then of its lack? What would cause this shame? Why is ventriloquism ashamed, but assimilation unashamed? (The unashamed is usually the open; but ventriloquists make no secret of their artifice—their artifice, precisely, is on display—while "assimilation" connotes digestion and therefore dissimulation.) Most Western critics see Walcott's successful poems in a similar light, but do not explain how such assimilation has taken place and at the same time left unmistakable traces.

Some postcolonial critics, although admitting that Walcott might seem to collaborate with the traditions of the oppressor, defend Walcott's openness to influence. J. A. Ramsaran, for example, suggests that "literature and art acquired through the European tongues . . . can help to quicken the West Indian imagination as their heightened awareness enables the native artist[s] and poet[s] to see around them, as if for the first time, a new world."[3] In this way the native poet can forge an "integrated" language through "self-exploration" of mixed heritages. Thus, Walcott "assimilat[es] *and transform[s]*" his English (Ramsaran, 134; italics mine).

By proposing that poets can grow only from maximum exposure to all kinds of knowledge and experience, Ramsaran's argument follows the Walcottian grain. Yet Ramsaran, like Vendler, implies by his chosen figures for influence that texts and poetic traditions must remain essentially separate. Vendler's "assimilation" and Ramsaran's "assimilat[ion] and transform[ation]" alike subscribe to a "transformative" metaphor, one of the oldest metaphors for influence in Western culture. As critical studies of Renaissance imitation have shown, the transformative metaphor is built upon a contradiction:

> [T]ransformation of the model into something new and different, especially when transformation is conceived as the means of hiding a text's relation to its model, calls into question the possibility of identifying the model. A thoroughly dissimulated transformation would not be understood even by "the silent searching of the mind"; the relation between text and model disappears.[4]

Whether critics argue, in defense of Walcott, that he assimilates and/or transforms his influences, or against him, that he does not but other poets can and do, they begin by assuming that the goal of one text is to consume and digest previous texts. Thus critics commend Walcott for assimilating and/or transforming disparate ingredients whose distinctness must be perceptible in order to know that assimilation or transformation has occurred, yet whose indistinctness is being praised. The fully assimilated or transformed influence would be invisible, the unassimilated/untransformed one would take the form of a quotation, and the numberless gradations between would frustrate consistent discrimination. On the one hand, the originality of the later poet diminishes when the critic inspects the later poet's grandparents and great-grandparents as well as parents and cousins; on the other, a poet, far from *willing* the adaptation of the past, cannot help such adaptation (even Pierre Menard is an original author). And if the transformative criterion for originality demands a radical shift of perspective in relation to one branch of the poetic family tree, but not to another, it fails to define any necessary characteristic by which we may identify the original.

Walcott's most interesting thought on influence inhabits and even embraces these problems. Although Walcott's poems do of course alter

DEREK WALCOTT'S POETRY

the texts they use, Walcott does not emphasize difference, much less stake a claim to originality upon it. On the contrary, the poems overwhelm with correspondences the "transformations" they at first set up, their frames of reference expanding to unveil more and more influences. But the nonexistence of originality in Walcott does not imply, as in Walcott's paraphrase of Naipaul, that because language "is mimicry, [it is] uncreative."[5] Rather, language is mimicry, and creative to the extent that it is. Aware that "the relation between text and model disappears," Walcott welcomes this disappearance.

The inexorability of influence permeates Walcott's poetry from its early days. Walcott declares that "Fear of imitation obsesses minor poets" ("MH," 25), and he has never thought of himself as a minor poet; the poems collected in *In a Green Night* already echo other texts in sophisticated ways. However, this volume engages mostly Walcott's canonical Western precursors, from Marvell to Baudelaire. As I indicated earlier, Walcott used more often to ignore "the crude, popular forms" of art. He rarely acknowledged the influence of Third World poets like Césaire and Neruda. At the same time, as Paul Breslin notes, "In most of his early poems . . . Walcott writes exclusively from a Caribbean perspective,"[6] so that even as he uses canonical Western forms and themes he almost always applies them to local details, as though testing their universality. In his later work, especially between 1979 and 1987, these values almost reverse; Walcott's subject matter ranges beyond Caribbean settings, but his style incorporates more folklore and creole. In *Omeros* Walcott once again focuses tightly upon St. Lucia, and his style is once again the nominally high style of Dantean or Shelleyan *terza rima*. But by *Omeros* Walcott has loosened his, and likely the reader's, definition of the high style. Achille's canoe, *In God We Trust*, has a grand name, but Achille's endearing misspelling of "trust" gently questions grandiosity, naming, God, and trust. In Walcott's first book this sort of wordplay, if it occurred at all, would probably have sounded cynical. In *Omeros* Walcott's incorporation of a "mistake" only intensifies the accuracy of his language, giving the word "trust" a depth and an ambiguity we would not otherwise perceive in it. Achille insists that the "error" is normative: "Leave it! Is God' spelling and mine" (8).

Walcott has gradually acknowledged a wider range of influences, owning that his frame of reference extends beyond "high" art to Carnival, calypso, and folklore; beyond generic boundaries to Latin American novels, all manner of visual art, and film; and beyond presumed national and linguistic borders to a generous selection of contemporary poetry in translation. Although some of these genres and traditions have always played into Walcott's poetry, the poems become willing to reveal their relation to an increasing number of them, and to shift— exposing more subjectivity, relaxing their tones, varying strategies more freely—with the open ebb and flow of influence.

M A N Y O F W A L C O T T' S early poems begin with such unequivocal markers of intertextuality as epigraphs, quotations, and conspicuous allusions. "In a Green Night" refers to Marvell, "A Sea-Chantey" to Baudelaire, "Orient and Immortal Wheat" to Traherne, "Ruins of a Great House" to Browne, Donne, and Blake, and "Lotus Eater" to Homer and Tennyson. These poems assert little stylistic difference from the Western canon (although, as we will eventually see, it is not possible that they assert *no* difference). This does not mean, however, that they have no point to make about the Western masterpieces. Instead of claiming originality, they claim a common mimicry. By this Walcott means to avoid what he sees in "The Muse of History" as a too frequent postcolonial misstep:

> [W]hile many critics of contemporary Commonwealth verse reject imitation, the basis of the tradition, for originality, the false basis of innovation, they represent eventually the old patronizing attitude adapted to contemporaneous politics, for their demand for naturalness, novelty, originality, or truth is again based on preconceptions of behavior. (18)

"In a Green Night," "Brise Marine," and "Ruins of a Great House" (*IGN*, 73–74; 56; 19–20) connect themselves precisely to the nonoriginality of French and British literary traditions. They are thus politically meaningful because and not in spite of the fact that they are not separatist.

DEREK WALCOTT'S POETRY

The title poem of *In a Green Night* unfolds from a phrase in Marvell's "Bermudas": "He hangs in shades the orange bright, / Like golden lamps in a green night."[7] By isolating Marvell's phrase the poem implies that it begins "in" an "isle . . . long unknown," like the one we barely glimpse in "Bermudas." Walcott sharpens the focus of Marvell's lens, offering a closeup of the area which had always in the British canon been either a vision in a dream or a speck on the horizon. Walcott zooms in even further upon Marvell's orange tree:

> She has her winters and her spring,
> Her moult of leaves, which in their fall
> Reveal, as with each living thing,
> Zones truer than the tropical.
>
> For if by night each golden sun
> Burns in a comfortable creed,
> By noon harsh fires have begun
> To quail those splendours which they feed.
>
> Or mixtures of the dew and dust
> That early shone her orbs of brass,
> Mottle her splendours with the rust
> She sought all summer to surpass.

Walcott emphasizes the "living" and therefore mortal quality of the tropical nature Marvell's voyaging speakers idealize as "eternal spring." Walcott's orange trees, "green yet ageing," suffer the "cyclic chemistry" of "moult," "dew and dust," "rust," and "blight." While Marvell's narrators recall England's religious intolerance and praise their island as a natural "temple" in comparison, Walcott's lyric seems to reprove Marvell's by pointing out that religion, nature, and art alike are perishable, and that "each living thing" is therefore "doom[ed] and glorie[d]" by its mortality (the same fires both "quail" and "feed" splendor).

Yet the poem's relation to Marvell is not so simple. Walcott echoes not only Marvell's characteristic tetrameter but also the structure of "Bermudas." Walcott's first and last quatrains stand apart from the intervening ones; the last almost exactly repeats the first, enclosing the poem in a sphere (like an orange) inside which the body of the poem reveals mortal imperfection. In "Bermudas" the first and last quatrains stand apart because they alone belong to Marvell's principal narrator; the lines between are in quotation marks, spoken by a group "From a small boat." The sanguine opinions expressed there do not belong to Marvell's narrator, let alone to Marvell. Marvell, like Walcott, plants the seeds of the fall within paradise. "Eternal spring" rather ominously "enamels everything," and

> He makes the figs our mouths to meet,
> And throws the melons at our feet,
> But apples plants of such a price,
> No tree could ever bear them twice.

In "Bermudas" paradise cannot be sustained, or "[borne] twice"; its "price" is inevitably another Fall. Although Marvell's pilgrims sound "holy and . . . cheerful," and claim that they are on the verge of a new Eden, "all the way, to guide their chime, / With *falling* oars they kept the time" (italics mine). Since "Bermudas" itself disavows the possibility of paradise within earthly "time," "In a Green Night" reflects much more than Marvell's meter. Along with local differences we find extensive sympathies. The two poems agree more than they disagree. Since Walcott's point is that creeds and oranges *inevitably* contain the seeds of their own fall, the poem can only gain credibility from the fact that Marvell's lyric comes to the same conclusion. Most of Walcott's early poems deal with canonical texts in the same way, establishing links of sensibility beneath a veneer of difference.

"Brise Marine" (*IGN*, 56) is the most complex of the early poems in its variety of influences. It seems to outline its difference from the Mallarmé poem whose title it reproduces, but also quotes Ben Jonson and stylistically echoes Hart Crane. Although the poem is ostensibly an unexceptional love lyric, its vision of influence is indispensable. "Brise Marine" not only describes the poet's stances toward the French, British, and North American traditions, but takes the relation between literary influence and influence in the largest, metaphorical sense—influx of experience—as its theme. While one might at first distinguish between Walcott's uncritical reference to Jonson, for example, and his apparent criticism of Mallarmé, his apparent criticisms, as in "In a Green Night," themselves turn up evidence of affinities.

The poem quickly raises the question of its relation to other poems. First, a poem in English with a title in a another language immediately transmits its doubleness, holding out the possibility that it might imitate or parody some mode from another culture. The title does not divulge whether the poem will do homage to Mallarmé or make fun of the exotic possibility it calls to mind. The possibilities in the balance here arise particularly often in Caribbean culture, where African, English, French, and other sources at the very least triple a poet's consciousness. Second, the reader will notice Walcott's anomalous style in "Brise Marine," since he is not prone to fragmentary statement or minimal punctuation. Here fragmentariness is bound up with the fallibility of memory:

> K with quick laughter, honey skin and hair,
> and always money. In what beach shade, what year
> has she so scented with her gentleness
> I cannot watch bright water but think of her
> and that fine morning when she sang O rare
> Ben's lyric of "the bag o' the bee"
> and "the nard in the fire"
>   "nard in the fire"
> against the salty music of the sea
> the fresh breeze tangling each honey tress
>   and what year was the fire?
> Girls' faces dim with time, Andreuille all gold . . .
> Sunday. The grass peeps through the breaking pier.
> Tables in the trees, like entering Renoir.
> *Maintenant je n'ai plus ni fortune, ni pouvoir . . .*
> But when the light was setting through thin hair,
> Holding whose hand by what trees, what old wall.
>
> Two honest women, Christ, where are they gone?
> Out of that wonder, what do I recall?
> The darkness closing round a fisherman's oar.
> The sound of water gnawing at bright stone.

The poet introduces events—that the woman sang on a beach, that she sang in the past—within the unanswerable questions he asks about them, questions which envelop the events in uncertainty. Details, traced backward, fade into an amorphous past. The speaker has lost the song's particular place and time; the first sentence, a verbless fragment, has no tense, and the following lines break down into sentences that never finish at all. What follows is only a series of lost facts and connections. The second sentence has not only no end, but no object: the woman has not scented the beach shade, but has scented something (missing now) *"In* [a] beach shade"; "year" may be either the thing scented or the period in which something else was scented. Because the first four lines are grammatically incomplete, the cause and effect relation implied between the fourth and fifth lines, which appear to tie the woman's scenting something to the poet's current state—"I cannot watch bright water but think of her"—also falls into doubt. The continual truncation of the sentences, a visible erosion like K's missing name, implies that time and the elements have worn the poem's events from the poet's memory. Adhering to this truncation as to a form, "Brise Marine," although it does not quite pretend to be a fragment, does pretend to fragmentariness. This incoherent air lends what details remain in the poem a sense of anonymous inevitability, as though, like many an ancient love lyric, it had been written by different hands. Walcott values a similar effect in Perse and Césaire ("MH," 14).

The central agent of erosion, the "bright water," has claimed the speaker's misplaced song; the Jonson lyric originally sung "against" the sea's rival "salty music" now forms part of the poet's experience of the sea. In this way the details that filter out of the poem (out of memory altogether) still influence the larger, more impersonal world they rejoin. Therefore, although the sea has swallowed up the singing's particulars, this one performance also forever alters the sea: "I *cannot* watch bright water but think of her." This interpenetration of song with sea transfers Bloom's apophrades, in which "the tyranny of time almost is overturned, and one can believe, for startled moments, that [poets] are being *imitated by their ancestors,*"[8] to the relation between artifice and nature: the sea which precedes the song is now redolent of the song as well as vice versa. The now partially forgotten experience of song has entered into a "correspondence," as Baudelaire would say, with the permanent sea, which now contains "lost" experience in a condensed form. Influence becomes something larger than the relationship between an inside and an outside, or between two individuals. It becomes the fluid and unavoidable medium in which life moves.

In Mallarmé's "Brise Marine" (1866), the poet feels an irresistible attraction toward the tropics, but realizes the journey's impossibility:

> La chair est triste, hélas! et j'ai lu tous les livres.
> Fuir! là-bas fuir! Je sens que des oiseaux sont ivres
> D'être parmi l'écume inconnue et les cieux!
> Rien, ni les vieux jardins reflétés par les yeux
> Ne retiendra ce coeur qui dans la mer se trempe
> O nuits! ni la clarté déserte de ma lampe
> Sur le vide papier que la blancheur défend
> Et ni la jeune femme allaitant son enfant.
> Je partirai! Steamer balançant ta mâture,
> Lève l'ancre pour une exotique nature!
>
> Un Ennui, désolé par les cruels espoirs,
> Croit encore à l'adieu suprême des mouchoirs!
> Et, peut-être, les mâts, invitant les orages
> Sont-ils de ceux qu'un vent penche sur les naufrages
> Perdus, sans mâts, sans mâts, ni fertiles îlots . . .
> Mais, ô mon coeur, entends le chant des matelots![9]

> [The flesh is sad, alas! And I've read all the books. To flee!
> Flee out there! I feel the birds are drunk at being amid
> the unknown foam and the clouds! Nothing, not the old
> gardens reflected in eyes, will restrain this heart which
> dips itself in the sea, O nights! Not the desolate clarity of
> my lamp on the blank paper, which its whiteness
> defends, and not the young woman nursing her child. I'll
> be off! Steamer balancing your mast, lift anchor for an
> exotic nature!
>
> An ennui, laid low by cruel hopes, still believes in the
> great goodbye of handkerchiefs! And, perhaps, the masts
> inviting storms are those a wind bends over lost
> shipwrecks, without masts, without masts, nor fertile
> islands . . . But, O my heart, listen to the sailors' song!]

The elements for which the poet longs, he knows, ultimately destroy the individual self in the shipwreck he foresees. Nevertheless, he pursues his vision at the risk of annihilation. Although he doesn't lift anchor within the frame of the poem, the poet turns in his last words toward the sailors' sirenlike song.

Again, by focusing his scene within the "exotic nature" that Mallarmé's poet only anticipates, Walcott's poem makes Mallarmé's hypothetical tropic more concrete, and takes for granted the danger Mallarmé's poem "discovers." While Mallarmé's poet vows he will not be kept from departing ("Rien . . . / Ne retiendra ce coeur"), Walcott's already drifts at the vagaries of the elements, time, and memory, and doesn't seem to have had a choice in the matter. Further, a native poet might point out that "exotic nature" is a contradiction in terms; nature is "by nature" not exotic, and in all nature the battle of elements is always as absorbing, as full of freedom and indeterminacy. The self-loss Mallarmé envisions as "shipwreck" quietly and continually permeates Walcott's "Brise Marine" in commonplace occurrences, in "The darkness closing round a fisherman's oar"—the loss at once more specific and less remarkable.

Mallarmé's poem itself, however, revises a poetic precursor, Baudelaire's "L'Invitation au Voyage" (1855),[10] in which the hero dreams of a pastoral tropic reflecting his idyllic love for a woman ("[un] pays qui te ressemble [a country that looks like you]") without considering the difficulty of getting there.[11] In the context of this comparison Mallarmé's avowals to disregard all human and physical barriers parody Baudelaire's would-be serenity, and his domestic ennui parodies Baudelaire's *acedia*. Most of Mallarmé's "Brise Marine" actually catalogues the temptations (the old gardens, the lamplight, the young woman nursing) that might keep him at home. Although the poet introduces each with a negative, if he introduces them at all he does not disregard them. In the final line the poet seizes upon the "chant des matelots," instructing his heart to listen to it as though it wished to do something else. When we read the poem beside "L'Invitation au Voyage," Mallarmé's vision of paradisal shipwreck seems not unlike Walcott's postcolonial knowledge that "the old vision of paradise wrecks here" ("MH," 6).

Nor can we stop here. Walcott calls "the isle of Cythera" a "sick . . . recurrence in French thought" ("MH," 6); Baudelaire's "Un Voyage à Cythère" itself, however, could hardly be more self-critical, ending as it does with a prayer for "le courage / De contempler mon coeur et mon corps sans dégoût [the courage / To contemplate my heart and body without disgust]." In 1862 Baudelaire published another version of "L'Invitation" in prose, calling the new piece by the same title.[12] As Barbara Johnson writes, "[T]he function of the prose poem is precisely to reveal what poetry is blind to about itself, not by in turn opposing the poetic as such, but by making its functioning more explicit."[13] In this second "Invitation" Baudelaire adds "c'est là qu'il faut aller mourir [There one must go to die]" to "C'est là qu'il faut aller vivre [There one must go to live]," likens the pastoral tropic's relation to other lands to that between art and nature, and emphasizes its inaccessibility: "plus l'âme est ambitieuse et délicate, plus les rêves s'éloignent du possible. . . . Vivrons-nous jamais, passerons-nous jamais dans ce tableau qu'a peint mon esprit, ce tableau qui te ressemble [the more ambitious and delicate the soul is, the more dreams recede from the possible. . . . Shall we ever live, ever pass into this picture my soul has painted, this picture which resembles you]?" This passage draws still further upon one from Pascal—"Nous ne vivrons jamais, mais nous espérons de vivre [We never live, but hope to live]."[14] The pessimistic and sedentary Pascal, as Bishop reminds us in "Questions of Travel," suggested that perhaps one is better off "just sitting quietly in one's room."[15] In Mallarmé's ironic echo of Baudelaire, and in Baudelaire's qualifying self-revision and reference to Pascal, these paradisal voyages contain their own foreknowledge of shipwreck. Lest we think that Walcott, Mallarmé, and Baudelaire concur only in their assessment of the elements' destructiveness, recall that Walcott's "A Sea-Chantey" unironically takes its epigraph from Baudelaire's first, "innocent" "Invitation" of 1855; recall also that Walcott's fusion of the beloved with the destructive elements, as he loses her song in the sea, and the sea in her song, occurs in Baudelaire's prose poem as well:

. . . ne pourrais-tu pas te mirer, pour parler comme les mystiques, dans ta propre *correspondance*? . . . Tu les [mes pensées] conduis doucement vers la mer qui est l'Infini . . . et quand . . . ils rentrent au port natal, ce sont encore mes pensées enrichies qui reviennent de l'Infini vers toi. (254–55)

[couldn't you mirror yourself, to speak as the mystics do, in your own *correspondence*? . . . You lead [my thoughts] sweetly toward the sea, which is the Infinite . . . and when . . . they re-enter their native port, my thoughts return enriched from the Infinite toward you.]

Walcott's lyric finally "owes" more to Mallarmé and Baudelaire than would at first seem. More important, the poem resists concepts of ownership and debt, and the separation that ownership—whether of a phrase, song, or memory—entails. "Brise Marine" does disclose its distance from Mallarmé's "Brise Marine," but as the Mallarmé and Baudelaire poems show, a poem can just as easily disclose distance from itself. Since both difference and correspondence are inescapable, difference per se is hardly remarkable. "Brise Marine"'s images of gradual seepage, of "the light . . . setting through thin hair" (16), "The grass peep[ing] through the breaking pier" (13), imply substances that are separable in abstraction but nonetheless interpenetrate upon closer inspection. All the while Walcott interpenetrates his precursors' texts by the very act of reiterating, as Johnson writes of Baudelaire, "the 'same theme' . . . in order to question both the idea of *same* and the idea of *theme*" (43).

At least this is where we end up if we pursue Walcott's allusive title. We end up somewhere else altogether if we pursue Walcott's allusion within the poem to Jonson's "A Celebration of Charis in Ten Lyrick Peeces."[16] The lyric Walcott quotes, "Her Triumph," gathers together several images of fragility: "a bright Lillie," "the fall o' the Snow," "the wooll of Bever," "Swans Downe," "the bud o' the Brier," "the Nard in the fire," and "the bag of the Bee" (92). That Walcott quotes two ("'nard in the fire,'" "'the bag o' the bee'") comes as no surprise, since "Brise Marine" too is about fragility, particularly of memory. Yet once again "there is something else going on." Walcott's reference to Jonson simultaneously refers to Pound, who echoes Jonson's "Celebration" in *The Pisan Cantos*:

> Serenely in the crystal jet
>   as the bright ball that the fountain tosses
> (Verlaine) as diamond clearness
>   How soft the wind under Taishan
>   where the sea is remembered
> . . . .
> This liquid is certainly a
>   property of the mind
> nec accidens est   but an element
>   in the mind's make-up
> est agens and functions   dust to fountain pan otherwise
>   Hast 'ou seen the rose in the steel dust
>   (or swansdown ever?)
> so light is the urging, so ordered the dark petals of iron
> we who have passed over Lethe.[17]

To all appearances, Walcott's "Brise Marine" "owes" even more to Pound, to whom he does not directly refer, than to Mallarmé or Jonson.[18] Walcott's sympathy with Pound, like his sympathy with Jonson, is in part thematic. In *The Pisan Cantos*, too, the sea's fluidity becomes a human property, the "element" of water an "element / in the mind's make-up." On the one hand, memories and ideas are difficult to hold in the medium of the mind, as though we had "passed over Lethe," and this perplexes the poet's task. On the other, we cannot completely extricate ourselves from recollection, as though we had passed *up* Lethe. Mental fluidity does not destroy memories, but it does keep them from becoming "dust to fountain pan otherwise," and provides a corrective to the desire for poetic form. In other words, the poet needs the Dionysian buoyancy and "diamond clearness" of Verlaine's fountain, a "light urging," as much as the order of "iron." We might say, combining the metallic and the watery, that the poet needs not a "fountain pan" but a "fountain *pen*."

Again, we expect thematic similitude from an allusion, but Walcott's sympathy with Pound is as much stylistic as thematic. "Brise Marine"'s fragmentation is patently peculiar for Walcott, who usually writes *of* fragmentation *with* coherence. In very few poems does he indent lines for no obvious reason, as he indents "'nard in the fire'" here; very few of Walcott's poems do with this little punctuation. These formal anomalies and other mannerisms such as the abridged questions ("what beach shade, what year")[19] are at once explained, in fact *only* explained, when we see the poem in relation to *The Cantos.* It is Pound whose mania is "always money," whose indentations are irregular, who often abbreviates names to initials like "K"—and Pound whose every other phrase echoes one from Verlaine, Jonson, or elsewhere, as nearly every phrase in Walcott's poem echoes one in Pound.[20]

Pound's attitude toward his own mimicry is fruitfully ambivalent. He writes, also in *The Pisan Cantos,* of "A swollen magpie in a fitful sun, / Half black half white" (521), commanding it to give up its vanity. The lines refer to the poet himself, and to artists in general (Walcott's further mimicry lends them a kind of mock-prophetic resonance). It would seem, here, that the magpie loses its dignity and even its identity by eating too many stolen delicacies. The last stanza of this famous passage, however, pivoting on a "But," ends by defending Pound's technique: "To have gathered from the air a live tradition" "is *not* vanity" (522; italics mine).

Walcott writes in "Culture or Mimicry?" that mimicry is the state in which "every sentence is a quotation" (6). By this standard "Brise Marine," going out of its way to mimic a mimic, would be the classic model. But the poem is also typical for the deviousness of its allusiveness. Walcott's title points us one way, his quotations from Jonson another, the style of the poem yet another. While my preceding remarks about Mallarmé, Baudelaire, and Pascal are true for what they're worth, in and of themselves they make "Brise Marine"'s poetic ancestry seem more stable than it is. Walcott does not, or not only, align himself with or against a certain tradition. Like Pound, he veers off in several directions at once—more an exploding pinwheel than an arrow. As Lowell writes of his own work, "[T]he echoes are so innumerable that [we] almost lack the fineness of ear to distinguish them."[21]

Thus a poem with a conspicuous French title may not be French through and through, however much it looks so. When we realize this, we realize that we come to poetry with a throng of ready-made assumptions, not to call them prejudices, about tones, forms, modes, and entire traditions we believe we can recognize. Reading Walcott with this attitude—the ordinary and inevitable attitude of experienced readers—can be fatal. We bite at the lure of the title only to find that, after all, Walcott's poet most resembles Mallarmé's in that he too has "read all the books."

I mentioned Vendler's praise of "The Season of Phantasmal Peace," her remark that unlike earlier poems which "borrowed theatrically" (23) from Yeats, it is "unashamed in its debt to Shakespeare, Keats, and the Bible; but . . . has assimilated them all into its own fabric" (27). In this context that observation is worth another glance. "The Season of Phantasmal Peace" begins,

> Then all the nations of birds lifted together
> the huge net of the shadows of this earth
> in multitudinous dialects, twittering tongues,
> stitching and crossing it. They lifted up
> the shadows of long pines down trackless slopes,
> the shadows of glass-faced towers down evening streets,
> the shadow of a frail plant on a city sill—
> the net rising soundless as night, the birds' cries soundless. . . .
> (*FT*, 98)

Vendler's comparisons to Shakespeare, Keats, and the Bible ring intuitively true—especially the Bible, perhaps because of Walcott's catalog of shadows. If Walcott's longer eighth line—so irregular as no longer to be iambic really, with its repetition of "soundless" and its trailing, descriptive dependent clause—does not too closely follow Shakespeare or Keats, assimilation is all about inexactitude. Mimicry is not. In Lattimore's *Iliad* we can read,

> These, as the multitudinous nations of birds winged,
> of geese, and of cranes, and of swans long-throated
> in the Asian meadow beside the Kaÿstrian waters

this way and that way make their flights in the pride of their wings, then
settle in clashing swarms and the whole meadow echoes with them,
so of these the multitudinous tribes from the ships and
shelters poured to the plain of Skamandros, and the earth beneath their
feet and under the feet of their horses thundered horribly.
They took position in the blossoming meadow of Skamandros,
thousands of them, as leaves and flowers appear in their season.

(88)

Where is peace more "phantasmal" than in *The Iliad*? In Homer even "nations of birds" are not peaceable; they are noisy, clashing "batallions" (thus Walcott insists on silence in his own poem). Moreover, the birds possess a doubly fictive life, more ghostly than the "tribes"'; there are birds in this passage only insofar as the tribes resemble them. These lines are also "phantasmal," in other words, because they are metaphoric. In "The Season of Phantasmal Peace" a metaphoric suspension, equivalent to the suspension of pastoral, overtakes the *whole* horizon (but does not last long).

Vendler's observation is accurate. But it is Lattimore, if anyone, who has assimilated Shakespeare, Keats, and the Bible, while Walcott has swallowed Lattimore whole. As when "Brise Marine"'s only reference to Pound *is* its reference to Jonson, this is mimicry almost in the biological sense, as when a butterfly prized by birds disguises itself as a leaf. Or mimicry's own mirror image, as when a large, guileless, brightly colored one tastes very bitter.

In "Ruins of a Great House" (*IGN*, 19–20) Walcott again plunges into a potentially infinite regression of mimicries, each of which possesses political resonance. Walcott places the British conquest of St. Lucia at the end of an originless chain of conquests including the Roman colonization of Britain. This almost archaeological probing of history ultimately undermines British claims to imperial authority by showing that the British themselves were once upstart postcolonials. Walcott links himself by epigraph and quotation to Browne and Donne, two canonical authors. But these canonical authors likewise

DEREK WALCOTT'S POETRY

remind England that it is only a former "colony" and an "island," and conceive systems of interconnections that challenge national and class boundaries.

Walcott's poem lies in the tradition of the medieval and Renaissance *ubi sunt* lyric. The poet, an outsider, a parasite among "the padded cavalry of the mouse," "climb[s] a wall" to examine the ruins of a colonial house and meditate on the demise of its "deciduous beauty":

> Stones only, the disjecta membra of this Great House,
> Whose moth-like girls are mixed with candledust,
> Remain to file the lizard's dragonish claws. . . .
> . . . .
> Marble like Greece, like Faulkner's South in stone,
> Deciduous beauty prospered and is gone,
> But where the lawn breaks in a rash of trees
> A spade below dead leaves will ring the bone
> Of some dead animal or human thing
> Fallen from evil days, from evil times. . . .
> . . . .
> The imperious rakes are gone, their bright girls gone,
> The river flows, obliterating hurt.
> I climbed a wall with the grille ironwork
> Of exiled craftsmen protecting that great house
> From guilt, perhaps, but not from the worm's rent
> Nor from the padded cavalry of the mouse.

Climbing "the grille ironwork" wall made by "exiled craftsmen" reminds the poet of his own complicity as a postcolonial artisan. Still, however such trappings of culture as craft may "[protect] that great house / From guilt, perhaps" while it thrives, craft cannot save it from death the leveler, "from the worm's rent." This thought sparks both a "coal of compassion" for the colonials as mortal individuals and a blaze of "rage" for their victims:

> Ablaze with rage I thought,
> Some slave is rotting in this manorial lake,

> But still the coal of my compassion fought
> That Albion too was once
> A colony like ours, "part of the continent, piece of the main." . . .
> . . . . All in compassion ends
> So differently from what the heart arranged:
> "as well as if a manor of thy friend's . . ."

The poet, seemingly caught between compassion for "the imperious rakes" and for the slave, simultaneously experiences the conflict as a difference within his own racially mixed identity. Again, he cannot be described as "between" conflicting emotions, since the two emotions can also be seen as one: the poet describes *both* emotions as species of fire, so that "compassion" is not, itself, unimpassioned.

Walcott approaches quietism here, always a danger in his work. "Ruins of a Great House" proposes no concrete solution, and does not seem "historical" except in the most generalized way. Still, the poem does propose an anti-imperialist literary tradition. The poem is markedly intertextual, framed by its epigraph from Browne's *Urn Burial* and its closing quotation from Meditation XVII of Donne's *Devotions*, and contains many other allusions.[22] Walcott's quotations here gesture toward ancient underlying traditions. Similarly, the poet's studies are casually archaeological, probing beneath surfaces to imagine the slave in the lake and perhaps even older corpses: "A spade below dead leaves will ring the bone / Of some dead animal or human thing / Fallen from evil days, from evil times." Walcott's attitude toward time here becomes paleological. Below the vegetable layer of leaves the spade will unearth a creature whose uncertain species recalls the interminable, vague period when "man" had not even taken its current shape.

By studying the ruins of civilization as archaeologist rather than as heir or slave, Walcott follows Browne, whose *Urn Burial* provides the poem's epigraph: "though our longest sun sets at right declensions and makes but winter arches, it cannot be long before we lie down in darkness, and have our light in ashes."[23] Since Browne believes the urns upon which he reflects are Roman, property of the one-time colonizers of Britain, he stands in relation to his urns as Walcott does to the "great house." Browne's preface muses upon history's ironic turn of events, and contrasts contemporary public reactions to the discoveries of Roman, as opposed to British, relics:

> When the bones of King *Arthur* were digged up, the old Race might think, they beheld therein some Originals of themselves; Unto these of our Urnes none here can pretend relation, and can only behold the Reliques of those persons, who in their life giving the Law unto their predecessors, after long obscurity, now lye at their mercies. But remembring the early civility they brought upon these Countreys, and forgetting long passed mischiefs; We mercifully preserve their bones, and pisse not upon their ashes. (116–17)

In his last sentence, which apparently bestows forgiveness on the former oppressors, Browne introduces several ambiguities. First, we don't usually say that "civility" is "brought upon" a country. A misfortune is more often "brought upon" one, so this civility sounds like a mixed blessing. Second, Browne can't really forget "long passed mischiefs" and declare them forgotten at the same time; if he had truly forgotten them, he wouldn't bring them up. The "mischiefs" are forgiven rather than forgotten, therefore, and ironically forgiven at that, since Browne relishes outdoing the ancient Romans in civility by forgiving them. In spite, then, of the "civility" the Romans "brought upon" them, the present-day British resolve not to revere Roman bones but merely to "preserve" them and "pisse not upon their ashes." For this the British may count themselves "merciful," and the Romans, since they "lye at their mercies," ought to be grateful. Browne's pseudocivilized promise itself echoes a Roman predecessor, however. In the *Ars Poetica* Horace is already concerned with ruins: "Man's structures will crumble; / so how can the glory and charm of speech remain perpetual?"[24] In this context, Horace wonders why the "mad" poet "persists in writing poetry. Is it / a judgement for pissing on his father's ashes, or has he profaned / a gruesome place where lightning has struck?" (203). For Horace poetry is necessarily ephemeral; poets "persist" in building what they know will fall. If they have profaned or vandalized their predecessors, they will surely also be profaned and vandalized simply by virtue of having written. This predicament cannot be avoided; it requires the perspectival shift of Horatian irony as acknowledgment. The "gruesome place," profanation of ancestors, ashes, and concern for historical and poetical ruins in this passage still echo, through Browne, in Walcott's "Ruins of a Great House."

Browne reserves some irony for his countrymen, too, since the kinship they assume to King Arthur's bones is delusory and self-centered. They "might think" that "they beheld therein some Originals of themselves," as if the bones held significance only because these ancestors made modern life possible. The selectively simplified genealogy that would recognize British descent from King Arthur, but not from the Romans,[25] misses the point of the discoveries, and glorifies the empire that Britain in its turn had become rather than grasping the danger in the whole concept of empire. Browne corrects this oversimplified perspective, asserting that empires are mere "morsell[s] for the Earth, whereof all things are but a *colonie*" (138; italics mine).

In the end "Ruins of a Great House" asks whether anything remains after human civilizations vanish and offers two answers, one bitter ("The rot remains with us, the men are gone") and one, immediately following and turning on its reference to Donne, ambiguously poised over the opposition of murderer-poet to slave-poet: "But, as dead ash is lifted in a wind / That fans the blackening ember of the mind, / My eyes burned from the ashen prose of Donne." The dead are like ash and the living, fire; still, Donne's "dead ash" has power to affect the living "ember" of the poet's mind, and "burn[s]" his eyes as though with tears. Although Walcott expresses his meeting with Donne as a contest between ash and ember, two fires battle *within* the poet as well. He is hardly less different from himself than from Donne, for he finds himself "Ablaze with anger" at the thought of the slave, while the "coal of [his] compassion"[26] returns him to a more ancient history which reveals that conquerors have also been subjects: "Albion too was once / A colony like ours, 'part of the continent, piece of the main.'" Here and in the poem's last line (" 'as well as if a manor of thy friend's . . .' "), Donne's words finish Walcott's thoughts. Walcott quotes the famous passage from Meditation XVII of Donne's *Devotions*:

No man is an *Iland*, intire of it selfe; every man is a peece of the *Continent*, a part of the *maine*; if a *Clod* bee washed away by the *Sea*,

DEREK WALCOTT'S POETRY

Europe is the lesse, as well as if a *Promontorie* were, as well as if a
Mannor of thy *friends* or of *thine owne* were; any mans *death*
diminishes *me*, because I am involved in *Mankinde*. . . . Neither can
we call this a *begging* of *Miserie* or a *borrowing* of *Miserie*, as though
we were not miserable enough of our selves, but must fetch in more
from the next house, in taking upon us the *Miserie* of our
Neighbours. Truly it were an excusable *covetousnesse* if we did; for
affliction is a *treasure*, and scarce any man hath *enough* of it.[27]

Donne refutes those who would ignore the misery of others by using
property as a figure for affliction, and robbery—"fetch[ing] in more
from the next house"—as a figure for pity. But he does so by employing
these same supposedly unseemly analogies. He discards the figure of
"begging" and the sentiment that produces it—"Neither can we call this
a *begging* of *Miserie"*—yet in the next breath makes a full turn, declaring not that the sentiment takes the wrong direction, but that it doesn't
go far enough: *"Truly it were* an excusable covetousnesse if we did; for
affliction *is* a treasure" (emphases mine). Walcott, whose poet literally
"trespasses," trespasses precisely upon Donne's notion of property.
That is, both Donne and Walcott contemplate the definition of the
"proper," asking in what the *selfsame* consists and finding that it depends upon the "other." Likewise, Walcott's quotations (including this
very quotation from Donne) question the idea of literature as property.
Walcott, using the same metaphor of housebreaking, applies Donne's
notion of *"begging* of *Miserie"* to the Third World, which is "miserable
enough of [itself]" to an extreme degree. The misery of colonial victims
(the "slave . . . rotting in [the] manorial lake") presses against the
poet's ability to pity their oppressors. But if on the one hand we hoard
our security, on the other we may hoard the sense of our own victimization. Both efforts are misguided insofar as conquest is an endless
regression (and is not this regression itself one meaning of the literal,
heraldic *mise en abîme*, the depiction specifically of *shields* within
shields?). Although Britons and postcolonials do not suffer *simultaneously*, imperialism harms both. Walcott's poet does not excuse "Ancestral murderers," but he does just manage to retain his ability to feel
compassion for them. He can do so partly because the archaeological

view of history shifts his focus from individuals to such concepts as imperialism, which have caused suffering from "Greece" to "Albion" to St. Lucia. By retracing part of the endless chain of conquests Walcott tries to avoid detaching a particular piece of history (piece of the main). He cannot account for all the empires that have ever existed, but he can at least set us thinking about the principles that lead back from one to another. Walcott appropriates pieces of the manners (manors) of Donne and Browne, stealing his ancestors' afflictions, and the ancestors from whom he steals encourage such theft. Perhaps, as Horace intimates, there is something inherently transgressive about writing poetry. If Walcott's poet is a trespasser and even a thief, so is Hermes, the inventor of language.

The lyric poetry of Walcott's middle period, dominated by *Another Life* and the spartan poems of *Sea Grapes*, usually engages prior texts less obviously. But in 1974 Walcott writes his two most important essays, "The Caribbean: Culture or Mimicry?" and "The Muse of History." In these pieces Walcott argues the impossibility of originality, attacking originality for its dependence upon linear time. "The Muse of History" develops a theoretical foundation for Walcott's uses of prior poems. Whereas "Culture or Mimicry?" addresses itself to an "interamerican" audience, "The Muse of History" addresses primarily Caribbean poets and critics; "interamericans" listen as eavesdroppers. It is therefore narrower, yet thematically more rambling, encompassing religion and history, epic and lyric. Still, because it begins as a defense of what Walcott calls the "patrician" (1) or "classic" (3) postcolonial style, it bears directly upon Walcott's stylistic openness to the West. In "The Muse of History" the immemorial impossibility of originality places all poets under the same burden and the same freedom, which burden and freedom, existing simultaneously, form a unity and not a contradiction—or, more accurately, a unity *and* a contradiction—in the figure of "the poet carrying entire cultures in his head, bitter perhaps, but unencumbered" ("MH," 3).

The essay, divided into six rather distinct parts, asserts that "patrician" writers "reject the idea of history as time" to see it instead as "myth" (2). Its first two parts describe and take a side in an ongoing dispute. On one side, poets who unduly adore "the muse of history "think of language as enslavement" (2). The literature of this muse "serves historical truth" and therefore "yellows into polemic or evaporates in pathos" (2); in addition, "as history it is forced to exclude certain contradictions, for history cannot be ambiguously recorded" (22). Belief in history as "myth," "fiction," and "simultaneity" (2), and in the object world as a series of renewals, in contrast, embodies "the revolutionary spirit at its deepest . . . recall[ing] the spirit to arms" (3). The poets Walcott admires (all American) are rhapsodically discontinuous, inspired by immanence rather than lodged in chronology. Whitman and Neruda are "exuberan[t]" (3), Césaire and Perse "elat[ed]" (17); even Borges "celebrates an elation which is vulgar and abrupt" (3). Further, the object world that enchants these poets is itself fluid, so that "[t]his is not the jaded cynicism which sees nothing new under the sun, it is an elation which sees everything as renewed" (3).

In the third part of the essay Walcott ponders the brutality of "New World history," its "tiring cycles of stupidity and greed" (4). At a parallel point in "Culture or Mimicry?," as we have seen, Walcott suggests that "the degradations have already been endured . . . to the point of irrelevancy" ("CM," 6), so that "[i]n the Caribbean history is irrelevant" and the loss of history produces "imagination as necessity, as invention" ("CM," 6).[28] In "The Muse of History" Walcott again welcomes the "amnesia" of the slave, because it forces the slave to reinvent his world: "That amnesia is the true history of the New World" (4). Slaves and the American poets who are their descendants must, like Crusoe, rebuild everything, "recreat[ing]. . . the entire order, from religion to the simplest domestic rituals" (5). Walcott doesn't specify here that this predicament can be seen as a metaphor for art, although he does imply that it is a metaphor for American poetry. This implication is clear, however, in Walcott's own Crusoe poems.[29]

The fourth and fifth parts of "The Muse of History" move on to discuss African-American Christianity in relation to "Eliot's pronouncement, that a culture cannot exist without a religion" (11). Can a culture then survive a conversion to its invaders' religion, and "can an African culture exist . . . without an African religion?" (8). By way of example Walcott explores some "revivalist poems[']" (9) potential to express resignation or defiance. "I'm going to lay down my sword and shield" at first seems "the most contemptible expression of the beaten" (10). On second thought, however, Walcott detects "a note of aggression" as well as "simple fortitude" (11) in the African-American repetition of Christian hymns. Through Christianity "the slave . . . wrest[s] God from his captor" (11). This movement recurs in the relation of the African-American poet to the Western poetic tradition. In fact, African-American poetic and religious traditions meet in the religious song: in the beginning of African-American Christianity "what we can look at as our poetic tradition begins" (13). Thus Walcott once again founds a species of American art upon an act of mimicry, at a beginning that by virtue of that act is not absolute.

To see what becomes of that unoriginal origin Walcott skips hundreds of years, down to Perse and Césaire, two Caribbean Modernists, "one from privilege, the other from deprivation" (13). Walcott finds "authority" and "form" in both poets, but also "sources . . . ancient and contemporary" and "the appearance of translation from an older epic which invests their poems with an air of legend" (14). Walcott, far from admiring the invisible assimilation of sources, admires the opacity of "original" poetry that *seems translated*. Walcott chooses his ancestors deliberately here. Perse and Césaire are the literary equivalents of Walcott's own familial and cultural lines, paternal and maternal, "white" and "black": "one patrician and conservative, the other proletarian and revolutionary, classic and romantic, Prospero and Caliban, all such opposites balance easily, but they balance on the axis of a shared sensibility" (16). Their pairing comforts Walcott, since his own identity cannot be composed simply of opposites when the Perse/Césaire relation is one of more than resemblance: "Sometimes they sound identical" (15). However, Walcott adds, "One is not making out a case for assimilation and the common simplicity of all men, we are interested in their differences, openly, but what astonishes us in both poets is their elation . . . in possibility" (17). The differences between Perse and Césaire *form* their "axis of . . . shared sensibility," joining and dividing them like the halves of Walcott's globe-fruit, "seamed by its own bitter juice" (27).

The final part of "The Muse of History," subtitled "On History as Exile," broadens the essay's scope and increases its polemical stridency. Once again Walcott sets up an apparent choice: on one side "the colonial in exile," cynical and envious of Western culture; on the other, "the generation after him, which wants to effect a eugenic leap" to Africa (21). And once again Walcott observes that the two sides are undone by their common assumptions. Both parties are "children of the nineteenth-century ideal . . . the hallucination of imperial romance" (22).[30] Even so, Walcott expends the strength of his attack on younger, leftist Caribbean poets, who, he believes, "begin to see poetry as a form of historical instruction" and form "as critical strategy" (22). Walcott suggests a definition of "blackness" more meaningful to him, one that crosses "racial" and cultural boundaries: "the term 'black' . . . impl[ies] a malevolence toward historical system" (24). Old World writers like Beckett and Ted Hughes, as well as New World writers like Wilson Harris, "write blackly," "[b]ut this blackness is luminous" (24). By constructing this anticategory Walcott half-parodies the ordering "process of the sociologist" (17) which peeves him so. And even as Walcott ponders the apparent choice between exiled colonial and native radical, his subtitle indicates that exile is not a choice at all but the condition of being in history.

Walcott's shrill indictments of political and didactic literature in "The Muse of History" tend to distract one from the essay's aesthetic interest—although, as his choice of Césaire may have been meant to indicate, he seems more provoked by what he perceives as the dominant style of Caribbean political writing than by its content.[31] Walcott's own shifting and sometimes contradictory terms, too, obscure his argument. Walcott uses the same informal critical metaphors for influence as his reviewers do, metaphors that imply either combat or digestion: New World writers may either "wrestle with [their] past" or "assimilat[e] . . . the features of every ancestor" (1). His ideas of history as myth, Borgesian "instant archaism," repetition and similarity grading into identity, immanence as ongoing renewal, and so on, are not done justice by these indifferent figures of speech (although Walcott does sometimes use them ironically). Still, the essay's re-examination of imitation and originality cannot be mistaken. "The Muse of History" suggests that Walcott sees his own intertextuality as part of a communal poetic "flux" (12). Although Walcott sometimes romanticizes that community, its character is in the end ambivalent: by participating in this "flux" the poet may be helping to weave a forever-unfinished tapestry, or breaking rocks in an endless chain gang.

WHILE MANY reviewers assert that Walcott "finds his voice" in the volumes since 1979, it is also only in the later volumes that reviewers believe Walcott entirely *loses* his voice to Lowell. "Old New England" serves as the chief example of this poetic capitulation, and it troubles Walcott's reviewers all the more because, contrary to the idea that poets outgrow their influences, it comes so late in Walcott's career.

"Old New England" appears in the first of two sections of *The Fortunate Traveller* devoted to the "North."[32] Here, Walcott (who now lives in Boston for most of the year) contemplates settings Lowell made famous and uses the strongly rhymed, heavily symbolic mode of *Lord Weary's Castle* as well. "Old New England" recalls Lowell's frenetic conflation of various types of violence in "In Memory of Arthur Winslow," his reiteration of Native American suffering in "At the Indian Killer's Grave," and, throughout *Lord Weary's Castle*, his disapproval of the Vietnam War, and perhaps even his meditation on black soldiers in "For the Union Dead":

> Black clippers, tarred with whales' blood, fold their sails
> entering New Bedford, New London, New Haven.
> A white church spire whistles into space
> like a swordfish, a rocket pierces heaven
> as the thawed springs in icy chevrons race
> down hillsides and Old Glories flail
> the crosses of green farm boys back from 'Nam.
> Seasons are measured still by the same
> span of the veined leaf and the veined body
> whenever the spring wind startles an uproar
> of marching oaks with memories of a war
> that peeled whole counties from the calendar.
>
> The hillside is still wounded by the spire
> of the white meetinghouse, the Indian trail

trickles down it like the brown blood of the whale
in rowanberries bubbling like the spoor
on logs burnt black as Bibles by hellfire.
The war whoop is coiled tight in the white owl,
stone-feathered icon of the Indian soul,
and railway lines are arrowing to the far
mountainwide absence of the Iroquois.
Spring lances wood and wound, and a spring runs
down tilted birch floors with their splintered suns
of beads and mirrors—broken promises
that helped make this Republic what it is.

The poem reflects the past's persistence in the present in its series of parallels, likening "Black clippers, tarred with whales' blood" in the first stanza to "Black clippers [that] brought . . . our sons home from the East" (that is, Vietnam) in the third; a "white church spire" to a "rocket pierc[ing] heaven"; and (implicitly) the past annihilation of Native Americans to contemporary racial intolerance.

New England's overinsistent novelty—"New Bedford, New London, New Haven"—indicates precisely its nonoriginality. The U.S., an imitation Republic, is a looking-glass land built on "beads and mirrors." These emblems of illusion, once traded for land, remain its base. Walcott views Old New England as through a transparency depicting New New England, and the two layers form a diorama depicting a scene of violent retribution. We cannot stop at two transparencies, either, since we need to recall why New England is called New England—it "originally" represented New Old England. Because New England refers us to Old England, we know that the "original" (or "old") Puritans did not invent the "broken promises / that helped make this Republic what it is." We can search if we like for the beginning of this chain in Old England; yet that will lead further back, to the early Christian era to which Walcott's ending image of crucifixion ("each shroud / round the crosstrees") refers, and still further, to the classical age upon which American Republics depend. As the very title of "Old New England" implies, "the idea of the New and the Old becomes increasingly absurd" ("MH," 6).

The poem places human violence within a larger natural pattern, among "swordfish," "marching oaks," "rowanberries bubbling like the spoor," and a "Spring" that "lances." When Walcott writes that "The war whoop is coiled tight in the white owl," he hints that human violence—in this case, the Iroquois's own—mimics nature's. Yet mimicry is more complex upon closer examination, for we project our own violence upon nature (in such nouns as "swordfish") and then mimic what we believe we see. Walcott's third and final stanza demonstrates this process:

> The crest of our conviction grows as loud
> as the spring oaks, rooted and reassured
> that God is meek but keeps a whistling sword;
> His harpoon is the white lance of the church,
> His wandering mind a trail folded in birch,
> His rage the vats that boiled the melted beast
> when the black clippers brought (knotting each shroud
> round the crosstrees) our sons home from the East.

As in nineteenth-century "arguments by design," Walcott chooses elements from a landscape, then infers a deity, "His wandering mind a trail folded in birch," from that already biased collection of choices.

Walcott's references to the old behind the new and the new becoming old show that New England has invented neither mimicry nor violence, but neither does the poem accept human despair by suggesting its inevitability. Although mimicry is in general a necessary part of life, cultures may choose to mimic in constructive or destructive ways. New England is neither alone in its imitation nor irresponsible for its invention of a violent God to imitate.[33]

Once again, juxtaposing two readings of this poem helps to reveal problems in the ways in which critics and reviewers are apt in practice to conceive influence. Calvin Bedient, for example, uses the poem to show Walcott's debt to Lowell and his newfound desire to speak as a sort of self-naturalized U.S. citizen. Bedient praises Walcott's "melodies" but worries about his "composition":

> Why complain that Walcott is not in fact a New England poet, that the "our" in "The crest of our conviction grows as loud / as the

spring oaks" or "our sons home from the East" is ersatz, when most American poets would sell their convictionless souls to be able to write like this? Still the poem is excessively written in proportion to what it has to say—is virtuostic merely. It reads like a smooth dream of phrases that not even Vietnam . . . can wake up. In a way that is its point, but the poet's hunger to absorb New England, and Robert Lowell, places him curiously inside the dream, insulated there, enjoying it. (32–33)

Bedient construes "our sons" as "New England's sons," but Robert Bensen, assuming that Walcott's "our" does not mean "New England's" but at the very least "the Americas'," terms this interpretation a "massive provincialism."[34] Bensen immediately becomes provincial too, however, in that his essay thwarts Walcott's aims and theories in the act of appreciating them:

what is revolutionary about the New World poet's concept of history as myth, according to Walcott in "The Muse of History," is [his] "contempt for historic time," [his] insistence on the simultaneity of past, present and future. . . . As Walcott describes him, the New World poet of St.-John Perse "moves through the ruins of great civilizations, . . . carrying entire cultures in his head, bitter perhaps, but unencumbered." What appears in Walcott's prose as a finished process, in his poetry becomes a lifelong struggle to disencumber himself of the myriad burdens that *obscure his progress and vision.* (31; italics mine)

"Finished process" is an oxymoronic enough phrase to describe Walcott's nonlinear "history," and "lifelong struggle," too, would do, if only that "process" or "struggle" remained free of the goal of *progress*—especially since a few pages later, Bensen notes that "[t]he emblem of temptation that the Old World offers the New . . . promises a 'vision of progress' " (35). Much as he advocates simultaneity, Bensen defends "Old New England" against Bedient's charge that Walcott wishes to "absorb" Lowell by proposing at least three ways by which Walcott distances himself from his precursor: by finding "the colonial past . . . simultaneous with the present" (35), by "find[ing] the Puritan God everywhere" while Lowell finds only godless modernity (36), and by "not, like Lowell, hold[ing] himself apart to judge. . . . Instead he claims a share in the suffering" (37). Here, Bensen merely replaces Bedient's transformative metaphor for influence (in which Walcott "hunger[s]" to "absorb" Lowell) with a more Bloomian model based on distantiation. In other words, Bensen celebrates Walcott for his "distance" and hence, originality, while Walcott's poem is a critique of origin. Further, although Bensen's observations of Walcott's poem are accurate, it would be provincial to believe Lowell incapable of the same sentiments. Lowell makes a particular effort to layer images of different eras into a more than linear history. When Lowell complains in "For the Union Dead" that "The Aquarium is gone. Everywhere," we can read this juxtaposition as a sentence in its own right asserting that what passes doesn't vanish, but disperses nowhere and everywhere (Lowell's enjambment even enacts this dispersal by using the beginning of a thought to end another). Lowell too was accused of being overwhelmed by language, and of violating the poetic past in *Imitations*. Walcott, far from distancing himself from Lowell, is influenced by Lowell's susceptibility to influence. In his *Paris Review* interview Walcott remarks, "I loved his openness to receive influences. . . . [H]e was not embarrassed to admit that he was influenced even in his middle-age by William Carlos Williams, or by François Villon, or by Boris Pasternak, all at the same time. That was wonderful" (Hirsch 1986, 226).

Most of all, however, Bensen's defense of Walcott, like Ramsaran's, suffers precisely from its attitude of defense, from the aura of guilty justification that impels its unnecessary attack on Lowell. Similarly, poststructuralist and feminist critics who most strongly criticize the Bloomian model of influence or the reification of literary canons occasionally write as though they believed most deeply in literary battles and in the physical reality of the canon—attacking Thoreau to "make room" for Fuller, for example, and thus devaluing certain authors even as they ponder the notion of value. To read "Old New England" and, I'd argue, other postcolonial and Postmodern literature, we need to give up justification along with originality. As Walcott puts it, "to condemn or justify is also the method of history" ("MH," 4).

In his later poetry Walcott is still developing his anti-imperialist network of poets, but the network outgrows the confines of British and French traditions and includes contemporary as well as canonical authors. In "Forest of Europe" (*SAK*, 38–41), for example, seventeen years after *In a Green Night*, Walcott links himself to Joseph Brodsky and, hence, Mandelstam. While most of Walcott's allusive poems reveal the effects of influence, "Forest of Europe" dramatizes influence at work. Brodsky recites a poem of Mandelstam's, one winter, to the listening poet:

> the wintry breath
> of lines from Mandelstam, which you recite,
> uncoils as visibly as cigarette smoke.
>
> "The rustling of ruble notes by the lemon Neva."
> Under your exile's tongue, crisp under heel,
> the gutturals crackle like decaying leaves,
> the phrase from Mandelstam circles with light
> in a brown room, in barren Oklahoma.

In the course of his meditation on Mandelstam's phrase Walcott draws another series of parallels, like those in "Old New England." The poem compares the suffering of Mandelstam and others like him to that of the Choctaws in Oklahoma, the Gulag Archipelago to "The tourist archipelagocs of my South." It next imagines Mandelstam on a train journey—probably on his way to exile in Voronezh—and the subsequent journeys of innumerable Russian emigrants and exiles:

> Who is that dark child on the parapets
> of Europe, watching the evening river mint
> its sovereigns stamped with power, not with poets,
> the Thames and the Neva rustling like banknotes,
> then, black on gold, the Hudson's silhouettes?

Finally, Walcott's "train" of thought ends where it began, with Brodsky's own exile:

> From frozen Neva to the Hudson pours,
> under the airport domes, the echoing stations,
> the tributary of emigrants whom exile

has made as classless as the common cold,
citizens of a language that is now yours. . . .

Brodsky counteracts the upheavals of his state and encourages the survival of Mandelstam's iconoclastic poetry. He passes the "divine fever" that afflicted Mandelstam on to the poet, so that it grows into a "fire" of language warming himself and Walcott through the "winter" of oppression:

Frightened and starved, with divine fever
Osip Mandelstam shook, and every
metaphor shuddered him with ague,
each vowel heavier than a boundary stone,
"to the rustling of ruble notes by the lemon Neva,"

but now that fever is a fire whose glow
warms our hands, Joseph, as we grunt like primates
exchanging gutturals in this winter cave
of a brown cottage, while in drifts outside
mastodons force their systems through the snow.

Mandelstam's poetry does not march through history as "mastodons" or as imperial or totalitarian armies do. The Mandelstam poem Brodsky quotes (untitled; #222) refuses the logic of power: "I saw the world of power through a child's eyes . . . / I owe it not one jot of my soul: / something alien to me, which I never wanted."[35] The "ruble notes" Brodsky mentions are being refused:

I never stood under the bank's Egyptian porch,
stupidly pompous, in a beaver mitre, glowering.
Never, never, above the lemon Neva, to the rustle
of hundred rouble notes, did a gypsy girl dance for me. (58)

Rather, Mandelstam "saw the poetry in forlorn stations," and wrote from a "space / so desolate it mocked destinations." Walcott, too, mocks destination and progress in his last stanza, which pulls back from the individual Mandelstam to one of the long vistas of time-that-can-hardly-be-called-time Walcott favors, and from which standpoint the present might as well be prehistory.

Mandelstam's phrase gains significance by virtue of more than one instantaneous transformation. First, Walcott imagines Mandelstam's composition of the phrase as a "breathing into life" which occurs in a single moment:

> As the train passed the forest's tortured icons,
> the floes clanging like freight yards, then the spires
> of frozen tears, the stations screeching steam,
> he drew them in a single winter's breath
> whose freezing consonants turned into stones.

Mandelstam "drew . . . in" a breath, and in that breath drew in a Russian topography of forests and train stations. He also "drew" or portrayed these scenes "in a single winter's breath," taking in the landscape and reproducing it literally in two halves of "the same breath" (although that breath lasts for a whole winter). The creation of breath coincides with that of voice: breath possesses "consonants" as soon as it is drawn (or draws) and these freeze at the moment they come into being, as breath freezes into mist in cold air. At least two instantaneous transformations take place here: perception of the object world into breath, thus voice, and breath into solid form akin to writing ("into stones").

Because it metamorphoses from breath into solidity and, in Brodsky's recital, back into breath, Mandelstam's poem exercises a kind of poetic exchange value. It circulates: "the phrase from Mandelstam circles with light / in a brown room." It is as though Brodsky had smuggled Mandelstam's poetic "ruble notes" into Oklahoma. As one river flows into another "from frozen Neva to the Hudson pours," the "tributary of emigrants" carries tradable phrases. A web of exchanges is a relational and differential system, as Michael Ryan observes, that "deploys the 'thing itself' along a chain of referential serial relations";[36] Walcott's monetary metaphor for language is structurally apt ("Money is a kind of poetry," wrote Stevens). That is, the poem recognizes that words and ruble notes are comparable even as, like Mandelstam's, it pointedly prefers words. In Walcott's concurrently running musical analogy the "note" joins the musical phrase as the tributary joins the river. Both musical and numerical notation are not customarily said to require translation, but between most cultures translation or at least explanation actually would be necessary; and money does undergo a sort of translation from one language to another. Mandelstam's phrase, too, does not emerge from the exchange process unaltered. In Oklahoma Mandelstam's lines are "as visibl[e] as cigarette smoke" instead of as freezing breath, and must be uttered in English as well as in Russian. The mimicry of Brodsky's recital is not exact. Indeed, the very inexactness of the process by which Mandelstam's phrase moves from speech to print and back again also keeps it fresh. We can't be so afraid of destroying poetry that we fail to use it: "what's poetry, if it is worth its salt, / but a phrase men can pass from hand to mouth?" "Forest of Europe" echoes "The Muse of History"'s vision of the poet "continu[ing] the pattern, hand to hand and mouth to mouth" (12). And by filling in the details of that vision with specific poets and phrases, Walcott puts his poetic money where his mouth is.

READING WALCOTT ALERTS us to the inadequacy of several common contemporary metaphors for influence—especially what would in Renaissance terms be called the "eristic" metaphor, in which the later poet overthrows the earlier poet in battle.[37] If the ape represents the failure to transform, the slave represents failure in combat. Derrida observes that "In the domain of 'criticism' or poetics, it has been strongly stressed that art, as imitation (representation, description, expression, imagination, etc.), should not be 'slavish' (this proposition scans twenty centuries of poetics)."[38] Indeed, the proposition has become so opaquely standardized that reviewers forget its literal application to much postcolonial literature. Any reviewer who suggests without irony that a Caribbean poet "struggle[s] with the dominating mad masters"[39] or even "fuse[s] the diction of his masters with his own,"[40] that he is "*at the mercy* of influence" (Vendler, 23) or "in a state of *helpless subjection* [to Lowell],"[41] appears to imply that Walcott's relation to his precursors reflects his literally "slavish" past. At times the master of the slave merges with the master of the apprentice, when reviewers speak of poetic craft. But the metaphor of apprenticeship is nothing to accept without commentary, either—nor is the coincidence of these two kinds of mastery.

Walcott uses the eristic and transformative figures, as he seems to use every proverbial metaphor in the language. As Walcott embraces the transformative metaphor's weakness—the place where "the relation between text and model" vanishes—he relishes the violence of the eristic metaphor, as in his review of the Australian poet Les Murray: "The barbarians approaching the capital bring with them not only the baggage of a cowhorned, shaggy army, but also the vandalization of the imperial language. . . . Let the shaggy, long horde of spiky letters and the dark-rumbling of hexametrical phalanxes rise over the outback toward the capital of the English language, and you have . . . Les Murray's poems" ("CD," 25). This passage, with its personification of the alphabet and its play on "capital," parodies literary "conquest" and hands victory to the barbarian. Walcott uses the slave/master figure similarly, at once resisting and perpetuating it: "This is not the grape-purple Aegean. / There is no wine here, no cheese, the almonds are green, / the sea grapes bitter, the language is that of slaves" (*AT*, 35). These lines are not from a poem of Naipaulian bitterness, but from "Gros-Ilet," a miniature mythic narrative of St. Lucian language. With these words the narrator advises Elpenor, one of Odysseus's men, to "keep moving, there is nothing here for you." The narrator uses a rhetoric as cleverly deceptive as Odysseus's to persuade Elpenor (a potential conqueror, but also a bumbler who died falling from Circe's roof) that he knows only a "language of slaves." The narrator's echo of classical formulaic phrasing ("grape-purple Aegean") alone belies his claim—unless Greek, too, is a "language of slaves." Indeed, it was, when "The Romans / acquired Greek slaves as aesthetics instructors / of their spoilt children" (*O*, 206). If Walcott berates sycophants of the muse of history for seeing "language as enslavement" ("MH," 2), Walcott's own work acknowledges that such linguistic enslavement remains a perpetual possibility.

Walcott's account of representation, which argues that mimicry is normative, obviously works against the grain of eristic and transformative versions of influence theory. In "Culture or Mimicry?" Walcott asserts that Carnival, the art form "which came out of nothing, which emerged from the sanctions imposed on it" (9), epitomizes American art's recognition of the mimicry inherent in existence. Whereas Naipaul declares that "nothing has ever been created in the West Indies, and nothing will ever be created," Walcott repeats him with a difference: "Nothing will always be created in the West Indies . . . because what will come out of there is like nothing one has ever seen" (9; italics mine). This sentence parodies the double bind of traditional concepts of representation, in which imitation (mimesis) forms the basis of representation and therefore culture, but one must also restrain mimesis from becoming mimicry in order to keep it from falling back *outside* culture. Lest we think there's no proper foundation of imitation or *likeness* in Caribbean art, Walcott asserts that there is: it is "like nothing." It "came out of nothing"; nothing is its mother, which it still resembles. Lest we think Caribbean art unoriginal in its mimicry, it is also "like nothing one has ever seen." By revising Naipaul's "has ever been . . . will ever be" to "will *always* be," Walcott makes "nothing" positive, a persistence rather than an absence. Derrida, too, conducts a critique of origin that finds mimicry to be language's necessary condition, and finds language the imitated as well as imitative term. In Derrida's reading of Mallarmé's "Mimique,"

> We are faced then with mimicry imitating nothing; faced, so to
> speak, with a double that doubles no simple, a double that nothing
> anticipates, nothing at least that is not itself already double. There is
> no simple reference. It is in this that the mime's operation does
> allude, but alludes to nothing, alludes without breaking the mirror,
> without reaching beyond the looking-glass. . . . Mallarmé thus
> preserves the differential structure of mimicry or *mimēsis*, but
> without its Platonic or metaphysical interpretation, which implies
> that somewhere the being of something that *is*, is being imitated.
> (*Dissemination*, 206)

Walcott's poetry is always conscious that it doubles what is "itself already double." However, as an American mimic Walcott sometimes feels *as though* he doubles authoritative and original texts, just as American culture as a whole expresses insecurity in its relation to European culture. Still, Walcott never, like Naipaul, internalizes Europe's illusory authority. Walcott reaches "beyond the looking-glass" in his poems and essays only to discover that he cannot get beyond it any more than his poetic precursors could. Because Walcott believes in the potentially enlightening capacity of poetic mimicry, he is more optimistic than many Postmodernists and poststructuralists who reach similar aesthetic conclusions. If linguistic traditions bind us in chains, the chains cannot be defined as either irons shackling "rock-pile convict[s]" or embroidery stitches in a tapestry. Neither resignation nor fortitude rules their continuance. But since they do not inherently debase, and can liberate, Walcott is not frightened by the infinite regressions of history and language.

"THE PAIN OF HISTORY
WORDS CONTAIN":
WALCOTT AND CREOLE POETICS

I heard them marching the leaf-wet roads of my head,
the sucked vowels of a syntax trampled to mud,
a division of dictions, one troop black, barefooted,
the other in redcoats bright as their sovereign's blood;
. . . .
but both, in bitterness, travelled the same road.

— *Midsummer,* LII

WALCOTT HAS SOME claim to several cultural traditions, and so to a range of languages. Walcott could conceivably write in St. Lucian French-lexicon Creole (or "patois"), "standard" English, the "English-lexicon creolized vernacular . . . emerging as a third strand" between French Creole and English,[1] or a combination of all of the above.[2] Inevitably, a critical argument erupts over Walcott's linguistic choices. Some Caribbean critics believe that a Caribbean poet's first priority is to sustain Caribbean creoles, while others believe that Caribbean English remains equally desirable. Western critics have also divided, and nearly as passionately, over the question of whether such a thing as linguistic purity exists, and if so, whether that purity fortifies or enfeebles a language (or both). Vendler, for example, maintains that Walcott's "dialect poetry" is "actually macaronic," and that while "dialect poetry" is an "experiment . . . worth trying," "a macaronic aesthetic, using two or more languages at once, has never yet been sustained in poetry at any length" (26).

Readers of postcolonial literature are accustomed to linguistic controversies. Since postcolonial poets whose homelands have suffered more than one colonization may be fluent in various languages, plus creoles of those languages, postcolonial critics realize the need to question whether we can indeed isolate a "native language" or "mother tongue" from others.[3] Creole languages offer insight into this query; they trouble the opposition between "native" and "foreign," demonstrating how much variance a "single" language actually contains and how thoroughly languages overlap.

Walcott, of course, grew up in a creole culture; in the thirties and forties, during Walcott's "sound colonial education" in St. Lucian schools and at the University of the West Indies, most of the St. Lucian population was bilingual or trilingual, but more comfortable in French Creole than in any other language.[4] His poetry, whether by decision or by cultural instinct, reveals the interpenetration of languages. Walcott deals with French-lexicon Creole by "taking that kind of speech and translating it, or retranslating it, into an English-inflected Creole" (Hirsch 1979, 289). It's obvious that he creates "English-inflected Creole" in some poems, less obvious that he creates Creole-inflected English in others. The poems that seem to fall into the general category of "standard" English are "tonally" St. Lucian: "*tonally* my basic language, is patois . . . underneath it all I think the whole thing is really a matter of tone" (Hamner 1977, 417; italics mine). Indeed, as Mervyn Morris observes, "There are . . . in Walcott's poetry interesting small examples of West Indian vocabulary placed unemphatically in a Standard English setting"[5] — so many examples, I'd say, that they destandardize Walcott's English; a constant embedding of "small examples" erodes the claim to normalcy of the medium in which they appear. Moreover, many poems weave a complex linguistic fabric by incorporating not only St. Lucian and Trinidadian inflections, but European languages and Latin. Walcott also uses figures that require the reader to consider animal and even inanimate sounds as parts of language (see "Cul de Sac Valley," *AT*, 9–15). In his interview with Ciccarelli Walcott describes "making an amalgam, a fusion, of all the dialects" (303) in his plays; in his "Note" to *O Babylon!*, he calls his adaptation of Jamaican Rastafarian speech "[m]y theater language."[6] Walcott's poetry, too, creates such a "theater language," which, taken as a whole, is difficult to characterize: it is no particular creole, but a creole of creoles. In this Walcott may remind us of many other poets' efforts to "write no language," or to write a multiplicitous language — from Spenser's poetic archaisms to Nicolas Guillén's *mestizaje*.[7]

Walcott does not speculate on the more distant repercussions of his Creole linguistic base. Nevertheless, it is useful to imagine what a creole poetic would be like, since creoles suggest not only a way to conceptualize postcolonial language, but a postcolonial way of conceptualizing language itself. Again, this shift of perspective in which the margin overtakes the center typifies postcolonial discourse. It would be tempting to say that Caribbean poets, for example, are particularly likely to evolve idiosyncratically polyglossic styles. But on second thought, as the linguists LePage and Tabouret-Keller point out, "in *any* community we find that language use ranges from the highly inventive and idiosyncratic to the highly conventional and regular . . . poets and writers *generally* are particularly inclined to be so, since they feel more strongly than most . . . the urgent necessity to draw on every possibility language affords" (12; italics mine). The polyglossia especially obvious in Caribbean poets and Caribbean communities can be found in all poets and communities when we examine their languages closely enough. Perhaps, once more, something generally true is more openly admitted in Walcott.

The change of perspective by which the eccentric reveals itself as the normative is "sensational," as Mervyn C. Alleyne puts it. According to Alleyne, "Caribbean language forms are crucial both to our understanding of the innate capacity for language with which human beings are . . . endowed, and to the unraveling of the mystery of the origin of language itself."[8] Indeed, Caribbean creole forms do reveal the nature of language; but they reveal precisely that language has no origin, that all languages arise from previous languages and change when they come into contact with others: "Many of today's internationally important languages (e.g., French, Spanish, and English) have diverged from their earlier form mainly because of contact with other languages" (Alleyne, 162).[9] Although in this sense all languages are creoles, the languages we now recognize as creoles would possess a privileged place in a creole poetic, insofar as only these languages recognize that they are creoles.[10] Finally, the creole model, since it incorporates difference in its very constitution, has a good deal in common with Western poststructural models of language. The idea of a Creole poetic helps us see the common ground and potential congeniality between postcolonialism and poststructuralism.

It would be fair to say, with Ramsaran (144), that while Walcott shows an interest in creole early on, he increasingly enlarges and thematizes that interest. *In a Green Night* tends to use traces of creoles for irony, or to serve thematic juxtapositions of cultures. While the effects are often interesting, Walcott does not seem as aware of their significance as he obviously is after *Another Life*. In what follows I would like to trace some of this by considering first a few of Walcott's early efforts at creolization; then some passages from *Another Life* and two poems from *Sea Grapes*; and finally "The Schooner *Flight*." The expansiveness of *Another Life* encourages Walcott to venture beyond the formal lyric and, likewise, to enlarge his poetic vocabulary, fully creolizing his own work. Further, in *Another Life*, "Names," and "Sainte Lucie" (*SG*, 40–42, 43–55), Walcott develops the possibility that creole repetitions of European words need not ironically diminish European meanings. Colonial repetition, as Bhabha points out, always contains difference, but difference can add as well as subtract an effect. Finally, "The Schooner *Flight*" (*SAK*, 3–20) exemplifies the nexus between Walcott's impulses toward creole and toward drama. In this dramatic monologue Walcott evokes a working-class, English Creole-speaking Trinidadian narrator who at once "speaks" and is written, both vernacular and literary, communal and individual. Here Walcott explores the paradoxical relation between the individual and the universal involved in the logic of creole. In this, as in so many of his poems, Walcott brings alive the tensions that pull language together and apart.

WALCOTT'S FIRST EFFORTS to draw upon creole(s) occur in his early sonnet sequence, "Tales of the Islands" (*IGN*, 26–30).

These ten sonnets employ at least three narrators, and offer glimpses of Chekhovian lives ("Miss Rossignol lived in the lazaretto / For Roman Catholic crones"). The "Tales"' ironies seem a bit heavy, but linguistically they compel. Two narrators speak either in St. Lucian English Creole or in Walcott's composite "theater language"—since both are second-order creoles, it's hard to tell. Yet even a North American reader unfamiliar with St. Lucian languages can discern that some process of translation has transpired (either from French to English Creole or from French Creole to Walcott's composite), since six sonnets (or "Chapters," in the sonnets' parlance) bear French or French Creole subtitles, but no sonnets—including two in the first person—are in either French or French Creole. Since Walcott transcribes Creole with gallicized spellings, as we know from "Sainte Lucie," each word in the subtitles looks identical to its French counterpart. Thus, Walcott gives us in the subtitles what appears "standard" French but is probably French Creole, in much of the narration what appears classical English, and in the dialogue what appears to be English Creole but may be a creole of creoles. On the level of idiolect Walcott adds "the fine / Writing of foam" (*Chapter X / "Adieu foulard . . ."*), literary allusions, and interminglings such as "They catch his wife with two tests up the beach / While he drunk quoting Shelley with 'Each / Generation has its angst, but we has none' " (*Chapter VI*).[11] This style will find finer expression in the Trinidadian Creole couplets of "The Spoiler's Return" (*FT*, 53–60), whose satire is more truly double-edged, pointed at the sentimentality of both cosmopolitanism and provincialism.

Nor can we determine which language has been "assimilated" to which simply by counting the number of words in each. The phrases become difficult to categorize as either English or English Creole, approaching Walter Benjamin's "pure language," in which "both the original and the translation [become] recognizable as fragments of a greater language, just as fragments are part of a vessel."[12] Walcott has said that in such early poems "[t]he aim was that a West Indian or an Englishman could read a single poem, each with his own accent, without either one feeling that it was written in dialect" (Hirsch 1979, 282). Walcott's comment subverts English purity, treating English as another "dialect"; but as Walcott phrases it here, he implies that readers remain linguistically unconscious, each safe in the assumption that the poem's language mirrors his or her own. To the contrary, in Walcott's poems we often register traces of various languages in rapid succession or at once, but these appear too fleetingly and ambiguously for *anyone* to claim them, to say with absolute certainty, "This is an English poem" or "This is a St. Lucian poem." Ironically, too often both Caribbean and Western readers have reacted to the poems' resistance to their linguistic comfort by surrendering to the surface of that resistance and rejecting the poems as foreign.

"Pocomania" and "Parang," also from *In a Green Night* (35–36, 37), are Walcott's first whole poems in English (or perhaps "theater") Creole. Yet these two poems about Caribbean rituals and forms remain special cases, since Walcott seems to have chosen their vocabulary in order to conjure their specifically Caribbean subjects. "Pocomania" juxtaposes Creole phrases with some that might be British English to enact the poem's thematic comparison between the pocomania ritual and European Christianity ("De bredren rattle withered gourds / Whose seeds are the forbidden fruit"). Yet the rhythms are often as difficult to categorize as those of "Tales of the Islands": "The waters of the moon are dry, / Derision of the body, toil." What purpose does the final comma serve? To elide something (maybe a repetition of the verb "to be")? To indicate a list of nonparallel phenomena? Since Walcott fractures all of his languages' grammars at once, it's hard to tell.

In "Parang" Walcott first produces a Creole monologue—the form that blossoms in many later poems—at more than sonnet's length ("Pocomania," in contrast, has an uncharacterized narrator rather than a true dramatic speaker). The speaker of "Parang" is an elderly former singer who retrospectively understands that "young men does bring love to disgrace":

> Oh, when I t'ink how from young
> I wasted time at de fêtes,
> I could bawl in a red-eyed rage
> For desire turned to regret,

> Not knowing the truth that I sang
> At parang and *la commette.*

According to Walcott, in "the thrum and cry of [Trinidadian] parang . . . with typical Spanish duality, the song of praise has the same pitch as the lament" (*JS/OB*, 4); apparently, in this case even the singer has been misled from his own meaning ("the truth that I sang") by treacherous pitch. The poem, like "Pocomania," uses its Creole vocabulary and its form to stage its theme. "Parang" uses "alternating rhymes of eight-[syllable] lines directly from the old Spanish" (*JS/OB*, 4), as do Walcott's first drafts of his equally Spanish-inflected *Joker of Seville*. The speaker's Creole, in this context of homage to a precise Spanish-Trinidadian milieu, becomes historically necessary. Even so, the poem remains polyglossic. First, as Vendler observes,[13] it evokes Yeats's English ("the wax and wane of the moon," "the falling of a fixed star"), but second and more important, its combination of Spanish form and Trinidadian Creole makes us realize that Trinidadian speech itself is polyglossic, suffused with what Walcott considers Spanish tonalities, among others (one of Walcott's addresses in Trinidad—"Duke of Edinburgh, Petit Valley, Diego Martin"—conveys some of this[14]). Walcott brings the same logic more explicitly to bear in his "Note" to *The Joker of Seville*: "there [is] no artifice in relating the music and drama of the Spanish verse to what strongly survives in Spanish Trinidad, or, debased as critics may think it, to the thrum and cry of the parang" (4). The "duality" of Spanish song, the dangerous ambivalence of love lyric, become characteristic of Walcott's own creole style in "Parang."

Still, in these early poems Walcott uses creole vocabulary to produce ironic effects. In "Orient and Immortal Wheat" (*IGN*, 48), for instance, in an example Morris picks out, "So is sin born, and innocence made wise, / By intimations of hot galvanize" rather than "intimations of immortality." (Lowell is fond of this "falling" effect, too, as when Mary Winslow resembles "A Cleopatra," but "A Cleopatra in her housewife's dress.")[15] Morris, who reads Walcott sensitively, recognizes the disadvantages and advantages of such usage when he recalls that while he once thought that Walcott's early efforts "borrow[ed] dialect for the literary middle-class," that estimation "fail[ed] to indicate ways in which meaning and apparent intention may make the 'borrowing of dialect' triumphantly artistic. Walcott and [Dennis] Scott are not trying to be faithful to dialect, they are trying to convey their complex perceptions" (19–20). Walcott's ironic uses of creole vocabulary, however, seem to accept the idea that English has "high" rhetorical connotations, and creole, comic ones. In contrast, by *Omeros* God appears, entirely without fanfare, and addresses Achille in English (or, again, composite) Creole:

> And God said to Achille, "Look, I giving you permission
> to come home. Is I send the sea-swift as a pilot,
> the swift whose wings is the sign of my crucifixion.

> And thou shalt have no God should in case you forgot
> my commandments." (134)

Although God speaks with humor, his speech is in no way ridiculous. Again, in "The Three Musicians" (*AT*, 28–32), a Creole narrator superimposes the story of the Magi upon that of a childless couple in Castries, and the superimposition highlights a genuine equivalence, not an ironic distance: "He was poorer than them, / no place for his bed; / 'My parlour is Jerusalem, / my table, Gilead' " (29).

In his 1968 interview with Dennis Scott, Walcott brushes off Scott's distinction between "a humanist poet" and "a folk poet": "This is a sociological statement that I am not interested in."[16] Walcott seems much more interested in his conversation with Robert Hamner (1977):

> I have not only a dual racial personality but a dual linguistic
> personality. My real language, and tonally my basic language, is
> patois. Even though I do speak English, it may be that deep down
> inside me the instinct that I have is to speak in that tongue. Well,
> I've tried to write poems in patois and feel that later on, maybe in
> my fifties, I will try to do something of that kind. On the other
> hand, it sometimes seems to me to be an academic thing, and I
> would not like to do anything consciously academic. . . .
> [U]nderneath it all I think the whole thing is really a matter of tone.
> . . . So one can—although it seems ridiculous sometimes—one can
> detect in the body of American poetry an American tone that is

quite different from the tone of an English poem: that is in terms of its feeling. (417)[17]

While most assume that creole poetry, so obviously centered around spoken language, must be anti-academic, offered to the working class which speaks it, Walcott wonders whether creole can become "sometimes . . . an academic thing," a particularly "conscious" poetry that pleases intellectuals. For Walcott it is less academic for an intellectual to write like an intellectual, in St. Lucian-inflected English, than to write in the French Creole he uses only on certain occasions or to craft dramatic personae to speak creole(s) for him. As Walcott explains to Hirsch, "I couldn't pretend that my voice was the voice of the St. Lucia peasant or fisherman" (Hirsch 1979, 287).

Conversely, Walcott reflects, "I have a poem . . . which is a translation of a St. Lucian song that feels very fresh to me.[18] Now I wouldn't mind getting a collection of those and doing some more translations of them" (Hamner 1977, 417). While an anonymous or communal folk song could never seem academic, one could still, however, call the service a translator provides academic. But then translation, including Brodskian self-translation, rarely pretends to naturalism. The translator makes a good model for Walcott's poet since, as we saw in the discussion of influence, one cannot at any rate *summon* a completely original poetic voice. Just as poets should recognize the pervasiveness of influence—"Young poets should have no individuality" (Hamner 1977, 419)—so too they should recognize the inescapability of their own linguistic complexity, their multilingual natures ("dual linguistic personality"): "Someone who knows what he is doing, a good poet, recognizes the language's essential duality. The excitement is in joining the two parts" (Ciccarelli, 305).

By suggesting that he might try more Creole poems in his fifties (this has not come to pass), Walcott implies that the experienced poet can more likely get away with intimacy. A truly naive poet, meanwhile, can sound academic; in Walcott's youth, he says, "West Indian verse seemed to have more of the flavor of a library than the most metropolitan verse not at all related to the Caribbean experience" (Hirsch 1979,

283). "The flavor of a library," then, afflicts both calculated Anglicized poetry (which Walcott has been accused of writing) and calculated creolized poetry, the genuinely naive and the genuinely metropolitan each slipping on the disguise of the other.[19] This is the comedy of what Césaire calls *bovarisme*, telling a story right out of Márquez's *Love in the Time of Cholera*:

> I still remember a poor little Martinican pharmacist who passed the time writing poems and sonnets which he sent to literary contests, such as the Floral Games of Toulouse. He felt very proud when one of his poems won a prize. One day he told me that the judges hadn't even realized that his poems were written by a man of color. To put it in other words, his poetry was so impersonal that it made him proud. He was filled with pride by something I would have considered a crushing condemnation. (73)

Césaire intends the anecdote to reveal the wretchedness of a consciousness that has not decolonized itself, and so it does, because the pharmacist was happy for the wrong reason. But we could still use more information. In what way were the pharmacist's poems impersonal? Were they gentle or merely insipid, austere or arid, delicate or slight? Most likely he wrote the "postcard poetry," filled with "references to bright blue seas," so familiar to Walcott (Hirsch 1979, 283). But what if he didn't—what if, although metrically redolent of Vigny, for instance, and not Martinican in theme, his poems seemed accurately observed, no works of genius, but sincere? The pharmacist's reaction to winning the contest betrays his colonial mentality, but would poems such as his inevitably belong to someone of that mentality? No definite barrier separates political statements from poetry, but neither is there always a one-to-one correspondence between them. I do not imply that decolonization is not an imperative goal, nor that Walcott would think it was not. Rather, Walcott would likely acknowledge its necessity and at the same time maintain that its achievement cannot take a single linguistic form, because there is no such thing as a univocal or unambiguous language of any kind, and no nation should have a single poetic vocabulary. We can't conceive poetic authenticity apart from myriad other ambivalence-producing considerations, including politics but also including the irrational inclinations of private experience.

Walcott's interviews of the last fifteen years submit that a poet doesn't have to write "exclusively" in French Creole, English Creole, or English—to choose a language and be done with it. Rather, Walcott includes all these languages in a poetic creole, in contradistinction to the fallacy of exclusivity: "On every island there is a dialect, a patois, which can become a world of fascination for someone who may want to write, *or* use, *or* absorb it into the whole West Indian idea of language" (Hirsch 1979, 286; italics mine). The following comments refer to drama but apply to Walcott's poetry as well:

> I can't create in pure Creole, French, or English, for all sorts of reasons. You might be in a situation where accents differ within a small area, among people who all speak French Creole. The same applies to English Creole in the Caribbean. . . . [B]ut since one considers the Caribbean—the English-speaking Caribbean—as a whole, as sharing one language with various contributory sources, one must try to find, using syntaxes from various dialects if necessary, one form that would be comprehensible not only to all the people in the region that speak in that tone of voice, but to people everywhere. It is like making an amalgam, a fusion, of all the dialects into something that will work on stage. (Ciccarelli, 303)

"One form that would be comprehensible . . . to people everywhere": the mirror image of creole, born from Walcott's appreciation of almost infinite difference, is universal language. Recall Benjamin's notion, once again, that "that which seeks to represent, to produce itself in the evolving of languages, is that very nucleus of pure language" (79). Indeed, in the visibly evolving creole languages of the Americas linguists have found "new insight into language universals" (Alleyne, 161). In Walcott's poetry creole becomes the key piece, the Rosetta stone, of a comprehensive albeit unattainable poetic language toward which the translator-poet builds. "Pure" language in Benjamin's sense implies neither grammatically "correct" classical language nor grammatically correct creole; it is what "no single language can attain by itself but which is realized only by the totality of their intentions supplementing each other" (Benjamin, 74). A poet's individual talent holds together tradition's disparate linguistic strands in a work that is a continual act of translation, not from one language into another, but from all languages into the creole of poetry itself. Walcott's creole poems occupy that territory where all the idiolects he knows intersect, and occupy it in such a way that we cannot miss the intersection. But even more important, we realize by attending to Walcott's creole poetry that his "English" poems, and in fact all poems, inhabit that same area. Yet this does not marginalize creole, making it, as Sartre made Césaire's Negritude, a minor term in a global dialectic. Of all the languages that pour into Walcott's poetry, creole alone does not have to redefine itself, does not have to realize it is a creole. Creole is not simply an *instance* of Walcott's poetic language, but the *model* of poetic language aware of its own nature.

Walcott believes on one hand that perfect translation lies beyond human reach, but on the other that we inevitably pursue the impossible. In his note to *O Babylon!*, which depicts "the life of a small Rastafarian community, squatters on a beach that faces the harbor of Kingston, Jamaica" (*JS/OB*, 155), Walcott faces translation's essential hopelessness and at the same time affirms that hopeless enterprise:

> In trying to seek a combination of the authentic and the universally comprehensible, I found myself at the center of a language poised between defiance and translation, *for pure Jamaican is comprehensible only to Jamaicans.* But the promulgation of a national language is as much a part of education now as it is of politics. When I considered that, *within that language itself, the Rastafari have created still another for their own nation,* I faced another conflict: if the language of the play remained true to the sect, it would have to use the sect's methods of self-protection and total withdrawal. This would require of the playwright not merely a linguistic but a spiritual conversion, a kind of talking in tongues that is, by its hermeticism and its self-possession, defiantly evasive of Babylonian reason.
>
> The Rastafari have invented a grammar and a syntax which immure them from the seductions of Babylon, an oral poetry which *requires* translation into the language of the oppressor. To translate is

to betray. My theater language is, in effect, an adaptation and, for clarity's sake, filtered. (155–56; italics mine)

So many adaptations stream into Walcott's "theater language": Jamaicans adapting English, Rastafari adapting Jamaican English, Walcott adapting Rastafarian Jamaican English. The logic of creole, as Walcott implies, raises the question of private language, the ultimate idiolect: if "pure Jamaican is comprehensible only to Jamaicans," by extension one is "purely" comprehensible only to oneself—which is to say, never comprehensible, since *meaningful* comprehension requires at least two minds.[20] Walcott's description of the "hermetic" Rastafari makes them resemble African *griots*, "guardians and manipulators of the word," who have "an attitude toward the word which forbids unveiling completely its attitude toward the word."[21] Faced with an anthropological and linguistic problem that resembles but is even worse than the problem Walcott himself presents to non-Caribbean interpreters, Walcott accepts the idea that since translation remains partial, translation means betrayal. But if writing = translation = betrayal, he has to betray, hoping for a linguistic miracle.[22]

W H I L E "Tales of the Islands" indicates an early interest in creolization, *Another Life* catalyzed that interest. *Another Life*, like Lowell's *Life Studies*, was carved out of a prose memoir, a method that not only allowed Walcott to explore his recurrent themes in more detail and to clarify their connections, but also generated questions too large for the work at hand to answer, questions for future work. *Another Life* forced Walcott to articulate relations between words and objects, languages and history, while making his style(s) more flexible; its composition— from prose to verse—encouraged interplay between narrative and lyric modes (besides, a long poem demands juxtapositions of styles if only to keep variety alive). In its evocation of an entire neighborhood with all its social strata, *Another Life* also demanded interacting voices, idiolects, and languages.

Another Life refers not only to prior texts but to communicative systems as diverse as Arawak hieroglyphics and *The Illustrated London*

News, Pasternak's *Safe Conduct* and *Pears Cyclopedia*, *Noa Noa*, and Williamson's *History of the British Empire*; to paintings, hymns, newspapers, novels, legends on coins, photographs, advertisements, Catholic litanies, maps, gravestones, and, of course, "the sky's tightened parchment" (17.i.6). Walcott plays these systems against one another, or draws unexpected parallels; more important, he entwines various linguistic strands, "code-switching" for tonal precision. In the episode dealing with the lycanthrope merchant Manoir[23] (IV "The Pact," i.4), for example, at least three languages voice competing prayers: "Saylie, / the wrinkled washerwoman, howled / in gibberish, in the devil's Latin," while "the young priest chanted: / *per factotem mundi* [*sic*], / *per eum qui habet potestatem* / *mittendi te in gehennam*" [by the creator of the world, by him who holds the power to send you to hell] over her. A little earlier, "a fly prayed at [Manoir's] ear-well" in minuscule two-beat Creole couplets:

Bon Dieu, pardon,
Demou, merci,
l'odeur savon,
l'odeur parfum
pas sait guérir
l'odeur péché,
l'odeur d'enfer,
pardonnez-moi
Auguste Manoir!

[Good God, forgive,
Demon, thanks,
the scent of soap,
the scent of perfume,
cannot cure
the scent of sin,
the scent of hell,
pardon me
Auguste Manoir!]

In these passages the Catholic Church and the devil speak inimical but equally exotic languages, whereas the fly, child of nature, gives thanks in Creole for Manoir's sweat, which attracts him. Each uses the linguistic system suited to his or her metaphysics; and Castries makes an unusual number of these available. Carrington explains that a St. Lucian polyglot's choice of language can depend on a dazzling array of considerations "such as place—urban or rural; occasion—private or public, formal, informal, or intimate; subject under discussion and the presence or absence of other persons" (7). The intricate combinations of languages available to a polyglot speaker, then, enable him or her to be very fastidious. Walcott observes, "Sometimes you can even hear a West Indian, if he's going to speak English, go up socially in his attack on the language for clarity or for communication or depending on the social situation" (Hirsch 1979, 287). In this passage the young priest cannot convince Saylie to name Manoir (the demon with whom she contracted) until he translates himself, climbing down the social scale from its divine apex, Latin—itself a language Western poets have thought universal—to meet her, if not in the devil's language, then in middle Creole ground, universal in another sense, that dogs, cats, and flies can speak: "Name! *Déparlez!*" The concept of code-switching assumes the essential separability of codes, but their dizzying interaction in practice troubles these separations. The priest's utterance shows that his English and his Creole have made contact; the imperative "Name!," without an object, is not "standard English." The concept of creolization encompasses what code-switching cannot: a creole is a language in which not the alternation but the interpenetration of languages is recognized as normative, constitutive of the language itself.

In another such intersection in *Another Life* schoolboys in Castries recite a secular catechism, including St. Lucia's Virgilian motto, and Walcott makes their mispronunciation of school English an opportunity for paronomasia. While according to Carrington such exchanges had to take place in English,[24] Walcott's phonetic spellings make it plain that the children's English remains subversively St. Lucian:

"Boy! Name the great harbours of the world!"
"Sydney! Sir."
"San Fransceesco!"
"Naples, Sah!"
"And what about Castries?"

DEREK WALCOTT'S POETRY

"Sah, Castries ees a coaling station and
der twenty-seventh best harba in der worl'!
In eet the entire Breetesh Navy can be heeden!"
"What is the motto of Saint Lucia, boy?"
"*Statio haud malefida carinis.*"
"Sir!"
"Sir!"
"And what does that mean?"
"Sir, a safe anchorage for sheeps!" (5.i.19–32)

Paradoxically, forcing the children to speak English only makes the ironies of their situation more obvious, as their innocent pronunciations deflect their textbooks' versions of political geography. Even though they don't realize it, their mispronunciations amount to reinterpretation. St. Lucia's motto is *Statio haud malefida carinis*, but the island's natives gave rather the opposite impression early in the seventeenth century, when they unhesitatingly dispatched 48 of the 67 passengers of the British vessel *Oliph Blossom*.[25] St. Lucia is indeed more of a safe anchorage for sheep, as the children say, than for ships.

Chapter 6 of *Another Life* goes on to validate the schoolboys' mispronunciation/reinterpretation by juxtaposing liturgical Latin and St. Lucia's Virgilian motto with descriptions of its landscape, which Walcott typically perceives as its own concrete poetry. The section works by literalizing the sanctity within the name "St. Lucia": Walcott finds the cabbage palms' gestures equivalent to "*alleluia!*," a rooster's cry to "*gloria!*"; Soufrière's volcano becomes a "sulphurous censer," and St. Lucia "Sancta Lucia, / an island brittle / as a Lenten biscuit." Combining the motif of sanctity with the children's suggestion, "the tinkle of a sheep's bell // draws the sea-flocks homeward." But "Sancta Lucia" is an ironic saint, because Louis's "green fusiliers boiled themselves like lobsters" in the volcano at Soufrière, that demonic "censer." Once again, beneath the would-be divinity implied by the Western name lies the history of colonial violence. The poet, probing the images associated with the name, exposes the distance between the would-be and the actual.

Homi K. Bhabha might call these instances of colonial mimicry, which produces a "metonymy of colonial desire . . . through the repetition of *partial presence*."[26] For Bhabha colonial discourse (both the colonizers' and the colonials') repeats itself "erratically, eccentrically," producing "disturbances of cultural, racial, and historical difference" in the "diminishing perspective" of a repetition "almost the same but not white" (128–29). Yet Walcott holds out the hope that while postcolonial mimicry can expose difference, it can invent plenitudes too, the way the steelband and calypso "supersed[e] [their] traditional origins" ("CM," 9). The idea that repetition diminishes is itself part of the logic of the West, which views creole languages as inferior *because* they are seen as secondary, belated, partial presences—"bizarre, aberrant, and corrupt derivatives" (Alleyne, 160).[27] Walcott has a finer sense of the paradoxical continuum between the repeated and the new, between mimicry and originality. As Kierkegaard's Constantius observes, "that which is repeated has been—otherwise it could not be repeated— but the very fact that it has been makes the repetition into something new."[28]

Two poems in *Sea Grapes*, "Names" and "Sainte Lucie" (40–42; 43–55), develop Walcott's logic of linguistic mimicry. Formally these longish poems, subdivided into sections of irregular stanza and line lengths, could well have fit into *Another Life*; in fact, they stand out from the rest of *Sea Grapes* and its rhetoric of destitution ("I shall unlearn feeling, / unlearn my gift"). "Names" deepens and details Walcott's ideas about the originlessness of language and its persistence through repetition. "Sainte Lucie," more autobiographical and less speculative, shows these ideas at work in a personal context.

Walcott divides "Names" into two parts, the first recounting a narrative of St. Lucian culture and language and the second reflecting on the linguistic condition in which that narrative has left St. Lucia. The first part, marked by a Roman numeral one, emphasizes the first person in a sort of visual pun. Yet as usual Walcott explores the tension between the one and the many. The poem is narrated by an "I" who first speaks of his culture, then *for* his culture: "My race began as the sea began" slides into "I began with no memory, / I began with no future." This movement from the plural to the singular (in which the

plural is ultimately found in the singular) echoes the poem's development of its theme. The poet tries to pinpoint the historical origin of his
culture, the pure beginning of the colonial period—"that moment /
when the mind was halved by a horizon"—and cannot find it, because
"the horizon / sinks in the memory." This throws the poet back on a
different concept of origin, the totality of individual beginnings of consciousness: "my race began like the osprey / with that cry, / that terrible
vowel, / that I!" The interjection occupies a unique space between nature and language, wordless emotion and phonetic sign, resembling
both a human birth cry and an osprey's call. Communal origin here
becomes no more than a series of individual realizations that one is in
the present, the "instant of self-recognition" that exists "for every individual American" ("CM," 7, 8) and initiates mimicry. The instant is
a kind of fortunate fall; we cannot distinguish "I" from "Ai," the interjection of grief (Apollo's wail over Hyacinthus later transcribed on
the hyacinth's petals). Becoming "another" ("CM," 8) with that "I,"
the poet "trace[s] our names on the sand / which the sea erase[s]
again." This popular metaphor from the British canon, whose *locus
classicus* is Spenser's *Amoretti*,[29] must remind us that this describes the
condition of all writing.[30] But the postcolonial Caliban, harboring no
illusions of pure origin or permanence, meets the sea's erasure with a
knowing "indifference."[31]

The second part of "Names" turns from this general discussion of the
origin of postcolonial language to the specific "names" that became
Caribbean: "when they named these bays / bays, / was it nostalgia or
irony?" Irony, the poet answers, "mockery" sprung from the "sour
apples / and green grapes / of their exile." Yet as Gregorias's miniature
Renaissance—"our false / spring"—is "real" in *Another Life*, native
mimicry retwists words already twisted into ironic shapes and invests
them with genuine lyricism:

> Their memory turned acid
> but the names held;
> Valencia glows
> with the lanterns of oranges.

The colonialists force the colonials to use these names, but exactly as soon as they do so, the colonials make the names their own (as writing poetry is, in "Forest of Europe," simultaneous with the poet's perceiving it in topography). "The African acquiesced, / repeated, and changed them"—the lines contain an ambivalence; "The African acquiesced" at first suggests that the African "changed" familiar names to European ones, "acquiesced, / repeated [after the Europeans], and changed them [the old names]." We can also read the verbs chronologically: Africans acquiesced, and as a result repeated the words, but later, gradually, changed them. Ramsaran reads the lines this way: "Walcott suggests that African acquiescence in naming things did not result in faithful mimicry of European nouns but in transforming them into creole with 'natural inflections' " (140). There is at least one more possible reading, however, in which Walcott *aligns* "repeated" with "changed"; *to repeat is to change*, since the speaker differs and time has passed between utterances. Repetition and change occur not consecutively but concurrently, as Kierkegaard and Bhabha know in their different ways. In "Culture or Mimicry?" Walcott calls mimicry an "order of life," of continuance, and thus, paradoxically, of change. In "Names" we re-encounter this paradox from its opposite side when Walcott implies that "bending" or changing language should be classed as a kind of acquiescent repetition. Further, the colonizers' metonymic "mockery" conforms to Bhabha's "partial presence," since naming a Caribbean region "Valencia" also mocks and *implicates* Spain's Valencia. But when the colonials repeat the colonizers' repetition, colonial language—like poetry—refills the oranges with juice, and more than that, with a brilliance they never had: "These palms are *greater* than Versailles, / for no man made them, / their fallen columns *greater* than Castille, / no man unmade them (italics mine)." "Names" returns to *Another Life*'s exuberant schoolchildren,[32] preferring their unorthodox astronomy to the classical nomenclature for stars:

> children, look at these stars
> over Valencia's forest!
>
> Not Orion,
> not Betelgeuse,

DEREK WALCOTT'S POETRY

tell me, what do they look like?
Answer, you damned little Arabs!
Sir, fireflies caught in molasses.

"Fireflies caught in molasses": the children poignantly suggest that
stars are as small, live, and vulnerable as fireflies in the matrix of the
universe. Fireflies are among the favorite creatures in Walcott's bestiary.
He first mentions them in poetry in "Lampfall" (*C*, 58–59), where they
represent a fluctuating, delicate curiosity: "Like you, I preferred / The
firefly's starlike little / Lamp, mining, a question, / To the highway's
brightly multiplying beetles" (59). In *Ti-Jean and His Brothers* the Firefly "lights the tired woodsman / Home,"[33] but annoys the Devil by his
mercurial gaiety (when *"The* FIREFLY *passes, dancing,"* the Devil barks,
"Get out of my way, you burning backside, I'm the prince of obscurity
and I won't brook interruption!" [151]). "Sainte Lucie" makes the
final association between fireflies and words, with its "text of fireflies."
In this context the fireflies' luminosity in "Names," too, conjures the
short-lived magic of the children's own Creole words, their way of
naming. The last image of fireflies therefore becomes attached to the
title, "Names." But the firmament in which words are trapped—language as a whole?—is also rather ordinary, like molasses, and itself
semi-fluid.

"Sainte Lucie," which follows "Names" in *Sea Grapes*, crests in Walcott's often-quoted invocation to Creole ("Come back to me, / my language").[34] Ramsaran's opinion that Walcott "seems of recent years to
give more attention to the African and French creole elements of West
Indian society" (144) finds support in this climax. "Sainte Lucie" expands upon "Names" ' linguistic focus, relating creole language to the
object world and, through its reference to Dunstan St. Omer's altarpiece, to visual representation as well. The poem enacts its sense of
linguistic interrelatedness by means of at least three strategies: first, by
Walcott's personal declaration of allegiance to St. Lucian Creole in the
context of a polyglossic poem that relates Creole to the polyglossic (or
small-c creole) spirit more generally; second, by translation, by pre-
senting both a French Creole folk song and an English (or perhaps

"theater") Creole translation of it; and third, by ending the poem with reflections on a piece of visual art. Elizabeth Klosty Beaujour argues that bilingual writers often seek "a third language," "separate from and additional to any of the natural languages the bilingual [or polyglot] may speak or write," with which to "reconcile the other two" (*Alien Tongues*, 54); she also suggests that for some bilinguals or polyglots, visual systems of communication (or visual elements within systems) provide such a third term.[35] I discuss Walcott's attraction toward the visual realm in succeeding chapters; for now, suffice it to say that it is no coincidence that Walcott caps his exploration of languages in "Sainte Lucie" with a celebration of St. Omer's visual art.

Walcott divides "Sainte Lucie" into five parts; the first, "The Villages," seeks "something always being missed / between the floating shadow and the pelican" (*CP*, 309), between object and reflection (a structure that reminds us of mimetic notions of language's relation to the object world, and of Plato's shadows which mark the limit of human knowledge). Since Walcott often compares the poet to a fisherman (see "Lampfall" [*C*, 58], "Night Fishing," and "To Norline" [*AT*, 56–57]), the "net rotting among cans" and "sea-net / of sunlight trolling the shallows / catching nothing all afternoon" here evoke a futile poetic fishing expedition for knowledge. The form of "The Villages" reinforces the notion of the poem as a net, fishing line, or, perhaps better, a plumbline to determine true depth: its twenty-three lines form one sentence falling down the page as though toward that "for which the dolphins kept diving, that / should have rounded the day." The surfaces of "The Villages" repel the poet's effort to penetrate them, leading him "no nearer" to the "secret" that always seems above, below, or "between" things.

If we understand the sections chronologically, we should expect the second part to look elsewhere for the "something" that escapes the poet. If this is so, then we can infer that the poet turns his attention from landscape to language—particularly St. Lucian Creole, as we might guess from Walcott's creolized title (Sainte Lucie, not St. Lucia). The second part is "a sinuous column of island names, snatches of speech, and a parade of creatures, products, crops, colors."[36] It seems as though Walcott were wondering with Rilke, "Are we *here* perhaps just to say: house, bridge, well, gate, jug, fruit tree, window . . . ?"[37] But Walcott is actually more concerned with his nouns as words, as though comparing their individual qualities. His list of nouns has the air of reverie, and alternates serenely between Creole and English as though each language led to the other:

> Pomme arac,
> otaheite apple,
> . . . .
> cerise,
> the cherry,
> z'aman
> sea-almonds
> by the crisp
> sea-bursts,
> au bord de la 'ouvière. (*CP*, 310)

Walcott wavers in this section between appreciating words for their purely physical properties, and choosing words for metaphoric and symbolic importance. He begins opaquely and repetitiously, "Pomme arac, / otaheite apple, / pomme cythère, / pomme granate, / moubain," but his choice of "Pomme" as his first word is already symbolically loaded. The apples, sea-almonds, "jardins," "scissor-bird," and fireflies that appear in this section are all old favorites, for mythological and personal reasons. Although the section begins with an apparent resistance to transcendence—trying to get down into the rough basement of Creole—nouns invariably lead to metaphors: "z'ananas / the pineapple's / Aztec helmet." Walcott tries not to let the metaphoric harden into the merely conventional, so he includes the "ciseau / the scissor-bird" in his bestiary as a substitute for the poetically conventional nightingale, which he does acknowledge, but only as a mystery: "no nightingales / except, once, / in the indigo mountains / . . . flicker of pimento." Yet it is obvious that nouns are already poetry, while, as in that "text of fireflies" (311), things cannot help exercising what Walcott calls "the right of every thing to be a noun" ("Names," 42). That metaphorization occurs in either Creole or English reinforces its human, psychological necessity; language cannot stay earthbound, and that is not a tragedy but a fact of life.

Walcott's attraction to certain images carries him, by means of associations, across linguistic boundaries. Here, self-translation is normative, both of the translator's languages are already metaphorical, and the object world cannot be seen except through metaphorizing eyes. Translation becomes, in George Steiner's sense, part of human perception. The second part of "Sainte Lucie," after discovering the intractibility of metaphor, develops its observations about Creole in human terms, rising from lists of flora and fauna to the social world that defines an individual by his relation to the community: "Oh, so you is Walcott? / you is Roddy brother? / Teacher Alix son?" (312). Finally, Walcott addresses himself to a plural, female personification of St. Lucia. Walcott defines his own stance through the same methods of metaphorization (and recovers his initial apple image) in a moment of open self-translation:

> O Martinas, Lucillas,
> I'm a wild golden apple
> that will burst with love
> of you and your men,
> those I never told enough
> with my young poet's eyes
> crazy with the country,
> generations going,
> generations gone,
> moi c'est gens Ste. Lucie.
> C'est la moi sorti;
> is there that I born. (314)

"C'est la moi sorti; / is there that I born" encapsulates the compositional method of Walcott's English Creole poems, "taking that kind of [French Creole] speech and translating it, or retranslating it, into an English-inflected Creole." Walcott practices his method visibly here, without erasures.

The third and fourth parts of "Sainte Lucie" stand in the same relation to each other as those two lines: the third part, "Iona: Mabouya

Valley," consists entirely of a St. Lucian Creole folk song, and the fourth part entirely of its translation. In other words, Walcott juxtaposes the song and translation rather than subordinating either to the other in a footnote or on a facing page. Sections III and IV both bear the same title, "Iona: Mabouya Valley," but even so Walcott assigns separate section numbers. In addition, only the "original" bears an explanatory note and only the translation a dedication (to Eric Branford), indicating that we should consider the song and its translation two complementary "originals." Once again, then, from Creole to English this time, Walcott reveals that repetition is more than the sum of what is repeated.

Walcott claims that "Iona" is a *conte* or "narrative Creole song" (314); the song compacts many years of family history into about sixty lines of varying stress, with frequent rhymes. Corbeau, the protagonist, marries Iona to care for the two children she has had in his absence, falls into bad company in Roseau, and dies there. Corbeau now haunts the river, while Iona remarries and, it's implied, continues to create drama around her. Since Walcott claims that "Iona" is a true folk song that he heard on the road down the St. Lucian coast, its inclusion is a sort of quotation from an anonymous author in which St. Lucia speaks chorically for itself; and as a song, it comes as close as print can to embodying a yet unconsidered means of representation, music. The song's focus on marriage, Corbeau's humanist universality ("'Corbeau came back and said, 'I know niggers resemble, / they may or may not be mine, / I'll mind them all the same!' '"), and his death in Roseau all prefigure Part V's description of a St. Lucian Adam and Eve in Dunstan St. Omer's altarpiece for the Roseau Valley Church.

After describing the surfaces of things in the first section, finding more insight into things through nouns in the second, and gradually deepening an understanding of human and social relationships in the third and fourth sections, Walcott finishes his examination of St. Lucia by considering St. Omer's rendering of it: "life / repeated there, / the common life outside / and the other life it holds" (319). Valerie Trueblood observes that "this is where you are taken to the center of the island," just as "Sainte Lucie" as a whole is "the central poem of *Sea*

Grapes" (10). At the same time, St. Omer's visual art completes Walcott's survey of the forms of linguistic understanding (description, free association in Creole and English, narrative, song, translation, and so on).

Walcott imagines the centrality of the altarpiece quite literally: "The chapel, as the pivot of this valley, / round which whatever is rooted loosely turns . . . / draws all to it"; the valley's "roads radiate like aisles from the altar." St. Omer's central altarpiece functions as a microcosmic Achilles' shield, a "dull mirror" that "repeat[s]" life right down to "the parish priest, who, in the altarpiece, / carries a replica of the church." But this infinite regression does not become a "diminishing perspective" (Bhabha, 128) in which colonial discourse disturbs a Christian text by producing a metonymy of it. Rather, repetition reaches its apotheosis, as when Brodsky's translation of one of his poems becomes "transfiguration" ("MI," 35); art's perspective is diminutive, but its concentration intensifies rather than diminishes, "turn[ing] the whole island" (320). St. Omer portrays "two who could be Adam and Eve dancing"; Walcott asks us to imagine the pair when no one sees them, on "A Sunday at three o'clock / when the real Adam and Eve have coupled" (321). Although Walcott seems here to oppose the "real Adam and Eve" to St. Omer's version, a moment later the altar's Adam and Eve are the "real" ones after all, "when the real Adam and Eve have coupled / and lie in rechristening sweat // . . . her sweat on his panelled torso." Since no original Adam and Eve exist, St. Omer's husband and wife are the "real" Adam and Eve. Typically, the altarpiece enables the poet to believe in art as "real" and therefore to perceive (in a perception indistinguishable, in the Blakean sense, from imagination) "the real faces of angels" peeking in the church windows. Walcott's habitual craftsmanlike literalism—what an artist shapes defines reality—coincides in this poem with his conviction that "[t]his is a society whose highest ritual is art" (Ciccarelli, 300), and whose political hopes should rest on art (Hirsch 1979, 284). Therefore, in this last section all roads lead back to St. Omer's altarpiece.

The "secret" and the "something" "that should have rounded the day" in "The Villages" are present in the altarpiece as a "silence." All of the various languages and forms of understanding seem to point to this "silence, // which comes from the depth of the world" but also "from the wall of the altarpiece" (322). St. Omer's altarpiece is a type of art, but also the prototype of art; the glimmering of this understanding beyond language which it offers is the only thing Walcott can imagine beyond "the deaths / of as many names as you want, / Iona, Julian, Ti-Nomme, Cacao." St. Omer's art here approaches Beaujour's "third term" which reconciles languages. But although visual art is given the last word, we have to remember that Walcott's poem follows St. Omer's example by aiming to represent everything, including St. Omer's representation and its own. In "Sainte Lucie" as a whole Walcott aims, as Beaujour claims polyglot writers often do, at "his own idiosyncratic, constantly shifting, active balance or flexible synthesis of all his languages" (105). And it expands notions of "language" along the way to include visual systems and even things themselves.

In "Dis and Dat: Dialect and the Descent," Henry Louis Gates proposes that the poet serve as "a point of consciousness of the language,"[38] not losing track, as those Harlem Renaissance poets who rejected dialect did, of the "responsibility to [his or her] language" amidst the "obligation to something called art" (187). Walcott does feel a particular obligation to art, as well as an "urge to the universal" (Gates, 186), which could either have pulled his poems away from Creole or engulfed and destroyed it. In "Sainte Lucie" Walcott draws creole and English, poetry, folk song, translation, and visual art into his own poetic creole or "theater language," a place from which all communication radiates. But Walcott's universalism is not the kind that "in practice . . . demand[s] the sacrifice of all that [is] not somehow Judeo-Christian" (187); "Sainte Lucie" gains its confidence, finds its clues, through Creole. Benjamin's "pure language" becomes imaginable in Walcott's poems, but only as a form of creole itself.

WALCOTT'S STATEMENT "I couldn't pretend that my voice was the voice of the St. Lucia peasant or fisherman" foreshadows the connection he would soon make between creole and dramatic poetry. Walcott exposes the sense in which poetry is a creole when writing in his own voice; dramatic monologues offer another way to explore creolization, since a cosmopolitan poet can thereby evoke a fisherman's voice without "pretending" that poet and fisherman are the same. In the last ten years or so Walcott has explored this new possibility to the full. Before *Another Life* only "Pocomania," "Parang," and two sonnets from "Tales of the Islands"—all English Creole or "theater language" poems—speak through personae distinct from Walcott's own. Nor are there many early third-person poems that focalize perspective through distinct single characters. But *Another Life* gathers disparate voices, and from then on—especially in *The Star-Apple Kingdom* and *The Fortunate Traveller*—many of Walcott's best poems have been dramatic monologues: "The Schooner *Flight*," "The Saddhu of Couva," "The Man Who Loved Islands," "The Liberator," "The Spoiler's Return," "The Fortunate Traveller." Third-person narratives like "Koenig of the River" and "The Star-Apple Kingdom" also evoke the interior lives of characters remote from the poet's persona. Of the six dramatic monologues, three are in Caribbean creoles, while another, "The Man Who Loved Islands," uses what we might call a Los Angeles idiolect—although all these poems ultimately form Walcottian hybrid creoles.

When Walcott's dramatic personae use what we think of as oral languages, we naturally want to imagine these poems spoken. But I would like to elaborate on D. J. Enright's response to Walcott's calling Creole "a tongue they speak / in, but cannot write" (in "Cul de Sac Valley")—that "Creole is at least a tongue that you can write *about*."[39] Walcott writes about his "theater language" in these poems, and about the interpenetration of the demotic and the classical. A poem written in creole is not an oral form, but a written form that calls attention to a mainly oral language. Likewise, Walcott's North American vernacular doesn't aim simply to emulate North American conversation. Vendler, who finds Walcott's American unconvincing because "[t]he person who would say ' 'cause there's no kick in' something or other would not say 'contemplation of silvery light,' " assumes that "the only point of using colloquialisms is to have them sound colloquial" (23). Walcott does not share this assumption:

If some critic of Brodsky's work says "this isn't English," the critic is right in the wrong way. He is right in the historical, in the grammatical sense, by which I do not mean grammatical errors, but a given grammatical tone. This is not "plain American, which dogs and cats can read." . . . [T]he same critic, in earlier epochs, might have said the same thing about Donne, Milton, Browning, Hopkins. ("MI," 35–36)

"The Spoiler's Return" (*FT*, 53–60), for example, is a playground for countless idiolects that ricochet against each other in the poem's couplets. Lines like "I see these islands and I feel to bawl, / 'area of darkness' with V. S. Nightfall" construct an eccentric, highly literary idiom often at odds with the vernacular "voice" one expects from a "dialect poem." As a phantasm, a calypso singer released from hell "to check out this town" (53), Spoiler is both less and more than an individual. He is a "real," though not live, historical singer, but also the floating consciousness of satire, who "pass[es] through" (59) Jesus, Dante, Rabelais, "Lord Rochester, Quevedo, Juvenal, / Maestro, Martial, Pope, Dryden, Swift, Lord Byron" (60), because "that is the style" (59). Spoiler's song has a refrain or "chorus"—the lines about V. S. Nightfall—but when he invites the satirists of the past to "join Spoiler' chorus" (54), the term applies to Spoiler's allusive, choric mode as well. Satiric calypso depends upon previous utterances for its own substance, having "emerged from a sense of mimicry" ("CM," 9), and is as inherently belated a mode as translation is. Every satirist writes in the language—or in a mockery of the language—his or her community uses. But since satire's critical function presupposes particular dates, proper names, and quotations, Walcott's impulse to allude coincides happily in Spoiler's polyglossia with satire's *need* to allude. In other words, the constant awareness in creole that one is in effect alluding to other languages and ringing changes upon them suits creole to satire— a language of mimicry for a mode of mimicry.

The relatively heavy ironies of "Tales of the Islands" turn ambiguous in "The Spoiler's Return," which hinges upon the ambivalent logic of parasitism. Spoiler derides "the scene / . . . passing over this Caribbean" by comparing it to the least admirable parts of the food chain—

sharks "ripping we small-fry off with razor grins," "crab climbing crab-back, in a crab-quarrel, / and going round and round in the same barrel" (54), or "Corbeaux like cardinals" (58). Here Walcott satirizes Trinidad's sometime failure to recognize its own mimicry, so that "all Port of Spain is a twelve-thirty show, / some playing Kojak, some Fidel Castro" (57). Spoiler's Carnival sendup of what is already "Carnival, straight Carnival" (57), however, is a mimicry of mimicry, which, in this case, as a double negative becomes positive, reflects irony ironically. The parasite, "a moralist as mordant as the louse" (55), is qualified to reveal this, and so to upset the hierarchies of the food chain:

> the gift of mockery with which I'm cursed
> is just an insect biting Fame behind,
> a vermin swimming in a glass of wine,
> that, dipped out with a finger, bound to bite
> its saving host, ungrateful parasite. . . .
> ....
> the flea whose itch to make all Power wince,
> will crash a fête, even at his life's expense. (55)

At the same time Spoiler's language, full of others' poetry, enacts a literary parasitism, alluding to earlier poets in their own satiric moments. The "writer chap" who quotes Shelley in "Tales of the Islands" *may* be exposing the distance between himself and Shelley; Spoiler deliberately aligns himself with Shelley ("all Frederick Street stinking like a closed drain, / Hell is a city much like Port of Spain"), Yeats ("for a spineless thing, rumour can twist / into a style the local journalist"), and especially Rochester's "Satyre on Mankind," which he quotes: *"I hope when I die, after burial, / To come back as an insect or animal"* (54). "[C]rown and mitre me Bedbug the First" (55), Spoiler agrees. As Walcott's narrator in "Ruins of a Great House" breaks into a mansion not only with "the padded cavalry of the mouse" (*IGN*, 20) but also with Browne and Donne, Spoiler is only "a vermin"—in the tradition of Jesus and Rabelais. Thus, Spoiler steals from Western tradition, but that tradition is itself parasitical. Through his poetic thefts he becomes a parasite of language in Michel Serres's sense—an "exchanger" and "transformer"[40] who "plays at being the same" and in that very play shows that the "I" is "another":

> The parasite plays the game of mimicry. It does not play at being another; it plays at being the same. . . . [Mimicry] is an erasure of individuality and its dissolution in the environment; it is a good means of protection in both defense and attack. I am a bird; look at my wings, I am a mouse; long live rats. I am an other, *a* and *b*, once again a synthetic judgment and the birth of the joker and the white domino. We are now returning to the former logic. I am another. Ulysses is a sheep when he leaves Polyphemus's cave. (202)

Rimbaud's phrase " *'Je' est un autre*," which Serres echoes here, is paradoxical. This statement of identity between "I" and someone else implies a difference inside the "I," implies that even the statement "I am I" is not symmetrical but schizophrenic. Our glimpses of linguistic unity always implode. Walcott's poetry stands on this tension like a luxury hotel in a country often rocked by earthquakes. Yet we shouldn't underestimate or deny Walcott's, and our, desires to coincide: "the claim to *have coincided* with the Other allows the Other to be different and apart from the subject, but when the subject renounces even the *desire* to coincide, the question of *knowing* the Other becomes problematic."[42] Christopher Miller finds deft cultural balance in Ahmadou Kourouma's novel *Les Soleils des indépendances*, whose creolized French contains "*calques*, traces, imperfect translations of Malinké" (294) which are both "revealing and teasing: on the one hand explaining things, and on the other reminding us we are outsiders" (295–96). I find a similar tension in Walcott's language, although Miller might find Walcott's degree of creolization insignificantly subtle in comparison to Kourouma's. Walcott "reveals and teases" by his linguistic choices, but also by thematizing the bidirectional pull of language, toward universal language on one hand and private language on the other.

Although calypso depends upon performance, Walcott balances its immediacy against Spoiler's reliance on precursors. (Of course, this is characteristic of calypso itself, and of Caribbean music generally.[41])

Walcott's dramatic creole poems always remind us that written words only rouse the illusion of voice. His self-reflexive emphasis on textuality diminishes the illusion of spoken language, which demands that we suspend our awareness of reading. Considering Walcott's many sailing metaphors for writing—"the craft I have pulled at," and so on—the reader familiar with Walcott comes prepared to view the Trinidadian sailor-narrator of "The Schooner *Flight*" as a poet figure, and his world as a paper reality. The past and present are textual creations, as in so many Walcott poems, though not less real for it: in the fifth section, "Shabine Encounters the Middle Passage," Shabine's crew meets ghostly slave ships whose bodies have become documents of the past, "with sails dry like paper" (10). Shabine personifies history as a "parchment Creole" (8); history has forced him, like Caliban, into poetry, because "that's all them bastards have left us: words" (9).

But, unexpectedly, Shabine is also literally a poet, and a romantic one who lives for poetry. He even surpasses Stephen Dedalus's refusal to renounce Byron in the schoolyard, stabbing the cook who mocks his poems: "[N]one of them go fuck with my poetry again" (14). "The Schooner *Flight*," he tells us, is a found manuscript, written in Shabine's "exercise book, / this same one here" (13). Shabine is thus a version of the young Walcott, who, as he tells Hirsch, "used to write every day in an exercise book" (Hirsch 1986, 207). "Exercise" recalls the tentativeness of poetic composition, but places that diachrony between covers, in the synchronic and spatial "book." Moreover, the "exercise book" yearns to reconcile the oral to the written—here a poem in a supposedly oral language emphasizes its status as a document. Walcott solves the problem of "pretend[ing] that [his] voice was the voice of St. Lucian peasant" by making his protagonist a poet who can deploy Walcott's own habitual metaphors: "my common language go be the wind, / my pages the sails of the schooner *Flight*" (5). Shabine meets Walcott halfway, being half autobiographical, half fictive; half creator, half creation; half poet, half sailor; half individual, half communal.

Thematically "The Schooner *Flight*" is a Caribbean universal history.[43] The poem relinquishes the quotidian world, journeys through the underworld of the Middle Passage, and prophesies Shabine's end in Maria Concepcion's *Book of Dreams*: " 'I'm the drowned sailor in her *Book of Dreams*,' " he exclaims, recalling Eliot's Phlebus the Phoenician (like Christ and Orpheus, a fertility offering). In "Out of the Depths" a storm lashes the *Flight*'s captain to his position, "crucify to his post," and casts Shabine in the role of Christ's companion thief: "I feeding him white rum, while every crest / with Leviathan-lash make the *Flight* quail / like two criminal" (18). Finally, in "After the Storm" (Revelations), "the noon sea get calm as Thy Kingdom come" and Shabine envisions Maria Concepcion/Earth marrying her bridegroom, the ocean (18).

The poem's details repeat a structure in which the individual doubles for the communal, or we find one inside the other. Shabine tells his mistress, "I loved you alone and I loved the whole world" (12); when he declares, "I had no nation now but the imagination" (8), the word "nation" is doubled inside "imagination." On one hand the *Flight*, sailing "by the last breath of Romantic quest" (Bedient, 33), seeks "a target whose aim we'll never know, / vain search for one island that heals with its harbor" (19); the *Flight*'s (and the poem's) speed *outward* seems relentless. But at the same time Shabine's healing target, his "one island," exists within him, is his own self, as much as it exists anywhere. Shabine could well write, with Walcott's preferred ancestor Browne, "wee carry with us the wonders, wee seeke without us."[44] Shabine carries his community like a gene. His very nickname is "the patois for / any red nigger" (4),[45] and as he explains in his famous formulation, he is at once "any red nigger," a "nobody," an Aeneas who contains his people's future:

> I'm just a red nigger who love the sea,
> I had a sound colonial education,
> I have Dutch, nigger, and English in me,
> and either I'm nobody, or I'm a nation. (4)

Brodsky reflects, "Given the nature of the realm . . . one thinks not so much about blood as about language. . . . And it's from this height of 'having English' . . . that the poet unleashes his oratorial power"

(165–166). Shabine does make his English a possession, something he has enveloped; but multiplicity as a whole is what gives him "height." He could not see himself as "a nation," the idea that generates the oratorial power, if not for his internal diversity. Shabine's either/or claim is really a reflexive proposition—not a cause and effect that unfold continuously but a constant tension, each part of which produces the other.

In the end of the poem Walcott expands the tension between individual and communal by pulling his perspective as far back as it can go. From his nearly posthumous distance Shabine reveals the universe as an infinite series of such tensions:

> There are so many islands!
> As many islands as the stars at night
> on that branched tree from which meteors are shaken
> like falling fruit around the schooner *Flight*.
> But things must fall, and so it always was,
> on one hand Venus, on the other Mars;
> fall, and are one, just as this earth is one
> island in archipelagoes of stars. (19–20)

The relation of earth to stars recalls and enlarges Shabine's nobody/nation pairing like a magnifying mirror. Venus and Mars "fall" together to couple (like Maria Concepcion and Shabine); Venus and Mars, man and woman, make one. The collected peoples of earth also make one, just as we can find a microcosmic "nation" in Shabine. But Walcott's line break shakes these human unities, and the earth's with the stars: when we pull back even further, the unities disappear in more disunities. From an already wide perspective "This earth is one," but from an even wider perspective it is only "one / island in archipelagoes of stars." As Shabine looks higher and higher up his universe-tree, the branches become more and more numerous, and he can't see the top. In "Cul de Sac Valley" Walcott looks down at the base of the linguistic tree (as I'll show in Chapter Five) and finds all the branches connected at the moment the tree disappears into the ground. Shabine, looking up at the stars, gazes at the opposite end of Walcott's spectrum,

DEREK WALCOTT'S POETRY

watching an eternal series of unities separate into branches. The equation works both ways; we have to keep in mind simultaneously that what we consider multiple can be seen as one, and that what we think single is multiple. "I am one, mee thinkes," writes Browne, "but as the world" (*Religio Medici* II.7, in *Selected Writings*, 76).

Shabine's "branched tree" recalls "Cul de Sac Valley"'s tree of language through their mutual resemblance to the Tower of Babel. Venus and Mars in their fleshly forms "fall" in love as Adam and Eve fell; but the mineral rubble of meteors that double as apples also evokes the Tower's crash from divine language. Walcott pursues language beyond its fall *apart*, however, to reveal that it "fall[s], and [is] one." If language simply fell, it would be one thing; but it falls and falls some more, splintering and recombining. Language can say, like Spoiler, "I decompose, but I composing still" (53). The phrases "broken English" and "broken French" disclose the belief that a creole is literally a "fallen" version of a former language. Brodsky remarks, "The realm this poet comes from is a real genetic Babel. . . . Instead of—or along with—'Dutch' [in "The Schooner *Flight*"] there could have been French, Hindu [*sic*], Creole patois, Swahili, Japanese, Spanish of some Latin American denomination, and so forth" (164, 165). The Caribbean is the floor upon which the shiny pieces of languages lie spread. And as such, more than any individual piece it reflects the lost, uninterrupted sheen of universal language. We don't have to speak of subsuming creole to universal language, because it already *is* that language, revealing unity and disunity by turns.

Shabine, compacting writing and voice again, declares his contentment with the paradox of his oral language manuscript: "I am satisfied / if my hand gave voice to one people's grief" (19). Shabine's phrase features a peculiarity of English grammar, by which "people" (plural) can constitute "one people" (singular). There are always more plurals to surround the singular, however, and this consciousness of a further plural induces Shabine to acknowledge his limit, his understanding of only "*one* people's grief." Shabine qualifies his accomplishment as if he could have done more, could have spoken for *more* than "one people"; but if he has only done what he "modestly" claims, he has composed an epic, the most ambitious kind of poem that Western literature can conceive.

Walcott has compared himself, in *Omeros* and elsewhere, to Homer, a comparison that makes his poetry seem an "egotistical sublime" indeed. Brodsky, not noted for humility either, has also made the analogy for Walcott: "the West Indies is a huge archipelago, about five times as big as the Greek one. . . . [I]f there is a poet Walcott seems to have a lot in common with, it's nobody English but rather the author of the *Iliad* and the *Odyssey*" (167). A basis for comparison does exist, in cultural situation if not in epic achievement. It is very likely that Walcott knows Richmond Lattimore's introduction to his translation of *The Iliad*:

> We do not know where Homer was born any more than we know when he was born. . . . But of one thing we can, I think, be sure. He was born on or near the coast of Asia Minor. Homer, therefore, comes after the Ionian migration; the Ionian migration comes after the Dorian invasion. . . . But the Iliad is pre-Dorian. Homer, himself an Asiatic Greek, deals with an age when there were no Greeks in Asia. The people of what in his day were Ionia and Aiolia fight in the Iliad on the side of Troy. . . . The conclusion is, I think, quite clear. Homer knew—how could he help it?—that the Dorians and the others had come and driven his people across the water to Asia. But he ignored this, because he went back to an age generations before, when the ancestors of his audience, doubtless his own ancestors as well, were lords of Greece and went to Asia not as fugitives to colonize but as raiders to harry and destroy. (19–20)

Lattimore hints at a nostalgia in Homer for the days when the Hellenic tribes were not "fugitives," but "raiders"; Homer fulfills an elegiac function. But neither could Homer have missed the resemblance between the Dorians and Thessalians, raiders in recent history, and the Achaians, raiders in ancient history. If the rapacity of the Dorian invasion was still fresh in memory, that memory helped to flesh out the rapacity of the Achaians themselves. The Dorians conquered the Ionians along with other Hellenes, but long before that, the Achaians also conquered the Ionians along with the Trojans. Although the Achaians were "doubtless his own ancestors," so were the Trojans; Homer was "poisoned with the blood of both . . . / divided to the vein" (*IGN*, 18). Various writers have realized the potential advantage of this position:

> "The man who finds his homeland sweet is still a tender beginner; he to whom every soil is as his native one is already strong; but he is perfect to whom the entire world is as a foreign land." The more one is able to leave one's cultural home, the more easily one is able to judge it, and the whole world as well, with the spiritual detachment *and* generosity necessary for true vision. The more easily, too, does one assess oneself and alien cultures with the same combination of intimacy and distance.[46]

As the "fortunate traveller" possesses an anthropological advantage, the poet who writes in something other than his native tongue, and thereby comes to see all tongues as foreign, possesses a poetic advantage. Indeed, according to Beaujour, neurolinguistics has found that bilinguals and polyglots show an "enhanced capacity to seek out and create structure, superiority in 'divergent thinking' and 'cognitive flexibility,' as well as increased metalinguistic awareness . . . 'greater awareness of the relativity of things' and high 'tolerance for ambiguity' " (102). Borges, who is himself certain that a text is "a thing among things," asserts that the poetic substantiality of a language bares itself most completely to the barbarian: "Studying a language, one sees the words with a magnifying glass; one thinks, this word is ugly, this lovely, this too heavy. This does not happen in one's mother tongue, where the words do not appear to us isolated from speech."[47] Sartre, too, augments Hugo by suggesting that the poet is the one to whom native words seem foreign: "white words stretch out *in front of him*, strange and unfamiliar. . . . Yet it is common knowledge that this feeling of a failure before language when considered as a means of direct expression is at the source of all poetic experience."[48] For both Borges and Sartre the uncommon visibility of words' dispositions in a poem elevates poetry above ordinary language; for both, *foreignness* helps to make words visible. To see a native word as "a thing among things," the native poet has to see the word as a foreigner does, when, in Stevens's words, the visible is a little hard to see.

My digression linking creole to classical Greek is typical of discussions of creole, because the etiologies of creoles interminably trace colonial to colonizer, self to other, and "purity" to impurity, or locate one of these terms inside the other. The infinite regress of colonialism envelops both Homer and Shabine, driving Ionians from Greece to colonize Asia Minor, and Africans to St. Lucia to help colonize the Caribbean. The local poet whose creole has not been legitimized and the international poet like Brodsky or Milosz who rejects his official language for political reasons close the ends of a circle: Walcott's internationalism is the other side of his creolization. By entering English Walcott feels St. Lucian contours as though he were an outsider, exploring its creole etiologies; but the English he enters is in turn inside creole. For the genuinely polyglossic poet outside and inside lose their conventional meanings. As Heaney has reason to know, "[Walcott's] fidelity to the genius of English now leads him not away from but right into the quick of West Indian speech" (7). We find creole and classical, native and foreign, individual and communal, singular and multiple, doubled one within the other; as a result, we have to see all of Walcott's poetry as creole poetry, for it incorporates myriad idiolects, glimpses of private language, and glimpses of universal language alike into a creole of creoles. We lose track ultimately of the separate linguistic branches, and also of the trunk of the tree. Yet the poetic result is not a lowest common denominator, a bland vocabulary, but diction and syntax that challenge both Caribbeans and non-Caribbeans. Walcott's readers will wish to ask—many of his reviewers *have* asked—"What language is this?" It is a fruitful question for a poet to provoke. As for the answer, Shabine reflects, "You would have / to be colonial to know the difference, / to know the pain of history words contain" (*SAK*, 12).

"FRESCOES OF THE NEW WORLD": WALCOTT AND THE VISUAL ARTS

The eye was the only truth, and whatever traverses the retina fades when it darkens. . . .

—*Midsummer,* XVIII

WALCOTT ONCE ASKED Lowell which painter he thought his complement; the logic of the question seems to identify Walcott with the traditional idea of the "sister arts," in which painting and poetry supplement each other's vacancies. Lowell named Vermeer. Indeed, Lowell's "Epilogue" contrasts Vermeer's solidity with Lowell's supposedly crude discursivity, and finds in Vermeer what Lowell feels he lacks.[1] Walcott's poetry, too, often considers the arts' interrelations. In *Another Life* the narrator claims to relinquish the visual arts to "Gregorias" (Dunstan St. Omer) and to reserve the verbal arts for himself, again implying that the two friends' arts complement one another. In *Midsummer* Walcott returns to the comparison and ponders whether the visual arts have more direct access to the object world or represent experience more completely than the discursive arts.

Walcott contemplates these traditional notions only as potentialities, however, not as truths. Even as the poems argue with themselves over the arts' relations, they quietly merge the verbal with the visual, highlighting their own physical substantiality and the spatial quality of figuration. This inability in practice to divide the visual from the verbal allows Walcott to express an internal aesthetic multiplicity. Walcott's culture—which refuses a firm distinction between past and present, does not treat words as property, and encourages creolization and "polymusicality"—also encourages this kind of artistic creolization. Carnival is an unclassifiable event that mingles spectacle, music, and words. According to Beaujour, polyglot writers such as Nabokov apply a "stereo-linguistic optic" to words, having developed a capacity for "psychological synaesthesia" through their multisided knowledge of language ("The stereopticon is . . . an instrument that creates a single, three-dimensional image by combining images from two separate points of view" [102]). Walcott is similarly well positioned to challenge genres[2] and art forms; his poetry not only takes account of other arts, but finds those arts themselves internally multiple.

Walcott's brief lyrics tend to assume aesthetic interpenetrations, freely applying questions of representation derived from the visual arts to poetry or vice versa. Walcott's associations between painters and writers in his interviews and classroom remarks[3] apply one logic to Lowell and Benjamin West (9/28/88), Marvell and Seurat (10/5/88), Zagajewski and Corot (10/12/88), Samuel Palmer and Edward Thomas (1/25/89). In his comments it becomes clear that the arts are not parallels in competition with each other, but fluid and ultimately uncategorizable means of expression. *Another Life* and *Midsummer*, Walcott's longer treatments of the arts' relations, begin by considering whether visual art *may* be more intimate with the object world, but in both poems this possibility is mainly a rhetorical excuse for meditations upon representation. Walcott's long poems, too, find the arts time-bound, figurative, and seamed by their common limitations.

WALCOTT'S EARLY POEM to Harry Simmons, "To a Painter in England" (*IGN*, 16–17), a background text for *Another Life*, already separates the two arts only to question their separation. In this rather formal blank verse epistle Walcott writes "to explain / How I have grown to learn your passionate / Talent with its wild love of landscape." "Your . . . talent" here refers to landscape painting; but the phrase also shows Walcott's characteristic impulse to locate his own "talent[s]" and others' in the same space, as the "I" learns "your . . . [t]alent." The reader may react to this claim by thinking, "I thought your talent was poetry." The lines make one wonder, that is, whether this poet has "grown to learn" a painter's talent in his own painting or in poetry.

While in *Another Life* writing sometimes seems methodologically indirect in its "sidewise crawling," Walcott indicates here that writing seems too "explicit" in its effect:

> So you will understand how I feel lost
> To see our gift wasting before the season,
> You who defined with an imperious pallette
> The several postures of this virginal island,
> You understand how I am lost to have
> Your brush's zeal and not to be explicit.

The poet would prefer, like the painter, "not to be explicit" (even though the entire epistle, by his own declaration, intends "to explain"). Writing is thus burdened with double liabilities—laboriousness of method, explicitness of effect.

The last stanza of "To a Painter in England," however, reverses the course of the poem and embraces the difficulty and "failure" it had previously lamented. At the same time it responds to the poet's sense of loss by conflating the art he misses with the one he possesses:

> But the grace we avoid, that gives us vision,
> Discloses around corners an architecture whose
> Sabbath logic we can take or refuse;
> And leaves to the single soul its own decision
> After landscapes, palms, cathedrals or the hermit-thrush,
> And wins my love now and gives it a silence
> That would inform the blind world of its flesh. (17)

Walcott's terms become paradoxical, resisting attempts to sort them out, even as rhymes emerge and, working in the opposite direction, hurriedly close off the poem. The stanza begins with a "But" that signals Walcott's rejection, at least in part, of the longing "not to be explicit" he has just stated. His "decision" now celebrates poetry's capacity to "explain" or "be explicit": he "would inform." Although we might want to call this "gaining a voice," Walcott attributes the capacity to inform to "silence" and allows "vision" as well to "disclose." The stanza brings up "architecture" and "inform[ation]," that is, only to provide each with negative markings. Walcott's network of paradoxical adjectives pollinates terms associated with one art with attributes associated with the other, and reveals the constitutional ambiguity of each: "vision" and "architecture" "disclose" and possess "logic," while "silence . . . would inform." "Vision" is forced to refer more broadly to the "discernment" that guides either art, "architecture" to structure in either. "To a Painter in England" never manages to break the ice of its formal tone, but it does show how metaphoric descriptions of both arts must be, and how, in W. J. T. Mitchell's words, "The burden of proof . . . is not . . . to show that some works have spatial form but . . . to provide an example of any work that does not."[4]

When Walcott imagines the interpenetrations of representation taking narrative form in *Another Life*, he has to represent a simultaneity as a development. Oppositions that are eventually shown to constitute each other must at first seem unrelated. Yet beneath the arts' apparent separateness lies a vast underground, which Walcott elsewhere imagines as a system of roots.[5] There entities believed distinct intertwine, and discoveries about one art pertain to the other.

In the early sections of *Another Life* the visual arts' potentially objectifying authority, "The clear / glaze of another life, / a landscape locked in amber" (1.i.18–20), entices the poet into painting and becomes his first model for art. The young student confronts an ancient problem, the difficulty of rendering a diachronic experience in an apparently synchronic form:

> All afternoon the student
> with the dry fever of some draughtsman's clerk
> had magnified the harbour, now twilight
> eager to complete itself,
> drew a girl's figure to the open door. . . .
> . . . .

                    This silence waited
for the verification of detail:
. . . .
and for the tidal amber glare to glaze
the last shacks of the Morne till they became
transfigured sheerly by the student's will,
a cinquecento fragment in gilt frame. (1.i.23–37)

The poet's art cannot (at least not yet) admit temporality: "In its dimension the drawing could not trace / the sociological contours of the
promontory" (1.ii.1–2). But even here in Chapter 1 Walcott hints that
objectifying rigor, far from resolving this classic problem, would dam-
age what it encountered, "glaz[ing]" perception and "lock[ing]" the
landscape, like "a cinquecento fragment," into a "gilt frame" (1.i.38).
The criminal connotations in both "gilt" and "frame"[6] intimate that
the painter's wish to "transfigure" and "frame" the landscape by
"will" would, if attained, actually violate the beloved scene. The poet's
hope to "verify" his experience like a scientific finding is a "dry fever,"
misconceived from the beginning. Although twilight's own "tidal amber glare" momentarily "verif[ies]" the artist's vision of an ambered
world, that vision cannot endure any longer than twilight itself; "twilight" has a visual aspect, the amber glow, but also a temporal aspect,
as a finite portion of the day. As it asserts its temporality, "The vision
die[s], / the black hills simplif[y] / to hunks of coal" (1.i.39–41). Walcott develops similar connotations for "twilight" in "What the Twilight
Says." There "dusk" heightens experience "like amber on a stage set"
(3), and coincides with Walcott's former fruitless rigidity in his direction of actors: "I insisted on a formality which had nothing to do with
[the actors'] lives. It made me believe that twilight had set me apart
and naturally I arrived at the heresy that landscape and history had
failed me" (32).

Harry Simmons, a "master" artist whose physical vision is imperfect,
stands against possessive mastery of the object world. Simmons's
"spectacles" are "thick as a glass paperweight," like the aged Monet's
or Degas's, and his eyes themselves resemble glass; he cannot pretend
to see through a "clear / glaze," and yet precisely this infirmity gives

him aesthetic independence. Walcott explains in his interview with Dennis Scott, "when I say the visual I don't mean a visual thing that has the solidity of the object. It's a way of looking, you know, a concentration that is calmer" (78–79). Simmons represents such internally directed concentration:

> with spectacles thick as a glass paperweight
> over eyes the hue of sea-smoothed bottle glass,
> the man wafted the drawing to his face
> as if dusk were myopic, not his gaze.
> Then, with slow strokes, the master changed the sketch. (1.i.75–79)

Simmons's confidence lies not in his manipulation of the object world, but in his own understanding; he reorders the sketch without looking at the scene that inspired it. If his gaze is "myopic," the "dusk"'s own clarity is suspect.

The poet soon accepts and even becomes overenthusiastic about nonrepresentational art. He envies Darnley, the village blind man, for the "great affliction" he shares with "Homer and Milton" (3.ii.38, 37). When the poet and Gregorias promise to render their island "in paint, in words" (8.ii.4), they pledge allegiance to an "astigmatic saint," El Greco (8.ii.2). The story of St. Lucia, whose passage toward beatitude leads her through blindness—"patroness of Naples, they had put out her eyes, / saint of the blind, / whose vision was miraculously restored" (12.i.56–58)—is yet another version of the Homeric or Miltonic exchange of physical for spiritual vision. Walcott, playing on the etymology of "astigmatism," hints that blindness is no "stigma" but a mark of authenticity like other saints' "stigmata." Now faulty vision, "defects in the lens of the eye" (*American Heritage Dictionary*), actually defines painterly or poetic perception.

Another Life later qualifies these values, however. Gregorias and the poet, taking literally "Baudelaire's exhortation to stay drunk" (12.ii.13), tread on dangerous ground, since their envy of physical blindness is as romantic and futile as trying to "frame" physical reality. "Astigmatism" at its worst can produce a merely oblivious art. For Walcott the best artists know that what they would render is itself fictive, but balance that knowledge against their aspiration toward precision *within* their fictive renderings. Magritte is Walcott's favorite surrealist because he gives us "exact dreaming, detailed reverie," unlike Dali, who becomes "too rhetorical," and Chirico, whose "languid perspectives [are] evanescent. . . . Magritte is tougher in terms of precision" (10/12/88). This sort of formulation redefines "reality" instead of jettisoning it, and demands "reality" within art while it points out the mimicry encompassing art: "Any corner of Magritte is real: only when assembled is it a metaphor. What is painted through the nonexistent head is real. Every bead of dew is itself a mirror" (10/12/88).

Another Life thus revises its goals for painting as its plot unfolds. But just as the poet and Gregorias arrive at their antirealist resolution, the poet abandons his painterly ambitions. He explains his reasons in Chapter 9:

> Where did I fail? I could draw,
> I was disciplined, humble, I rendered
> the visible world that I saw
> exactly, yet it hindered me, for
> in every surface I sought
> the paradoxical flash of an instant
> in which every facet was caught
> in a crystal of ambiguities,
> I hoped that both disciplines might
> by painful accretion cohere
> and finally ignite,
> but I lived in a different gift,
> its element metaphor. (9.ii.1–13)

This announcement seems surprising and sudden in a poem filled with ardent declarations of love for painting. Pamela Mordecai, by way of explanation, gives a thorough reading of Chapter 9 in terms of what she calls Walcott's "prismatic" vision or his "disposition to perceive and construe experience in sometimes unresolved pluralities."[7] Mordecai argues that the poet actively chooses words over paint, contrary to his rhetoric of failure, because "[t]he prison of the canvas is a linear (planar) prison" unsuited to Walcott's "prismatic" thought (97). Indeed, Chapter 1's observation that "in its dimension" the poet's drawing cannot represent "sociological contours" foreshadows Walcott's craving in Chapter 9 for "facet[s]." Walcott's remarks to Hirsch also support Mordecai's interpretation:

> What I tried to say in *Another Life* is that the act of painting is not an intellectual act dictated by reason. It is an act that is swept very physically by the sensuality of the brushstroke. I've always felt that some kind of intellect, some kind of pre-ordering, some kind of criticism of the thing before it is done, has always interfered with my ability to do a painting. (Hirsch 1986, 206)

Walcott feels that his clumsy rationality can't adapt to the immediacy of painting, but by the same token, may assume that painting can't accommodate "intellect" and "criticism" very well. In Chapter 9 Walcott's poet obviously assumes that painting cannot accommodate "metaphor" (at least, not easily). Yet this need not mean that painting is inferior, as Mordecai implies. Her analysis rests on an assumption that painting effects a "simple translation/transformation of visible world to replica in paint" (101), an assumption Walcott would not share. She understands the poet's choice between visual and verbal arts as one between "simply . . . interpret[ing] the world" in painting versus "redefin[ing] the word" in the "larger battle" of literature (101). But Gregorias, as well as the poet, pledges an antirealist "astigmatism." Walcott would not agree that "For Gregorias the flat canvas is sufficient" (101) if by that we assume that flatness precludes redefining the world. To the contrary: the flat canvas *necessitates* redefinitions of the object world.

Rather, while the visual arts have their limitations—"A bird's cry tries to pierce / the thick silence of canvas" (9.i.24–25)—the verbal arts and "real life" share these. Take the case of the bird's cry: even a poem, although it may give us a phonetic "score" for the reproduction of certain sounds, does not *emit* sound. Writing therefore seems indirect, a "sidewise crawling," in comparison to painting, and the narrator "envie[s] and underst[ands]" Gregorias's "derision" of it (9.ii.33, 32). As Mordecai shrewdly suggests, however, "sidewise crawling" (identified with the sea crab, another symbolic animal from Walcott's "Tropical Bestiary" [C, 21]) is not necessarily a disadvantage, since "obliquity" is "a kind of guerilla strategy" (103). Both arts, then, are oblique. In Chapter 9 the poet lets go not of visual art per se but of an absolute division between visual and verbal. That is, we can read the line "A bird's cry tries to pierce / the thick silence of canvas" as a complaint about painting's restrictions, but we can also see in it the arduous and admirable *attempt* to approach the nonvisual in paint—and it is far from clear that this attempt is absolutely unsuccessful. The very next lines show us a reciprocal attempt within verbal art: "the wild commas / of crows are beginning to rise" (9.i.26–27). Wishing to make the arts "cohere" presupposes their fundamental division; situating both arts along a spectrum does not.

Walcott suggests the subtlety of this spectrum in various ways. First, he makes a practice of referring to already textualized paintings. Svetlana Alpers has shown that Dutch artists frequently represent texts within paintings, allowing the visual arts to include the verbal;[8] Walcott's references to paintings in books enact a similar openness from the corresponding side, embedding pieces of visual art within texts and those texts in turn within his own text about visual art and poetry. Although the poet's first glimpses of painting and poems are local and direct—Simmons's correction of the poet's sketch, and a quotation from one of George Campbell's poems ("Holy")[9]—he encounters Western classics indirectly, through Leonardos and Verrocchios "In [Thomas] Craven's book" (4.2).[10] The poet calls Craven's book "[Gregorias's] museum," and of course, St. Lucians would need to turn to their bookshelves, not to museums, for paintings. Indeed, anywhere in the world one more often sees paintings reproduced than not. Walcott emphasizes what we take for granted, that we usually *experience* a painting through a book's mediation: its size, its condition, its ordering, its commentary. Thomas Craven makes precisely this point in his introduction, and by means of a startlingly familiar phrase: "I cannot buy Rembrandts and Holbeins and Daumiers; nor can you nor anyone—save the wealthy collectors. The bulk of the great art of the world is inaccessible to all—save the most fortunate travellers" (14). Yet the poet finds substitutes for the inaccessible masterpieces in his father's "volumes of *The English Topographical Draughtsmen*" (9.iii.5) and Gregorias's "turpentine-stained editions / of the Old Masters" (8.i.52–53). The individual histories of Gregorias's reproductions even increase their authority: like the "originals," they are redolent of turpentine. Each painting varies from others and so, more subtly, does each reproduction vary from other reproductions. Thus, the poet does not ask Gregorias if he remembers Constable's "The Hay Wain"—Gregorias has never seen "The Hay Wain"—but rather, " 'The Hay Wain' / in [his] museum, Thomas Craven's book" (12.iii.9–10).

Second, Walcott emphasizes the physical substantiality of written words, demonstrating that words share the aspect of material presence with images and that both painter and poet practice within the looser category of craft. Gregorias and the poet are "[d]runk, / on a half pint of joiner's turpentine" (8.i.63–64), "joined" by their dedication to building: "we swore to make drink / and art our finishing school, / join brush and pen and name / to the joiner's strenuous tool" (12.iv.24–27). It is in this context that Walcott elaborates a much-loved metaphor, comparing language to a tree and the poet to a carpenter. As early as "Crusoe's Journal" (*C*, 51–52) the Crusoe-poet turns "the bare necessities / of style . . . to use," "hewing a prose / as odorous as raw wood to the adze" (51). More than twenty years later Walcott would say, "At this period of my life and work, I think of myself in a way as a carpenter" (Hirsch 1986, 206), and would reuse the carpenter metaphor in *The Arkansas Testament* (for example, 9–15). In *Another Life* the poet renounces painting only to connect poetry to the craftsmanship of carpentry:

> I watched the vowels curl from the tongue of the carpenter's plane,
> resinous, fragrant
> labials of our forests,
> over the plain wood
> the back crouched,
> . . . .
> sweat-fleck on blond cedar. . . . (12.i.1–8)

At the heart of the *paragone* between visual art and writing lies the opposition between nature and culture, and thus physical and mental labor. It therefore comforts Walcott's poet to see that nature and culture—in terms of representation, the originality of the object world and the mimicry of art—are linked, whether or not he wills it, through craft. This emphasis on craft can become grandiose, since the poet-carpenter resembles Jesus: "the rain driv[es] its nails . . . / into his hands" (16.i.70–71). But it also leads Walcott to accept art's temporality. If language is like wood it is a material presence, but like all material presences, perishable. The fire of Castries (June 19, 1948) drives this point home by interrupting the young artists' romantic notions with its "fierce rush" of "history" (12.iv.32–33). Nor does the rest of reality exist in any more permanent fashion. The young artist struggling to render his landscape feels overwhelmed by the object world's "furnace"-like presence (9.i.70–72), but the fire of Castries disfigures that object world as well. Amid such all-consuming transience the artists' short-lived ecstasies do not seem particularly fragile or limited; transience even flushes art with a kind of feverish light. "[E]ach steeple [is] pricked / by its own wooden star" (21.ii.34–35), and Walcott ends by celebrating Gregorias's "crude wooden star, / its light compounded" by the "mortal glow" of the fire that will consume it (23.iv.22–23).

Another Life implies that the best art recognizes its vulnerability while not completely surrendering to flux. Walcott's model of artistic balance is the Flemish painter who renders "the world," but in a drop of water. For Walcott, Stevens and Monet lack form in comparison, Eliot is like a "broken bundle of mirrors," and "cubism [is] shattered faith" (11/9/88). At the other extreme, "Flaubert tried to let the object itself do all the work, . . . denying that the writer is a writer" (10/19/88). Walcott's own preferred metaphors for art, like the waterdrop or the "text of fireflies," inhabit the ground between these poles.

W H I L E *Another Life* unfolds its implications for visual art and poetry gradually and dramatically, Walcott's lyrics, even very early ones, contain those conclusions from their beginnings. Meditations on visual art allow Walcott to talk about writing and yet maintain a sensual and descriptive surface. One of Walcott's earlier formulations about visual art, "A Map of Europe" (*C*, 42),[11] enacts the relations between perception, representation, and the object world. In this poem the object world is not meaningfully distinct from perceptions or representations of it and recognizable only from previous representations; human perception of that world therefore remains figurative.

In the first stanza the poet's "flaking wall . . . / Maps Europe with its veins" when he perceives it according to "Leonardo's idea" that familiar shapes appear in the object world's random patterns—that "landscapes open on a waterdrop / Or dragons crouch in stains." Following Leonardo's suggestion, Walcott arranges a "landscape" out of the room's accoutrements, centered around a beer can whose "gilded rim gleams like / Evening along a Canaletto lake,"

> Or like that rocky hermitage
> Where, in his cell of light, haggard Jerome
> Prays that His kingdom come
> To the far city.

The poem's associations lead both outward, from the room's objects to new metaphors for them (stain → dragon, flaking wall → map of Europe), and backward, from the room's objects to previous representations of similar objects (loaves of bread in Vermeer and Chardin):

> The light creates its stillness. In its ring
> Everything *IS*. A cracked coffee cup,
> A broken loaf, a dented urn become
> Themselves, as in Chardin,
> Or in beer-bright Vermeer,
> Not objects of our pity.

In either case the room's objects assume significance from the associations the poet makes to them. There are no "things themselves," only a stain that becomes a dragon when seen through "Leonardo's idea" or "A broken loaf, a dented urn" that "become / Themselves" when we perceive them "as in Chardin."[12] Objects must undergo as much transformation to "become / Themselves" as to become other. Perception encompasses transformation here; when the poet praises "the gift

DEREK WALCOTT'S POETRY

/ To see things as they are," he is praising the "light" by which painters like Chardin and Vermeer see, not the object world in its unmediated solitude:

> In it is no lacrimae rerum,
> No art. Only the gift
> To see things as they are, halved by a darkness
> From which they cannot shift.

In this passage the object world and its representations, "things as they are" and things perceived, interrelate in tangled ways that mimesis cannot explain. In the last two lines Walcott selects the very feature of painting we might think most obviously artificial—its flat surface, or ability to represent only two-dimensional, "halved" things—and equates that artificiality not with "art" but with "things as they are." Further, "To see things as they are" (see them in this "light") requires a "gift," and means seeing them "halved by a darkness / From which they cannot shift"—like painted images against a black background. "Art" and "things" and "the gift / To see" now oppose, now enclose each other, resisting our desire to string them into a familiar formula ("the gift / To see" + "things" = "art").

Moreover, in "A Map of Europe" Walcott demands that we see objects "Themselves," "Not objects of our pity" (not substitutes for people). Although this formulation seems to reject figurative interpretations of still life, the rest of the poem redefines objects "Themselves," so that objects become "Themselves" only through Chardin-like perception. This redefinition obviously qualifies any rejection of figuration in still life. And indeed the poet does make figurative interpretations of the still life he imagines, suggesting the condition of its nouns as well as merely naming them. The background of "darkness" in a Chardin-style still life seems to "halve" things so that we can't see the "other side" they lack. But by noting the same effect in his room, the poet reminds us of the "darkness," in the sense of "ignorance," that circumscribes the things of the world, and of space and time that also lock real objects into the few dimensions they dominate, "From which they cannot shift." Walcott makes the same point more explicitly in *Mid-*

summer: "the depth of *nature morte* / was that death itself is only another surface / like the canvas, since painting cannot capture thought" (XVIII). In this case the limitations of still life, particularly that of its "surface," point to severe limitations in reality: "death itself is only another surface." The poet of *Another Life*, too, decides that he "can no more move [his mother] from [her] true alignment, / . . . than we can move objects in paintings" (2.iii.65–66). Painted figures can't escape from space, but this fact leads to a question the visual arts often raise: are living things so superior, who can't escape from time?[13] Such moments break down the barriers between physical depth and surface, literal and figurative expression. The poem rejects Virgil's figure of the "lacrimae rerum," yet characterizes "things as they are" by an equivalent figurative use of "darkness."[14] Although this time figurative darkness coincides with the actual color of a painting's background, and of shadows in a room, the poem doesn't really claim this innocent reading; and its last phrase, "they cannot shift," personifies "things" rather than leaving them in their strangeness. When we see "things as they are," we still see through figures: at most, we see figuration itself.

Finally, although it is in itself a minor lyric, "A Map of Europe" introduces Walcott's enthusiasm for works of art that balance precision and figuration, permanence and temporality. Detail is once again the hinge of these qualities. The poem implicitly praises Canaletto, Chardin, and Vermeer for their detail—as we can better comprehend by exploring some of the associations, for Walcott, of that landscape-containing "waterdrop." The image of the droplet haunts Walcott's poetry. As early as "Origins," Walcott's surrealistic attempt to sketch in the "mythopoeic coast" of unrecorded Caribbean history, he praises "those [who] . . . / Harvest ancestral voices" by attending to nature's immanent prophecies: "Those who conceive the birth of white cities in a raindrop / And the annihilation of races in the prism of the dew" (*SP*, 55). In *Midsummer* Walcott explicitly links a waterdrop to detail:

The Dutch blood in me is drawn to detail.
I once brushed a drop of water from a Flemish still life
in a book of prints, believing it was real.

It reflected the world in its crystal, quivering with weight.
What joy in that sweat drop, knowing others will persevere! (XVII)

The drop of water is at once an image of gemlike precision and, like
the carpenter's "sweat-fleck on blond cedar" (*AL*, 12.i.8), of the effort
it takes to achieve that precision. Similarly, about a phrase in Adam
Zagajewski, "when dew / gleams on a suitcase,"[15] Walcott has said,
"What gleams on the wet suitcase is a precision that doesn't need to
be there—crystalline and clear," and then compared Zagajewski's
"dew" to Magritte's precision ("Every bead of dew is itself a mirror"
[10/12/88]).[16]

"Precision that doesn't need to be there," as Walcott puts it, is the
defining characteristic, for Norman Bryson, of "realism." Apparently
random details—"precision that doesn't need to be there"—lend a
work rhetorical verisimilitude.[17] By pointing out Magritte's use of random detail Walcott reminds us that in spite of this rhetorical realism,
the structures that enclose precision remain fictive. Walcott typically
negotiates the tensions between verisimilitude and figuration, permanence and temporality, solidity and fluidity, by balancing them against
each other in this way, allowing at most *either* the work's internal mi-
nutiae *or* its larger structure to aspire to verisimilitude and permanence, but not both at once. If the work "reflects the world," it does
so in a dewdrop; but a dewdrop is very ephemeral (indeed, an emblem
of ephemerality), so that its exquisitely reflective details exist in an
imperfect and transient form. The dewdrop's message is "that *others*
will persevere." Likewise, "light" in "A Map of Europe" creates a hermetic magic circle, a "cell" (like St. Jerome's) or a "ring" (perhaps
guarded or threatened by stain-dragons) in which objects achieve
"Themselves." At the same time, however, an uncertain dark background encircling the ring highlights its fragility (as "the far city" likewise contextualizes Jerome's cell), and this uncertainty constitutes its
luminosity.

Walcott's even earlier sonnet on Rembrandt's "The Polish Rider"
(*IGN*, 70) provides additional clues into his poetic, and this time relates
human emotion to form. In this poem the artist's rage for form is sub-
liminated passion:

The grey horse, Death, in profile bears the young Titus
To dark woods by the dying coal of day;
The father, with worn vision portrays the son
Like Dürer's knight astride a Rozinante;
The horse disturbs more than the youth delights us.
The warrior turns his sure gaze for a second,
Assurance looks its father in the eye,
The inherited, bony hack heads accurately
Towards the symbolical forests that have beckoned
Such knights, squired by the scyther, where to lie.
But skill dispassionately praises the rider,
Despair details the grey, cadaverous steed,
The immortal image holds its murderer
In a clear gaze for the next age to read.

Walcott here addresses problems of empathy and form similar to those Vendler discusses in her reading of Keats's "Ode on a Grecian Urn":

> Keats's response to the urn . . . becomes a classic case of the dilemma which the psychologists of perception . . . call the dilemma of figure and ground. If the spectator focuses on one aspect, the other recedes into the background, and vice versa. In this case, the dilemma is that of subject matter and medium, of "men" and "marble." While Keats pressingly interrogates the urn's figures, he cannot think of them as other than real. . . . On the other hand, as soon as he allows his consciousness of the marble medium to arise, he loses his sense of the figural representations as "real," and a disjunction in tone marks the breaking of the spell.[18]

Walcott's beholder of "The Polish Rider" experiences a similar vacillation between levels of aesthetic understanding. Walcott indicates at first that the painting's empathetic and formal qualities are separate, or can at least be considered separately: on the empathetic level, for example, "The warrior turns his sure gaze for a second," while on the formal level "skill dispassionately praises the rider." Walcott further breaks empathetic properties into two kinds, literal and allegorical. Allegorically, "The grey horse" corresponds to "Death" and "The warrior" to "Assurance," and the forests are "symbolical" (presumably of the dangers that lead to death). Although Rembrandt's painting contains these various readings simultaneously, the poet can't describe them simultaneously, and so must pause to make correlations between possible readings. But with its final paradox the poem makes an effort to superimpose the literal and the allegorical: "The immortal image holds its murderer / In a clear gaze." The literal object of representation, the model, is a mortal human being; but as either Assurance (or even Mortality) or a painted image, it is "immortal." The now-dead individual model and artist and the "immortal image" somehow co-exist.

The painting's discursivity conveys passion, "But skill dispassionately praises." "Dispassionate praise" is something of a contradiction in terms, however. Although we may make an effort to see the painting's empathetic or formal qualities at a given moment of observation, emotion and "skill" ultimately reside in each other; it is "Despair" itself that "details the grey, cadaverous steed." Grasp of detail and outline, requirements of technique, sublimate despair and passion, which in turn literally "inform" form.

Walcott explores these relations between verisimilitude and figuration, formality and empathy, and permanence and temporality most exhaustively in a beautiful and ambitious lyric, "The Hotel Normandie Pool" (*FT*, 63–70). Although this poem is not directly about visual art, it shows the tensions of visual perception and interpretation at work within autobiography; Walcott here reveals why such tensions arise, how they move the poet, and why he manipulates them as he does. The poem concludes that perception must take the form of self-reflection. Walcott plots the versions of self-reflection by aligning groups of apparently correspondent images—images of reflection, like water, mirrors, and the surface of the eye, which in turn reflect one another. But the experience of reading the poem frustrates our figurative expectations: instead of a stable descriptive surface and a parallel figurative "level" beneath that, we sense multiple metaphoric "levels" which sometimes parallel, sometimes contradict one another. "The Hotel Normandie Pool" is uncomfortably quasi-allegorical, like Lowell's "Falling Asleep Over the Aeneid," and as difficult as Lowell's poem to grasp. James Dickey worries that Walcott may have developed a "chronic inability to state, or see, things without allegory,"[19] and the observation certainly applies to this poem. But that perception can be only figurative ("allegorical" in de Man's sense), and unstably so, is itself an essential insight of Postmodern poetry.

Walcott's multiple analogies make summary both difficult and necessary. The poem is set on "New Year's Morning," and so the poet broods upon his upcoming fiftieth birthday (January 23) and the consequent changes he suffers (divorce, aging, and withdrawal from his family, from romance, and from the Caribbean). In Part I the poet discloses his solitude, depicts his youthful daughters, and wishes for transformation: " 'Change me, my sign,' " he addresses the water, " 'to someone I can bear.' " The poet, an Aquarius—"the water bearer"— can no longer bear himself; one might say that his image no longer "holds water." Ovid, the poet of metamorphoses, appears in response to this call for transformation. Considering the phrasing of the poet's plea, we understand that the modern poet "bears" Ovid within his own consciousness—Ovid is "someone [he] can bear," yet himself at the same time.[20] Given Ovid's presence, the numerals dividing the poem's sections are appropriately Roman; and, as in "Names," section "I" is devoted to the solitary self while "II" introduces further characters, in this case precisely the I's double. The poet's invocation resurrects his precursor from the dead, as Walcott reminds us by references to Ovid's "pallor," "graveness," "shades," and gesture of "bur[ying] his room key" in his robe pocket. Ovid is a figment of the poet's imagination, a "species" or secondary reality whose countenance seems to have been influenced by the poet's memories of Roman sculpture or profiles on Roman coins. Ovid's language, Latin (which the poet conveniently knows), has a "mineral glint," and his features tan to "a negotiable bronze." While it is also a measure of Ovid's secondary nature that one often cannot distinguish him from the poet, this doesn't imply the poet's contrasting primacy. He too speaks in the "dead language" of Latin, and his own body, like a statue's, is "vein[ed] . . . in stone" at the sight of the apparition. Furthermore, Walcott as poet has been formed by the author, Ovid, as much as he now forms the character of Ovid. The very motif of "turning to stone," for instance, has its *locus classicus* in the *Metamorphoses* (VI. 298 ff.). Finally, in Part II Ovid offers a stoic comfort to the poet by issuing a Dantean "prophecy"-which-has-already-happened:

["]Romans" — he smiled — will mock your slavish rhyme,
the slaves your love of Roman structures, when,
from Metamorphoses to Tristia,
art obeys its own order. Now it's time."
Tying his toga gently, he went in. (69)

"The Hotel Normandie Pool" links these autobiographical concerns to aesthetic ones through its double-edged play on "reflection": Walcott likens the surface of the pool variously to a mirror, a page, and to the surface of the eye, all of which reverse or invert the images they encounter. While water, mirrors, and the eye invert phenomena physically, the page (a figure for the writer's mind) does so metaphorically, like Freud's dreamwork. It is conventional for allegory to parallel physical structures to figurative ones, but in "The Hotel Normandie Pool" we encounter multiple varieties of physical reversal itself, and slightly disorienting differences arise between these. For instance, water (usually a horizontal surface, as in the pool) inverts an image by reproducing it upside down, while a mirror (usually a vertical surface) reverses the image not top to bottom but side to side, reproducing left as right. Again, the pool divides the poet from a shadow-world beneath it, as Acheron divides the living from the dead; but the poem equates the space *across* Acheron with the space *beneath* the water, and aligns a horizontal with a vertical. The reader has often to turn images of the pool or mirror around, or upend them, imagining a vertical surface on its side or vice versa, to grasp the resemblances Walcott proposes between them. Figurative reality does not exactly coincide with physical reality; yet these are disconcertingly *said* to coincide in Walcott's tropes. We begin to become conscious of the leaps of faith we make in order to accept traditional spatial metaphors.

Elsewhere in the poem Walcott asserts the possibility of "visual rhyme," equating verbal rhyme with the relation between object and reflection and also between similarly shaped objects: "the rubber ring that is a / red rubber ring inverted at the line's center" forms a "rhyme in water," and Ovid's fringe of "foam hair" is "repeated by the robe's frayed hem." Walcott thus calls attention to "rhyme" in its broadest sense as a possible nexus between verbal and visual systems. Obviously, "The Hotel Normandie Pool"'s network of metaphors is overwhelmingly spatial (or, in Mitchell's terms, "tectonic"), but in spite of this the poem's parallelisms work against exact spatial resemblances, as though testing how accurately spatial conceptualizations can correspond to one another and to kinds of conceptualizations more likely to be considered nonspatial. (The poem's emphasis on image may further explain Walcott's choice of Ovid as his muse since, according to Jean Hagstrum, Ovid has "long [been] considered the most pictorial of poets."[21]) In the poem's most revealing conceit, Walcott compares his stanza to a pool: nine lines of blank verse contain a finite "weight," namely forty-five poetic feet, without spilling over, while a swimming pool contains so many feet of water. The surface of the stanza changes as the poet fills it up: when he introduces his children's names into the stanza, "the next line rises as they enter it," as the water level rises in a pool when someone steps in. Here Walcott playfully literalizes one of the most common ways of speaking about a text. As Mitchell reminds us,

> A closer look at this curious object ["the work itself"] inevitably reveals it as a complex field of internal relationships, the most common of which is the phenomenon of stratification, or what is usually called "levels" in literature. We usually discern at least two levels in any literary work, labeled by such binary oppositions as literal and figurative, or explicit and implicit, but there seems to be a tendency to want more strata than this as a way of fulfilling some hierarchical model of inclusiveness, importance, or ideality. (281–82)

The image of stratification that Walcott brings into the poem by imagining the volume of his stanza literally thus returns us to allegory, to the notion of literal and figurative "depths." The poem certainly expresses and fulfills a need for "more strata" than two, but teases us by placing the strata slightly out of alignment (the poem is not as transparent as a pool; a pool does not reverse the image in the same way as a mirror) and by finding the "literal" or "explicit" strata themselves figurative (no reflection is completely transparent; the objects of representation are also representations).

Walcott contextualizes these aesthetic questions by implying that, politically as well as poetically, the poet's world no longer allows him to *believe* in correspondence: "each idea has become suspicious / of its shadow." When one suffers the "exile of divorce" (a "divorce," as in Williams's *Paterson*, from community as well as from a single partner), reflecting surfaces return "disfiguring" images. To believe in transparency against the evidence of experience would indulge the authoritarian wish for a frozen reality: "Only tyrants believe / their mirrors, or Narcissi." Although the poet prays "that this page's surface would unmist / after my breath as pools and mirrors do," he knows that the page is no more cooperative than self-knowledge: "all reflection gets no easier." And perhaps the most intense experiences, such as pain, remain out of reflection's reach altogether, "beyond words."

Walcott's elaborate series of analogies offers a quasi-allegory that refers to other and still other quasi-allegories beyond. From one secondary reality we view another, a structure that recalls Plato's paradigm for human understanding in Chapter VII of the *Republic* (except that Walcott does not stop the regress at two realities). Walcott probably does have Plato in mind, since "The Hotel Normandie Pool" begins with an image of shadowy figures. On New Year's Eve, the poet confides, he had watched "soundless waltzers dart and swivel" from his window, his isolation evoking "the great chapter in some Russian novel / in which, during the war, the prince comes home."[22] Walcott then arranges still another network of correspondences in which, in the poet's personal "war" against time and alienation, his smoker's cough becomes a "fusillade" of gunfire; snow, the "gauze" wrapped around his injury; and the "ribboned" drapes that part him from the waltzers, his soldier's medals (here the reader is likely to remember Dickey's concern about Walcott's allegorical method). The waltzers' "light-scissored shapes" echo (or rhyme) against the mothlike "splayed shadows of the hills" the poet views from his table, which in turn literally "foreshadow" the shade-realm from which Ovid will soon emerge. The cutout-like waltzing silhouettes, then, exist at once in the "real world" of paired-off sexual generation—the "war between the sexes" that worries the poet—and, like Plato's shadows, in a "secondary" world. Walcott's identification of dancers *with* distant shadows implies that the vibrant sexual dance from which the poet has withdrawn is from the outset a secondary reality, while Walcott's "disfigur[ations]" between levels imply a language "exiled" from resemblance.

The image of Plato's cave resonates as well in passages of "What the Twilight Says," in which Walcott revises Plato in at least two ways. First, Walcott instructs his actors to fall backward through even deeper darkness rather than to struggle toward the source of light: "The darkness which yawns before them is terrifying. It is the journey back from man to ape. . . . [B]ut the darkness must be total, and the cave should not contain a single man-made, mnemonic object" ("WTS," 5). Walcott would have his actors persist in their darkness until they become wise, rather than attempting, as much of the Western tradition urges, progress toward enlightenment. Second, Walcott's "story-tellers" do not passively observe history's shadows, but imaginatively control them: "ancestral story-tellers fed twigs to the fire" ("WTS," 5–6). And imaginative listeners and perceivers in turn invest fiery shadows with significance: "I was drawn, like a child's mind to fire, to the Manichean conflicts of Haiti's history. . . . The fire's shadows, magnified into myth, were those of the black Jacobins of Haiti" ("WTS," 11). In this view history, though it may be fictive, is not vanity for that; it is revelatory myth. When the poet complains in "The Hotel Normandie Pool" that, given his personal estrangements and Caribbean politics, "exile seem[s] a happier thought than home," Ovid responds, "on a tablet smooth as the pool's skin, / I made reflections that, in many ways, / were even stronger than their origin" (68). Thus, against Plato's claim that artistic mimicry of already unideal objects produces even more debased representations of the ideal, "The Hotel Normandie Pool"'s object world is already composed of representations, but art's mimicry of mimicry limits as well as causes their vitiation.

Walcott usually sends his audience clear allusive and formal signals when a poem is large-scale. In "The Hotel Normandie Pool" Walcott's meditative, nine-line, irregularly rhymed stanzas and reliance on invocation suggest the "greater Romantic lyric." Its third and final section, a two-stanza envoi, fulfills that suggestion and closes the poem's central theme of reflection with a glimpse of an unmediated nature that is, like Keats's "Ode to a Nightingale"'s, literally "beyond words" and beyond images, too. At the end of the first section Ovid arrives preceded by the poet's vision of his daughters "rid[ing]," like Venus, "on the rayed shells of both irises." Walcott links the eye's iris, mediator of all perception, to Iris, the gods' messenger. So as Iris the messenger ushers us into the poem's exploration of perception, the "envoi" ("a sending away") ushers us out into a world without mediation, in which reflections are finally exact:

> At dusk, the sky is loaded like watercolour paper
> with an orange wash in which every edge frays—
> a painting with no memory of the painter—
> and what this pool recites is not a phrase
> from an invisible, exiled laureate,
> where there's no laurel, but the scant applause
> of one dry, scraping palm tree. . . . (70)

This is the dominion of pure presence, in which the pool reflects or, in the poem's terms, silently "recites" a watery sky empty of all but "an orange wash"—an image of the innocent but vacant reflection "beyond words" which had eluded the poem. There is a kind of Zenlike ecstasy in the perfect circularity of pool and sky, the ecstasy of "one palm clapping." Nature is authorless—there is no "invisible, exiled laureate"—yet somehow *seems* like representation even so. The poet cannot express total immanence; even his reference to an "invisible, exiled laureate" who does *not* exist clings to a remnant of anthropomorphism. Nature looks to the poet's eyes more like an unconscious representation—"a painting with no *memory* of the painter"—than "originality" or unpainted reality. Nature's immanence does not for all practical purposes exist for linguistic beings. A wordless, imageless suspension would mean oblivion:

Dusk. The trees blacken like the pool's umbrellas.
Dusk. Suspension of every image and its voice.
The mangoes pitch from their green dark like meteors.
The fruit bat swings on its branch, a tongueless bell. (70)

The fruit bat, literally "suspen[ded]" from its branch, resembles a funeral bell tolling, and the mangoes "pitch[ing] from their green dark like meteors" indicate both the death of an important person (Ovid has disappeared again) and the death of consciousness. Although "pitch" intensifies the "dark," it also underscores the sticky vegetable and animal richness of the mangoes and fruit bat: this is "nature," but nature without mediating images or words is death for human perception. In the story of Philomela nature's most eloquent speaker, the nightingale, has a tongueless woman for a sister: even nature's most articulate expressions cannot make up for the mutilation of human language.[23] Nature can convey to us only undifferentiated sorrow at an absence of human language. By closing "The Hotel Normandie Pool" on an image of unmediated nature, Walcott suggests that after individual poets and perhaps entire civilizations expire, nature is likely to get the last "word," but it will be a silent one. Poets and painters sometimes aspire to that condition, but not for long.

WALCOTT'S LOOSE LYRICAL sequence, *Midsummer* (1984), revisits *Another Life* ten years later and asks for a last time whether the poet has a "choice" between verbal and visual art. At the time Walcott wrote *Midsummer*, he tells Hirsch, "I felt that for the time being I didn't want to write any more poems. . . . I was going to concentrate purely on trying to develop my painting" (Hirsch 1986, 229). Unlike most of Walcott's work, these poems are structurally and syntactically casual. Not that Walcott allowed himself to be completely formless: "you can't leave things lying around with unjoined shapes, little fragments and so on" (229). *Midsummer* doesn't have the polish of Walcott's other volumes, yet it is by no means plotless or styleless. Still, Walcott's observations on its composition suggest that he wanted to distance himself from literariness, to push writing toward some alternative means of expression "against the idea of writing poems" (229). Since Walcott

DEREK WALCOTT'S POETRY

was painting a good deal at the time, it would make sense if he asked again whether the visual arts could represent that alternative, as they at first seem to in *Another Life.*

Midsummer's frequent references to the visual arts have caught the attention of many of its readers, some of whom suggest that its relative plotlessness and casual arrangements of detail make it resemble still life.[24] Indeed, while *Another Life* alludes principally to Italian Renaissance painters (reflecting the poem's theme of personal renaissance, but perhaps also its narrativity and psychologism), *Midsummer* alludes more often to Northern painters, to Breughel (VIII), Dürer (XV), Vermeer, and Ruysdael (XVII) — and, in the French tradition, to Chardin (XVII) as well as the more expected Gauguin. Although these painters were, of course, capable of historical and psychological works, their names at least trigger associations with still life and its attendant stasis and reticence. Still life is more often dominated by composition than by history or psychology: "[In still life] an aesthetics of silence reigns, no statement is allowed to issue from the objects brought together within the frame, and if there is allegorical intent, it is arcane" (Bryson, 23). *Midsummer* aspires toward such "an aesthetics of silence" in that its poet tires of the stridency and hypocrisy of language. But the volume demonstrates once again that silence is inaccessible even through visual art.

Walcott sometimes envies the visual arts for what he sees as their relative freedom from politics and the cacophony that too often typifies polemical language. *Midsummer* bristles with grievances against words: "[W]hether one chooses to say *'ven-thes'* or *'ven-ces'* / involves the class struggle"; in language one must always "be discreet" (XLIII, "Tropic Zone," i). Of his early work the poet concludes, "Every word I have written took the wrong approach" (III); "More skillful now" but "more dissatisfied," he complains, "everything I read / or write goes on too long" (IX). Where "children lie torn on rubble for a noun" (XXII), the poet has to wonder "if I sound / as if my voice were flattering the flag" (XL). It is difficult to find a correlative in the visual arts for such problems of intonation; language has too much specificity and can reveal too much. But on the other side of the verbal double bind, words can seem "Neanderthal" (XL), crudely denotative, belonging to "the charred cave of the television."[25] There seems no way out: "Was evil brought to this place / with language?" (XXIV).

In XL the poet glimpses a free immanence floating beyond words:

> Before its firelit image flickers on
> your forehead like the first Neanderthal
> to spend a whole life lifting nouns like rocks,
> turn to the window. On a light-angled wall,
> through the clear, soundless pane, one sees a speech
> that calls to us, but is beyond our powers,
> composed of O's from a reflected bridge,
> the language of white, ponderous clouds convening
> over aerials, spires, rooftops, water towers.

These images of clouds—and they are, like the visual arts', secondary or "reflected" images—are not empty. They are a pure sort of "speech," like a passionate cry (an "O"), and although human beings don't have the power to answer in the same language, the poet comprehends its seductive superiority to human communicative, religious, domestic, and public works ("aerials, spires, rooftops, water towers"). But this immanence is no more accessible to the visual than to the verbal arts. The clouds are "reflected" transparently through a "clear" and "soundless" medium, as Walcott knows paint, language, and, indeed, consciousness are not. For better and worse, "everything becomes / its idea to the painter with easel rifled on his shoulders" (XVIII). As a painter-writer Walcott must deal with "The overworked muck of my paintings, my bad plots" (XIII). The cloudscape does not imply that images surpass words because they reproduce presence; rather, it lifts presence above both arts onto a flawless but impracticable plane that images and words alike sometimes wish to reach, but invariably cannot.

Midsummer's yearning for "the language of . . . clouds" is sometimes also a yearning for the permanent and timeless. In the very first poem, "clouds . . . keep no record of where we have passed" and "light has never had epochs," whereas "the honey of time will riddle" Brodsky's poems (II) and Walcott's "lines will wilt like mayflies" (XII). There is a freedom in the "language" of light and clouds the poet respects: "Go, light, make weightless the burden of our thought, / . . . be untranslatable in verse or prose" (XLVIII). But light is an "untranslatable" language, whereas the poet needs a translatable one.

Midsummer's poems on Gauguin and Watteau suggest a provisional resolution to this conflict: the artist may memorialize the object world *in* rather than *from* its corruption. "Gauguin," a miniature first-person monologue in the manner of some of Lowell's sonnets, is in two parts of seventeen and twenty lines. In the first part Gauguin scoffs at the "white-ducked colonists" of Papeete who "pretend . . . / that a straight vermouth re-creates the metropolis"; Gauguin stresses how thoroughly he left that metropolis behind, and issues a command: "Get off your arses, you clerks, and find your fate. . . . / Pack, leave! I left too late" (XIX, "Gauguin," i). The main purpose of the first part, however, is to identify Gauguin with the poet. The painter describes his face as an ambiguous mask:

> I saw in my own cheekbones the mule's head of a Breton,
> the placid, implacable strategy of the Mongol,
> the mustache like the downturned horns of a helmet;
> the chain of my blood pulled me to darker nations,
>
> . . . .
> I am Watteau's wild oats, his illegitimate heir.

Gauguin becomes associated with Bretons, Mongols, and "darker nations" at once—becomes, like the statue in "Bronze," creolized. Walcott has made much of his own "illegitimacy" in the Western tradition, calling himself "this neither proud nor ashamed bastard, this hybrid, this West Indian" ("WTS," 10), but the European Gauguin is similarly illegitimate.

In the second part Gauguin explains his attitude toward the tropics and the representation of its landscape, and in doing so brings *Midsummer* closest to the imagery of *Another Life*: "I have never pretended that summer was paradise, / or that these virgins were virginal; on their wooden trays / are the fruits of my knowledge, radiant with disease." "Gauguin" 's "fruits," "sea-almond eyes," "furnace," and especially the "sulphur" and "volcano that chafes like a chancre" and so recall Soufrière—all belong to *Another Life*'s complex of images. "Gauguin" also resurrects *Another Life*'s "amber" metaphor for the painterly desire to reify. While paint might, like amber, paralyze, Gauguin's amber doesn't capture a romanticized landscape like the one *Another Life*'s student painter had coveted:

> No, what I have plated in amber is not an ideal, as
> Puvis de Chavannes desired it, but corrupt—
> the spot on the ginger lily's vulva, the plantain's phalloi,
> the volcano that chafes like a chancre. . . .
> . . . .
> I placed a blue death mask there in my Book of Hours
> that those who dream of an earthly paradise may read it
> as men.

Walcott refers to his own work here, reiterating through Gauguin's mask that the best American art "does not pretend to such innocence, its vision is not naive. Rather, like its fruits, its savor is a mixture of the acid and the sweet" ("MH," 5). The "spot on the ginger lily's vulva" plated in amber is, like the "Polish Rider," an invulnerable likeness of imperfection (the mirror image of the world in a waterdrop—a vulnerable likeness of perfection). Artists who seem uncritical, like Puvis de Chavannes, of their Midas-like power to "plate" fall prey to irony: in the very moments they believe they immortalize their subjects, they cooperate with "Death, the engraver"[26] to rigidify it. More sensitive artists like Rembrandt and Gauguin acknowledge that they cannot preserve the object world from corruption, and "never [pretend] that summer was paradise." Gauguin memorializes only decay itself, "plat[ing] in amber . . . / the spot on the ginger lily's vulva." These tensions between permanence and transience generate Walcott's paradoxical metaphors for art: "fruits . . . radiant with disease," gold-plated bodies, "a blue death mask . . . in my Book of Hours," and finally "frescoes in sackcloth to my goddess Maya."

Walcott is particularly keen on frescoes (he subtitles Chapter 10 of *Another Life* "Frescoes of the New World," and the poet in Chapter 4

146   DEREK WALCOTT'S POETRY

"envie[s Leonardo and Verrocchio] their frescoes"). Like Walcott's favorite medium, watercolor (with which he "sketch[es] on . . . fast-drying paper" [L]),[27] frescoes force the artist to work rapidly and, as a result, preserve a heightened fluidity. Gauguin did not produce frescoes; Walcott uses the term metaphorically here, which encourages the reader to extend the term to poetry. Now these metaphoric frescoes, which seem to hold in tension permanence and fluidity, are done "in sackcloth,"[28] indicating their elegiac function (and perhaps that even an artist in frescoes has something still to atone for). Finally, Walcott consecrates them to "Maya," the principle that all is illusion. This complex metaphor reveals Walcott staking out his differences from various canonical aesthetic positions—for example, Keats's in "To Autumn," which likens art to nature (a "wailful choir" of "small gnats"), and Yeats's in "Sailing to Byzantium," which locates art in artifice ("hammered gold and gold enamelling"). Walcott's metaphors for art tend to combine these positions, placing transience within the longing for permanent form.

"Watteau" follows "Gauguin" in *Midsummer*, reversing chronology as Walcott works backward from "illegitimate heir" to ancestor. "Watteau" considers its subject's more "tremulous" style critically, yet finds advantage, too, in its fragility and uncertainty. Walcott identifies with Watteau as well as with the renegade Gauguin; Craven encourages this mirroring by noting that Watteau, "the son of a Flemish artisan, wandered to Paris in his youth" and was thus "[t]hrown between two civilizations" (374).[29] As Watteau's heir, Walcott inherits a "hollow" and "tremulous" legacy:

> The amber spray of trees feather-brushed with the dusk,
> the ruined cavity of some spectral château, the groin
> of a leering satyr eaten with ivy. In the distance, the grain
> of some unreapable, alchemical harvest, the hollow at
> the heart of all embarkations. Nothing stays green
> in that prodigious urging toward twilight;
> in all of his journeys the pilgrims are in fever
> from the tremulous strokes of malaria's laureate.
> So where is Cythera? It, too, is far and feverish,

it dilates on the horizon of his near-delirium, near
and then further, it can break like the spidery rigging
of his ribboned barquentines, it is as much nowhere
as these broad-leafed islands, it is the disease
of elephantine vegetation in Baudelaire,
the tropic bug in the Paris fog. For him, it is the mirror
of what is. Paradise is life repeated spectrally,
an empty chair echoing the emptiness. (XX, "Watteau")

Watteau's "Cythera" or America, like Baudelaire's, is a projection, "far and feverish," "near / and then further." The Old World itself, as in *Omeros's* Lisbon, is no less unreal; the "hollow" of the embarkation only doubles the "cavity" of the "spectral château." Cythera is "the mirror / of what is," yet "repeat[s] spectrally," so the specular logic of mimesis must be "spectral" logic of imperfect repetition. The Old World is another manifestation of the same logic, as we infer when Cythera, "*too*, is far and feverish." The New World faces the Old like "an empty chair echoing the emptiness," as one mirror facing another creates an infinite regression. Walcott's language is itself an echo-chamber, doubling and redoubling its motifs. Both connotations of "spectral," ghostliness and incandescence, operate here; and "spectral" in combination with "mirror" recalls "speculum," an instrument to "dilate" (as Cythera "dilates on the horizon") or to reflect. Walcott's half-rhymes suggest the inexactitude of mimicry, falling from "groin" to "grain" to "green": "Nothing stays green," indeed.

In his interview with Ciccarelli Walcott ties poetic "resonance" in its widest sense to perceptual ambiguity of this kind. The poet *uses* the instability of perception to gain insight into "resonances":

> Once a gong has been struck, the visible resonances of figure, sound, and image will all be concentric and will be subject to all kinds of true and perhaps contradictory perceptions. If one looks hard at any bright object it will multiply itself, will send out dimmer images around it. (299)

Here "figure, sound, and image" all have "visible resonances"—as though in Beaujour's "stereolinguistic optic." In addition Walcott, who likes to handle verbal figuration "literally," materializing clichés, reads even the most unliterary details in Watteau's painting figuratively. He muses that "Nothing *stays* green" in the "Pilgrimage," lending Watteau's treatment of color a temporal dimension. Watteau's "spray of trees" is "amber," a color that for Walcott symbolizes the attempt to preserve. Like Blake, Walcott allegorizes technique: Watteau's "tremulous strokes" are appropriate for "malaria's laureate." We understand such incessant metaphorization better when we see it as an effect of Walcott's belief that a poem, or even an entire play, "is essentially one metaphor with many components" (Ciccarelli, 299).

IN " WATTEAU " Walcott is about as far as possible from the "separate but equal" theory of the arts. Although Walcott is "content to be a moderately good watercolorist[,] [b]ut . . . not content to be a moderately good poet," he is "in fairly continual practice," and "[w]hile painting . . . would find lines [of *Midsummer*] coming into [his] head" (Hirsch 1986, 207, 206, 229). Walcott, *un*like Blake here, does not exercise his talents by illustration, calligraphy, or hand printing, the most explicit ways of underscoring words' visuality.[30] Yet his sensitivity to visual art and vision does inform his poetry. Walcott's "perceptual polyglotism," like other bilinguals', manifests itself in "greater awareness of the relativity of things" and "tolerance of ambiguity."[31] Since Walcott thinks of language as material to shape, he sees poetry as a "craft" that shades into painting and shares its goals and limitations. As a result, he maintains an awareness of the spatial and visual properties of writing. For Walcott, visual art is not a separate and competitive system, but a part of poetry itself, even as metaphor, semiotics, and narrative shape visual art.

THE CULTURE OF NATURE AND THE
NATURE OF CULTURE

The right verb leapt like a fish from its element,
the tadpole wriggled like an eager comma,
and the snake coiled round its trunk in an ampersand.

—*Midsummer,* XXIV

FROM THE PERSPECTIVE of the Old World, it has seemed that nature overpowers culture in America, especially in its poorer regions. In the realm of poetics the correlative of the nature / culture opposition is that between the object world and representation. If a place seems culturally empty, it is because representation seems to lag behind the object world there. When the nineteenth-century "imperialist pamphleteer,"[1] J. A. Froude, writes that in the Caribbean "[T]here has been romance, but it has been the romance of pirates and outlaws. . . . [T]here are no people there in the true sense of the word,"[2] he ties a lack of *people* to a lack of *material* for a certain kind of representation, romance. According to most Western indices of culture, "there are no people" without representation, although there may be human beings; there is only an object world which includes human beings. Two pages later Froude continues, "To the man of science the West Indies may be delightful and instructive. Rocks and trees and flowers remain as they always were, and Nature is constant to herself; but the traveller whose heart is with his land, and cares only to see his brother mortals making their corner of the planet into an orderly and rational home, had better choose some other object for his pilgrimage" (349). As a self-proclaimed defender of the Americas Walcott works against this logic. Walcott's poetry cannot conceive of a world without representation; America could not completely drown culture in nature even if it tried, and there are no human beings waiting to become a people.

Of course, on the other hand, there is no culture without nature. For Walcott, as for many other poets, Adam is the prototypical natural man; Walcott emphasizes the duplicity of Adam's role, however, in that this natural man must also have been the inventor of culture. American poets have always been fascinated by the figure of Adam. As John T. Irwin has shown, Whitman, for example, thinks of himself as a kind of Adam, making an "effort to recapture the language of physical objects in his role as poet of the Edenic New World" (29). When Walcott writes that the "vision of man in the New World is Adamic," "elemental, a being inhabited by presences" ("MH," 2–3, 2), he, too, seems to believe in a "language of physical objects." Yet the very idea of a "language of physical objects" already means that Adam is *not* an inventor but a perceiver of language (not that there is always a difference between invention and perception). Irwin adds, "This work of naming, whereby physical nature is translated into phonetic signs, is possible only because nature already possesses a linguistic structure" (71). In this sense nature contains language, seeming to precede language and to make it possible. Still, we can apprehend nature, including the fact that it contains language, only through representations of it, by virtue of its being contained in language. Thus each of Adam's words is indeed a beginning; but these are beginnings *over*, not primal beginnings. If we wrap either nature within culture or culture within nature, we will find ourselves "doing the chicken and the egg until dawn."

Since Walcott cannot avoid this double bind (or germinative dance), he invites its movement. If instead of trying to hold nature within culture or vice versa, one searches out both nature and culture in unexpected places, one is at least voluntarily dancing, and this has always been Walcott's method. As a very young poet Walcott discovered that the writers of the English Renaissance describe nature in cultural terms, reading the world as a divine text. Walcott's first published poem, printed in the local paper when he was fourteen, likewise "talk[s] about learning about God through nature and not through the church" (Hirsch 1986, 207). An extremely early sonnet, "A City's Death by Fire" (*CP*, 6), already finds intersections between books' "leaves" and trees', the poet's papery "tale" and the equally tenuous "wooden world" with its visible stories ("All day I walked abroad among the rubbled tales," the young poet declares). Since then Walcott's poetry has consistently described the world as representation (nature as culture) and vice versa. In these complementary ways Walcott constructs, in Irwin's terms, "a human language that is continuous with the language of nature because its elements are borrowed from that language" (Irwin, 33). But, again, we can see even in the phrase "language of nature" that as language is natural, nature is linguistic.

The Castaway and *The Gulf* begin to articulate the interpenetration of the object world with "the bare necessities / of style" (*C*, 51), and to connect a poetic based upon this interpenetration to Caribbean history. "The Castaway," "Crusoe's Island," "Crusoe's Journal," and "Air" try in various ways to represent pure nature, and in doing so demonstrate the impossibility of their efforts.

"The Castaway" imagines a scene and a circumstance as nearly elemental as possible. Yet its title already indicates that this scene and this circumstance are not primal, that they have been preceded by other, presumably more "cultured" conditions. We believe that nature precedes culture, but if the paradigm of the castaway is normative, culture may always precede any happenstance that seems to escape it.

In "The Castaway," as in *Robinson Crusoe*, the purer the protagonist's apprehension of nature, the more nature resembles a prison:

> The starved eye devours the seascape for the morsel
> Of a sail.
>
> The horizon threads it infinitely.
>
> Action breeds frenzy. I lie,
> Sailing the ribbed shadow of a palm,
> Afraid lest my own footprints multiply.

The castaway experiences the seascape as a hunger, an absence. Like Froude, he finds "nothing" on this island—"Nothing: the rage with which the sandfly's head is filled." Unlike Froude, however, he grapples with nothingness as a positive presence, and this grappling pushes him in certain directions. First and foremost, he feels a nonspecific impulse to "act." He resists this impulse, for the prospect of action as reaction to nothingness inspires him with an unexpected fear—a fear that his "own footprints" might "multiply." Robinson Crusoe shivers with mingled terror and relief when, discovering Friday's footprints, he discovers that he is not singular. If in the New World Crusoe is a type of Adam, the quintessential Adamic experience is thus the realization, for the first time, that one is *not* first. This experience recurred with each European expedition, whose explorers found culture after culture where they expected none. By contrast, Walcott's castaway, as a postcolonial, is not terrified at the prospect of the other per se, but by the prospect that the other will only turn out to be another. To avoid this fear the castaway avoids Crusoe's famed industry. Crusoe projects parts of himself everywhere to recreate British culture in miniature, busily trampling the island underfoot in a kind of "frenzy" from which Walcott's castaway swerves. Instead, he "lie[s], / Sailing the ribbed shadow of a palm." By choosing this path, however, he fends off the multiple projection of his own footprints by means of an equally projective, hallucinatory use of the imagination. His fictive "Sailing" is a "lie" in Plato's sense that all poets are liars; and the castaway's hope to escape the fear of "frenzy" by means of this lie is itself a lying hope. Although he can abstain from certain actions, then, the narrator cannot abstain from the frenzy of culture, for he joins it in the act of lying.

As "The Castaway" progresses, it unearths the seeds of transcendent myths within the most humble, minimal, and supposedly earthbound of images. Like the protagonists of some of Beckett's novels, Walcott's castaway feels reduced to the sum of his bodily functions:

> Pleasures of an old man:
> Morning: contemplative evacuation, considering
> The dried leaf, nature's plan.
>
> In the sun, the dog's feces
> Crusts, whitens like coral.

We end in earth, from earth began.
In our own entrails, genesis.

"Evacuation" is only a small pleasure within a vacuous existence. Still, the "contemplation" that accompanies and possibly springs from it is anything but vacuous. Most immediately, the castaway's epigrams ("We end in earth, from earth began. / In our own entrails, genesis") bring the ambiguous borders of the life cycle into focus. Insofar as origin and ending are questioned, the idea of cultural or natural origin is also suspended here. The contemplation continues, even more grandiosely,

> Godlike, annihilating godhead, art,
> And self, I abandon
> Dead metaphors: the almond's leaf-like heart,
>
> The ripe brain rotting like a yellow nut
> Hatching
> Its babel of sea-lice, sandfly, and maggot,
>
> That green wine bottle's gospel choked with sand,
> Labelled, a wrecked ship,
> Clenched sea-wood nailed and white as a man's hand.

How easily and almost automatically "contemplation" magnifies "evacuation" into annihilation, and the bodily into the spiritual. The castaway's claim to "abandon / Dead metaphors" is followed by a list of metaphors to be abandoned—and thus, the poem does not exclude them after all. It is as though once the castaway uses the word "genesis," even in its lower-case sense, he *has* to proceed through "babel" to the "gospel" of crucifixion. Life begins in earth, and live metaphors grow from dead ones. The elaborate, familiar plot of Christian mythology "hatches" from nearly nowhere, apparently spontaneously generating. True, Walcott marks each element with a minus-sign: the gospel is "choked with sand" and cannot speak, what is "nailed" is only driftwood, and so forth. Yet to staple "Dead metaphors" with minus-signs is not the same as to *"abandon"* them. As the castaway's hope to escape the frenzy of culture is a lying hope, his wish to abandon dead metaphors (to evacuate them, to *cast them away*) is haunted by their return, as "Labelled" by cliché as the wine bottle by its brand name. Like the return of the repressed, whatever is *cast away* comes back. (According to yet another cliché, castaways send off messages in bottles—so how did that bottle get back on the beach?)

"Crusoe's Island," a poem in three parts from the same volume, specifies that its castaway is Crusoe, but at the same time makes Crusoe loosely metaphoric of the Caribbean postcolonial intellectual. Its title, too, is telling, for it emphasizes that the island is Crusoe's property, that Crusoe claims his solitude. Much of the poem criticizes the Crusoe-poet's embrace of intellectual solitude and intimates that he cannot really separate himself from his community. Still, neither can we stand apart from the speaker's solitude. Standing apart from solitude would mean finding somewhere to stand that is not also an island. This may not be possible, and if not, people who live on islands shouldn't throw glass bottles. Like "A Far Cry from Africa," "Crusoe's Island" shows the double difficulty of standing apart, either to reject community or to judge the hermit-intellectual who rejects it.

In the first section, "The chapel's cowbell / Like God's anvil / Hammers ocean to a blinding shield." The poet-narrator moves away from the people who answer this religious cattlecall: "*I* labour at my art. / *My* father, God, is dead" (italics mine). As he understands it, he has lost his faith in bitterness over his own father's early death ("He gathered my father. / Irresolute and proud, / I never could go back"). Angry at God, the poet turns away from his local church and therefore from a large part of his neighborhood. Although he momentarily believes he has achieved "heaven without his kind" ("Two paradises 'twere in one / To live in Paradise alone," writes Marvell[3]), he isolates himself unbearably by spurning the popular faith. The internal exile that results is precisely the kind of unproductive reaction to betweenness Walcott most fears:

> Past thirty now I know
> To love the self is dread
> Of being swallowed by the blue

Of heaven overhead
Or rougher blue below.
Some lesion of the brain
From art or alcohol
Flashes this fear by day:
As startling as his shadow
Grows to the castaway.

The poet believes himself between Christianity ("the blue / Of heaven overhead") and nature (the "rougher blue below"). "[D]read[ing]" both, he simply doesn't look up or down, but "love[s] the self," justifying himself exactly where he stands. In "The Castaway" the poet does not want action to become a mere reaction to fear, and hopes that the self will remain singular. In "Crusoe's Island" inaction in its turn proves a mere reaction to dreaded alternatives, and the hoped-for singularity of the self only embodies the castaway's loneliness, then splits into duplicity after all.

This voluntary castaway from heaven and earth assumes a solitude he never actually possesses. Although he buries "dread" in "art or alcohol" (especially, we can infer, by night), these remedies create a "lesion of the brain," a change in the structure of his mind. The "lesion" or self-division brings back "by day" the "fear" he casts away by night. In the sobriety of daylight, as the shadow grows from the body, the other grows from the self. And this shadow-other expresses precisely the poet's repressed longing for community: "He watched his shadow pray / Not for God's love but human love instead."

The appeal of islands is "the cure / Of quiet," the idea of "be[ing], like beast or natural object, pure." But since "no man is an island," the search for natural purity ends in disarray. In the second section of the poem the duplicity of the self reaches its crisis point:

I have lost sight of hell,
Of heaven, of human will,
My skill
Is not enough.
I am struck by this bell
To the root.

DEREK WALCOTT'S POETRY

Crazed by a racking sun,
I stand at my life's noon,
On parched, delirious sand
My shadow lengthens.

By now the "cowbell" of simple faith has taken on grander powers.
Although a bell may "strike" noon, no one is ever "struck by" a bell—
rather, by lightning. Like lightning then, the bell is divine, cleaving the
poet, showing him that he is a forked animal. As the castoff desire for
community returns, so too does religious fear. The bell displays its divinity in part through its disdain for logic. When it is literally noon,
one sees no shadow at all; but at his "life's noon," like Dante at the
beginning of *The Divine Comedy*, the poet's shadowy sense of duplicity
unnaturally increases.

The third and briefest section of "Crusoe's Island" contains a great
deal of delicate maneuvering. The poet renounces art's power to transfigure, yet remains loyal nevertheless to what remains of art. In his
very last lines the poet observes young girls returning from church and
remarks, "Nothing I can learn / From art or loneliness / Can bless them
as the bell's / Transfiguring tongue can bless." The ending of the poem
thus seems to lapse, with a sigh, into silence. But two stanzas earlier
the third section had opened with a most ambiguous "condemnation"
of art:

Art is profane and pagan,
The most it has revealed
Is what a crippled Vulcan
Beat on Achilles' shield.
By these blue, changing graves
Fanned by the furnace blast
Of heaven, may the mind
Catch fire till it cleaves
Its mould of clay at last.

Walcott's shield obviously recalls Auden's "The Shield of Achilles." In
Auden's poem Vulcan does not transfigure the world, for as Auden
writes in his elegy for Yeats, "poetry makes nothing happen." Vulcan

"only" represents the world in all its mundane horror. Walcott agrees, here, that art must be "profane." And Walcott, like Auden, suggests that poets are hurt into poetry, beating out art to compensate for their own injuries.

Still, how much of a renunciation is this? Neither Auden's Vulcan nor Walcott's lacks power, encyclopedic breadth, or accuracy; "the most [art] has revealed" is everything that we know. Then too, since the poet has already decided that he cannot "be, like beast or natural object, pure," it would be absurd for him simply to reject art, whether or not art transfigures. Indeed, the body, a natural object, is already a mortal sculpture, a "mould of clay." The very phrase "natural object" is, once again, almost oxymoronic, for living things are the most "natural," while "object" rings of inanimacy and perhaps artifice. And even as this stanza "prays" to heaven, it envisions heaven as a "furnace blast"—in which case God resembles Vulcan, an artist. The equivalences with which the poem began (God has an anvil, the ocean is his hammered shield) hold water after all, despite the crisis of its second section. In effect, the artist prays only for the ability to use his conflicts well. His duplicity, tortuous as it is, lets him "Catch fire," and lightning symbolizes not only divine retribution but poetic inspiration. When the mind, burdened and inspired by self-division, finally "cleaves / Its mould of clay," the body, obviously, expires, and the mind with it. Stripped of its metaphoric magniloquence, the poet's prayer is unregenerate: "Let me write poems till I die."

While "The Castaway" and "Crusoe's Island" seem to fight their own attraction to culture, throwing the bottle out and watching it return, "Crusoe's Journal" (C, 51–53) accepts this attraction and, in the poem's words, "assume[s] a household use" for it. Walcott explains that he wrote "The Castaway" at "a beachhouse by [him]self" in Trinidad, where "[t]he beaches . . . are generally very empty—just you, the sea and the vegetation around you." At that beach house, he conceived "an image of the West Indian artist as someone who was in a shipwrecked position" (Hirsch 1986, 213). "Crusoe's Journal" takes up at the scene of such a beach house:

> Once we have driven past Mundo Nuevo trace
> safely to this beach house

perched between ocean and green, churning forest
    the intellect appraises
objects surely, even the bare necessities
    of style are turned to use,
like those plain iron tools he salvages
    from shipwreck, hewing a prose
as odorous as raw wood to the adze;
    out of such timbers
came our first book, our profane Genesis
    whose Adam speaks that prose
which, blessing some sea-rock, startles itself
    with poetry's surprise,
in a green world, one without metaphors;
    like Cristofer he bears
in speech mnemonic as a missionary's
    the Word to savages,
its shape an earthen, water-bearing vessel's
    whose sprinkling alters us
into good Fridays who recite His praise,
    parroting our master's
style and voice, we make his language ours,
    converted cannibals
we learn with him to eat the flesh of Christ.

The position of the beach house in "Crusoe's Journal" evokes Walcott's own precarious position, apparently "between worlds." Here, although the sense of betweenness persists, nature (ocean and forest) seems at first to have overtaken *both* sides. The "drive" to this isolated spot, "past Mundo Nuevo trace," is thus a minuscule version of Walcott's other imaginary journeys into the past, from "Origins" to *Omeros*, beyond the trace of the meridian, to a place untouched by the corruptions of Old World language and indeed, any language—to "a green world, one without metaphors." Life's clutter cleared away, "the intellect appraises / objects surely." Walcott's multiple layering of fictions and histories again superimposes Crusoe, Adam, and "Cristofer," various figures who would have experienced this primal greenness.

Even in a green world, "style" is a "bare necessit[y]" and counts among the Crusoe-poet's "objects" in the sense that it is both his tool and his *aim*. While the narrator of "The Castaway" shies from self-multiplication, the narrator of "Crusoe's Journal" finds it human and inevitable:

> All shapes, all objects multiplied from his,
>   our ocean's Proteus. . . .
> . . . .
> So time, that makes us objects, multiplies
>   our natural loneliness.

Four years later, in "Culture or Mimicry?" Walcott would explicitly articulate the logic of such beginning, in which loneliness is the mother of invention:

> The stripped and naked man, however abused, however disabused of old beliefs, instinctually, even desperately begins again as a craftsman. In the indication of the slightest necessary gesture of ordering the world around him . . . in the arduous enunciation of a dimmed alphabet, in the shaping of tools, pen or spade, is the whole, profound sigh of human optimism. (13)

To apply this passage to "Crusoe's Journal" we must remark, right off, its insistence. It would not be surprising if in this passage "ordering the world" constituted culture; few would argue that point. But Walcott states much more than that here, since "the *indication* of the *slightest* necessary *gesture* of ordering the world" contains "*the whole*" of "human optimism." The "whole" of culture, apparently including its end, exists in the first *indication* of the *slightest gesture* toward it. This is because the beginner begins "again," having through "abuse" been "disabused" of some previous culture. The "sigh" with which "human optimism" begins is also the last breath of lament for a world destroyed.

According to Irwin, Adam spoke nouns: "when the language of words derived from the original language of objects, the words that derived first and that are still closest to that original language were concrete nouns" (32). Adam's speech was thus purely denotative, pure "prose." In "Crusoe's Journal," denotative language *is* metaphoric. Prose "startl[es] itself" into poetry—or is startled to find that it *is* poetry, as Adam and Eve are startled to find themselves naked. The first utterance in the "green world" at once denotes and metaphorizes, as functional ("as raw wood to the adze") as it is decorative. In this passage and in "Crusoe's Journal," the "world . . . without metaphors" almost immediately reveals itself as the world *of* metaphors. The poet cannot imagine the "green world," nature in the absence of rhetoric, without imagining it through rhetoric. Greenness itself is conventionally metonymic of natural purity, and Adam's words are, further, "mnemonic as a missionary's" (another property supposedly specific to *poetic* language). Walcott reaches for the "green world" over and over, because, as he writes at the end of "Crusoe's Journal," "all of us yearn for such fantasies / of innocence." "[S]ince the intellect demands its mask," in other words, we *"pos[e]* as naturalists, / drunks, castaways, beachcombers"* (italics mine), neither able to cast away our yearning to cast away metaphor, nor to fulfill it.

"The Castaway" and "Crusoe's Journal" reply indirectly to Froude. The epigraph of "Air" (*G*, 69–70) finally reproduces Froude's remark. The entire quotation reads: "There has been romance, but it has been the romance of pirates and outlaws. The natural graces of life do not show themselves under such conditions. There are no people there in the true sense of the word, with a character and purpose of their own." From the first Froude's statement bristles with contradiction. First, the "romance of pirates and outlaws" discounted here arises in many British contexts (in Byron, for example) as the height of romance. Second, Froude implies that precisely the "conditions" of nature inhibit the *"natural* graces of life." And finally, the qualifying phrase, "character and purpose *of their own,"* leaves open the possibility that Caribbean people do serve the purposes of other, non-Caribbeans; in which case, no one could ascribe the alleged failure of Caribbean "character and purpose" to Caribbeans alone.

Although "Air" responds to its epigraph, its response is less predictable than the one I have just outlined. We might expect a postcolonial poet to answer Froude's statement by dramatizing Caribbean culture, preferably of Froude's time. We would, at any rate, expect a poem about "people." Instead, an absence of culture, of people, dominates

"Air," the ending of which rather vacantly echoes Froude: "[T]here is too much nothing here." However, while for Froude absence connotes passive emptiness, "Air"'s absence results from the erasure of entire "peoples":

> Long, long before us,
> those hot jaws, like an oven
> steaming, were open
> to genocide; they devoured
> two minor yellow races, and
> half of a black;
> in the Word made flesh of God
> all entered that gross un-
> discriminating stomach. . . .
> . . . .
> a faith, infested cannibal,
> . . . eats gods, which devoured
> the god-refusing Carib, petal
> by golden petal, then forgot,
> and the Arawak
> who leaves not the lightest fern-trace
> of his fossil to be cultured
> by black rock. . . .

As he does in "A Far Cry from Africa" and "Old New England," Walcott attributes what we think of as a human "open[ness] / to genocide" to nature, here the rain forest. The steaming forest somehow prefigures Nazi "ovens" "long before" them. In "Natural History," a sequence of emblematic animal poems in *Sea Grapes* (36–39), the continuity of nature and culture is similarly embittering: "History / is natural; famine, genocide, / as natural as moonlight" (38–39). Likewise, in *Omeros* "Battles were natural as storms; they needed no cause" (82).

Walcott's desire to place genocide in a natural context flirts with resignation. Moreover, by charging the Arawaks' disappearance to the rain forest, Walcott not only writes of erasure but erases history himself. As it happens, the Caribs ravaged the Arawaks, and Western settlers wiped out the Caribs (eradicating their culture and then observing that there was no culture about). Even so, as Walcott mentions elsewhere, the Arawaks did leave some traces—most notably, traces of written language, a sign of "advanced culture." In "Air," however, the Arawaks' eradication seems both "natural" and complete.

In spite of these possible liabilities, "Air" really does counter Froude, and I would offer at least three defenses of its logic. First, in the Froude quotation the belief that cultural habits are "natural graces," and that those who don't possess them are therefore not "people in the true sense of the word," is bound up with a fuzzy and sentimental conception of nature itself. "Air" ironizes nature and short-circuits this sentimentality. Its wordplay points to the nature that suffuses the very word "culture"—a word that encompasses all organic growth as well as human artifice. Second, Walcott's poem, unlike Froude's statement, gives no indication that Walcott fails to lament certain genocides, or "[disavows] / . . . human pain," as he puts it. And third, the poem does draw a distinction between natural and human genocides: the stomach of nature is "gross" and "un- / discriminating." Nature's inhumanity lies precisely in its nondiscrimination, which allows the extinction of tribes and species. Because nature is "open," it is "open / to genocide." Still, if we distinguish humanity by its discrimination, we must recognize that the double edge of that discrimination also makes humanity's own more calculated genocides possible. Thus, on the one hand, Walcott pays for "Air"'s picture of pure nature with deliberate erasures. On the other, the picture itself in its terrifying purity reflects the worst in culture.

In "Homage to Edward Thomas" and "Wales" Walcott gradually reveals that what is particularly obvious and politically significant in Caribbean writing is also significantly present elsewhere. "Homage to Edward Thomas," contemplating a particular poet's relation to his landscape, suggests a paradigm for other poets:

> Formal, informal, by a country's cast
> topography delineates its verse,
> erects the classic bulk, for rigid contrast
> of sonnet, rectory or this manor-house
> dourly timbered against these sinuous
> Downs, defines the formal and informal prose

of Edward Thomas's poems, which make this garden
return its subtle scent of Edward Thomas
in everything here hedged or loosely grown.
Lines which you once dismissed as tenuous
because they would not howl or overwhelm,
as crookedly grave-bent, or cuckoo-dreaming,
seeming dissoluble as this Sussex down
harden in their indifference, like this elm. (55)

In Walcott's opening proposition ("Formal, informal, by a country's
cast / topography delineates its verse") landscape and poetry are not as
original object and secondary representation. Thomas's English countryside provides a "cast," suggesting either sculpture or printing—in
either case, controlled arrangement. Walcott attributes the capacity of
"delineation" to "topography," which is ordinarily considered static
and thoughtless, but is here an art not unlike calligraphy. To "deline-
ate" means to represent and to write, so when topography "delineates," it acts out the writing or "graphing" latent in itself.[4] "Topography delineates" simply by being, as mountains sculpt their self-
portraits, streams etch their signatures into stone. So when "topography delineates its verse," we must ask whether "verse" refers to Thomas's work—a native's verse, which the country claims by familial
right—or to the topography's own concrete "poetry"; to the assertions
Thomas "hedged," or to the hedges that grow here. The question is not
answerable insofar as the two overlap. And we may judge how far that
is by the fact that the very term "topography" may refer either to the
place described or to the act of describing it.

Similarly, "sonnet, rectory or this manor-house" alike possess "rigid
contrast[s]." Since Walcott has already punned on "manor" and
"manner" in "Ruins of a Great House," we should look closely at the
phrase "this manor-house." The demonstrative pronoun, in particular,
seems curiously displaced. "This" is a sonnet we're reading, but "sonnet" passes unspecified, just another part of the countryside, while
Walcott draws us to the house. "This" makes us wonder whether
"this" may not refer to the sonnet on the page after all, metaphorized
as a manor house. The two are obviously similar. The house is "tim-

bered against these sinuous / Downs" because it is made out of timber;
Thomas's poems and this sonnet are also "timbered," first because a
sonnet is written on paper, and second because the poet matches its
tone, its "timbre," to that of the surrounding Downs. The equation also
works in reverse: "the formal and informal prose / Of Edward Thomas's poems . . . make this garden / return its subtle scent of Edward
Thomas." Walcott's line break hints that Thomas's poems not only
make the garden return an impression, but "make this garden," in that
we recognize the garden because it matches our own previous representations of it. By the time Thomas's lines "harden in their indifference, like this elm," "indifference" connotes not only the lines' and
elm's nonchalance but their *non*difference.

In "Homage to Edward Thomas," Walcott's statements about language (which he does not separate from poetic language) are typically
mimetic, although mimesis is always a two-way street for him. His
"Eulogy to W. H. Auden" confides, "Our conjugations, Master, / are
still based on the beat / of wings that gave their cast to / our cuneiform
alphabet" (*AT*, 63). Elsewhere Walcott hints that Brodsky's Cyrillic alphabet not accidentally resembles his native forestscape ("MI," 6). Remarks like "The pace of strolling is iambic pentameter. Right?" (Hamner 1977, 418) roll easily off Walcott's tongue. Indeed, the relationship
he posits between landscape and language is more than close; landscapes already *are* linguistic. In *Another Life* "inlet[s] / [mutter] in
brackish dialect" (8.ii.7–8), "each ochre track . . . / los[es] itself in an
unfinished phrase" (8.ii.12), "the water rat takes up its reed pen / and
scribbles. Leisurely, the egret / on the mud tablet stamps its hieroglyph"
(22.i.14–16), "a bush would turn in the wind / with a toothless giggle,
and / certain roots refused English" (23.i.19–21). These are not similes, not parallels, but metaphors that imply continuity.

Walcott is more persistent on this point than on any other. The near-
sonnet "Wales" (*FT*, 87), seven years after *The Gulf*, still uses terms
very reminiscent of "Edward Thomas"'s to explore and question the
continuity between the Welsh landscape and the postcolonial rebel-
liousness of the Welsh language.

> Those white flecks cropping the ridges of Snowdon
> will thicken their fleece and come wintering down

through the gap between alliterative hills,
through the caesura that let in the Legions,
past the dark disfigured mouths of the chapels,
till a white silence comes to green-throated Wales.
Down rusty gorges, cold rustling gorse,
over rocks hard as consonants, and rain-vowelled shales
sang the shallow-buried ax, helmet, and baldric
before the wet asphalt sibilance of tires.
A plump raven, Plantagenet, unfurls its heraldic
caw over walls that held the cult of the horse.
In blackened cottages with their stony hatred
of industrial fires, a language is shared
like bread to the mouth, white flocks to dark byres.

Walcott hints in Cratylan fashion that among "alliterative hills" divided by caesuras, poetry cannot help being alliterative, that in rocky regions, people speak with hard consonants, and so forth. People like to believe that their landscapes and languages show national character. In this case Wales and Welsh alike seem to convey a "stony hatred / of industrial fires." The native language counters invading "Legions" and upholds independence, like the "stubborn bilingual sign[s]" in another poem about Wales ("Streams," *AT*, 80). Walcott asserts with his sacramental "bread" simile ("like bread to the mouth"), too, that the Welsh language consecrates community and makes the nation more than the sum of its parts. The poem's extra line embodies this linguistic generosity, overflowing formal bounds. Like "Forest of Europe," then, "Wales" hopes that "What keeps [civilizations] at such times from disintegration is not legions but languages" (Brodsky, 164).

The idea that a national language consecrates community certainly approaches naive patriotism. Pride in postcolonial language may recommit the errors of Empire, overglorifying the very language being praised for expressing a hatred of false glory. "Wales" makes very high claims for Welsh, arguing that it is as essential as bread and as spiritual as communion. Walcott also limits his hymn to Welsh, however, by comparing this essential, spiritual language to silence and noncommunication. At the risk of some repetition, we need to read "Wales"' language and landscape more closely.

First and most obviously, landscape resembles language. Hills are "alliterative," full of "gap[s]" and "caesura[s]." To some extent the proposition is reversible: the words on the page also resemble landscape. As the Welsh panorama descends from peak to valley, so does the poem. Its first line is its "[ridge] of Snowdon," and the rest of the poem "come[s] wintering down" the page. However, as snowlike sheep descend "over rocks hard as consonants," it is the *space between* words (white like sheep or snow, not black like ink[5]) that descends over consonants hard as rocks. The same language that is "like [white] bread" and "white flocks" therefore also resembles "white silence." Similarly, "byres" shelter "flocks," but mouths in the act of eating bread-words alter as well as preserve them. In the process of perpetuating language, we consume it, and vice versa. Although sacred silence can speak louder than words, the idea that "a white silence" will come to "green-throated Wales" occludes that of Welsh as an eternal monument.

It is important to note as we read through Walcott's linguistic landscapes that Walcott's conception of nature as language and vice versa does not reify language. That is, he does not treat words *as though* they were things, or aim to transform them into things. Either would presuppose that objects precede words or exist at a higher level of reality than words. Rather, poetry manifests both the inherent substantiality of words and the world's already textual character, "the right of every thing to be a noun" ("Names," 42). Although we live in a textual world, this world need not be hypothetical or ephemeral, since texts themselves are substantial. In poetic practice this results in a dizzying reciprocity within mimesis: "trees and men / [labour] assiduously, silently to become // whatever their given sounds [resemble]" (*AL*, 8.iii.26–28). In this line from *Another Life*, signifieds ("trees and men") and signifiers ("their given sounds") aim toward an undefined third term ("whatever"). The signifiers resemble *something*, but not something identical with their signifieds, since the signifieds too must "[labour] . . . to become" it. The world and its representations thus share something—it is hard to know whether to call it a common root, a common aim, both, or neither—and the poet's consciousness of this something-shared keeps poetry alive to reality's linguistic structure on the one hand and the physical structure of words themselves on the other.

Because Walcott's interest in the continuity between nature and culture is so strong in the first place, it scarcely shifts over time. But Walcott's anxiety about the question does seem to sharpen over the years. Sometimes Walcott's very early efforts seem, by their very insistence, to take the continuity between nature and culture for granted. In "The Castaway" and "Crusoe's Island" Walcott stages the temptation to keep nature and culture apart. But in later poems like "The Sea Is History," "A Latin Primer," and "Cul de Sac Valley," even the willing beholder struggles to perceive their continuity, and battles doubts about the status of his culture and his own position within that culture. Of these poems "The Sea Is History" is most celebratory, its struggle most easily resolved.

"The Sea Is History" (*SAK*, 25–28) is, like many of Walcott's earlier poems, completely structured from its title on by pairings that identify nature with culture. However, typical of Walcott's later style, the poem is at once loose-limbed (its varying diction allows for humor) and dramatically complex. In this imaginary dialogue, as in *Another Life* and "Names," the schoolmaster-poet, perhaps speaking for a group of adults, asks questions, and schoolchildren, or perhaps one representative child, answer him. Together they enact a mock catechism on Afro-Caribbean history. While schoolmasters usually know the answers to their own questions, this one does not. Again, as in "Names," he is educated by the children's folk wisdom:

> Where are your monuments, your battles, martyrs?
> Where is your tribal memory? Sirs,
> in that gray vault. The sea. The sea
> has locked them up. The sea is History.

The children fill the schoolmaster-poet's request for "monuments, . . . battles, martyrs" with a series of scenes from the African diaspora, each linked to some corresponding Biblical scene. The beginning of slavery is an ironic Genesis announced by "the lantern of a caravel"; "Then there were the packed cries, / the shit, the moaning: // Exodus." Next, the poem imagines slaves drowned in passage. "Bone[s] soldered by coral to bone" are "the Ark of the Covenant," and "white cowries clustered like manacles / on the drowned women, // . . . the ivory bracelets / of the Song of Solomon." Myth and nature soak through the history narrated here so that it is hardly recognizable as the coherent sequence in history textbooks, in which one finds "no joy . . . except their love of events" (*O*, 95). Caribbean history is "locked up," sunk in suppression, and susceptible to myth. Still, what we might call "myth" usually has an empirical, historical component. And all history resembles Valéry's sea, "forever rerenewed," because memories are never recorded without sea changes.[6]

About a third of the way through the poem the schoolmaster-poet offers a comparison of his own: "the tidal wave swallowing Port Royal, / . . . that was Jonah." The poet, catching on, accepts the logic of the children's preceding metaphors, then shifts focus slightly by requesting some evidence of Caribbean cultural history. Given Walcott's preoccupation with Froude's and Naipaul's remarks about Caribbean cultural poverty, his question sounds mocking and anxious:

> . . . the tidal wave swallowing Port Royal,
> . . . that was Jonah,
> but where is your Renaissance?

The children respond to the poet's turn towards cultural history with elaborate evidence of natural art, in a manner that is itself "Renaissance."

> Sir, it is locked in them sea sands
> out there past the reef's moiling shelf,
> where the men-o'-war floated down;
>
> strop on these goggles, I'll guide you there myself.
> It's all subtle and submarine,
> through colonnades of coral,
>
> past the gothic windows of sea fans
> . . . .

and these groined caves with barnacles
pitted like stone
are our cathedrals. . . .

Walcott's underwater panorama recalls *The Tempest*, and these interpenetrations of nature and culture recall *The Winter's Tale*: "over that
art, Which you say adds to nature, is an art / That nature makes"
(IV.iv.90–92).

The poem gathers evidence of Caribbean history and culture, then,
and also asserts a central redefinition, proposing that "The Sea *Is* History." Still, the children repeatedly distinguish between their own evidence of history and a history still to be sought: "the ocean kept turning blank pages / looking for History"; "that was just Lamentations, /
it was not History"; "but that was not History, / that was only faith."
This kind of splitting also occurs in "The Muse of History," where Walcott uses at least two definitions of the word, disparaging history as a
linear record but respecting it as a communal consciousness suffusing
perception. One kind of history, history as a continuously recorded
sequence, *is* probably lost to the Caribbean, and that is just as well,
since as Spoiler remarks, "he ain't recognize me." A second history, a
history embedded in the forms of the object world, can never be lost.
History still "resides in the body's memory" as a deepening spatial and
vertical entity,[7] a "replete" text. We can see history in the rings of a
tree, in our palms, or in words, in every material form that has been
led by its own experience to take its present shape and no other. In this
sense "The sea is History" because the sea is the repository of earth's
oldest forms of life—of fossils, coelacanths, and other hidden treasures.

The children search beyond this, however, for a third and most elu-
sive history, a history of Caribbean independence. After "Emancipa-
tion," after "each rock broke into its own nation," the poem moves
quickly through the development of independent Caribbean politics:
"then came the synod of flies, / then came the secretarial heron, / then
came the bullfrog bellowing for a vote." Rita Dove explains that "Only
with the break-up of the British Empire does the clock start to tick. . . .
History begins with self-determination."[8] History can take a lesson

from biology in this regard. "The Sea Is History" identifies the independent "History" just "really beginning" with organic life, placing it in the same tidepools in which "natural history" begins:

and then in the dark ears of ferns

and in the salt chuckle of rocks
with their sea pools, there was the sound
like a rumor without any echo

of History, really beginning.

An echo repeats the form of a sound as a shadow repeats a shape, and lends sound a sort of three-dimensionality. The future, although anticipated by "rumor," does not itself anticipate anything. Nothing can follow the future except more of itself; it has no echo. Locating history in the future therefore frees it from repercussions. History remains amorphous and ambivalent, something one must always approach. When we put an ear to its secret places and tidepools, we hear a soft, ambiguous "salt chuckle," undefinable as either tears or laughter.

In "A Latin Primer" (*AT*, 21–27), the poet's discovery of native and "natural" linguistic power coincides with his own poetic empowerment. In truth, the poet *re*discovers a knowledge once believed, then shaken by doubt, and it is a discovery in itself when the poet realizes this. At the beginning of the poem the apparent cultural poverty of the young poet's surroundings compels him to seek "help" in "distant literatures." At the same time, in the back of his mind he already accepts "help" from the language of nature:

I had nothing against which
to notch the growth of my work
but the horizon, no language
but the shallows in my long walk

home, so I shook all the help
my young right hand could use
from the sand-crusted kelp
of distant literatures.

The very words in which the poet complains about isolation admit that it *is* possible to notch poetic growth against "the horizon" and that "the shallows" do have "language." It likewise admits that "literatures" are so much "sand-crusted kelp." Since his complaint forms against the background of an unconscious continuity between nature and literature, it is no surprise that the poet soon "[finds] [his] deepest wish / in the swaying words of the sea."

For a time the poet seems to believe nature larger than culture. Insofar as he too simply sides with nature, he cannot see much value in his position as an instructor of basic Latin. Nature is full of "swaying words" that respond to one's "deepest wish," while Latin forms and the devices by which the poet understands them seem oppressively artificial:

> I hated signs of scansion.
> Those strokes across the line
> drizzled on the horizon
> and darkened discipline.
>
> They were like Mathematics
> that made delight Design,
> arranging the thrown sticks
> of stars to sine and cosine.

Latin serves as a sort of hardest-case for the poem. "[H]at[ing] signs of scansion" himself, the poet even more deeply doubts their relevance to his students, who "would die in dialect." If Latin—a language no one grows up speaking or ever knows for certain how to pronounce, a language spoken and written only as an academic exercise—can be "natural," then probably any "literary" language is natural, including that the poet desires to write.

Latin is old and dry. Still, there is a place for the old and dry: "the old words dry / like seaweed on the page." The sea, too, is like a Latin poet; it not only has "a page," but "scan[s] its own syllable," and "the boys' / heads [plunge] in paper / softly as porpoises" even amid the useless activity of learning Latin. But the poet achieves the final shift of perspective he needs while following the flight of a frigate bird. Walcott has been drawn to the frigate bird, "my phoenix" (*AT*, 21), at least since having included it in "A Tropical Bestiary," Walcott's sequence of emblematic poems in *The Castaway*. There the frigate bird emblematized the poetry of earth: its "easy wings / Depend upon the stress I give such things / As my importance to its piercing height." Now, the frigate bird exemplifies nature's impulse toward language. Its wings poised in flight form their own V-shaped ideogram:[9]

> a frigate bird came sailing
> through a tree's net, to raise
>
> its emblem in the cirrus,
> named with the common sense
> of fishermen: sea scissors,
> *Fregata magnificens,*
>
> *ciseau-la-mer,* the patois
> for its cloud-cutting course;
> and that native metaphor
> made by the strokes of oars,
>
> with one wing beat for scansion,
> that slowly levelling V
> made one with my horizon
> as it sailed steadily
>
> beyond the sheep-nibbled columns
> of fallen marble trees,
> or the roofless pillars once
> sacred to Hercules.

As the poet repeats the bird's names in the three languages familiar to him, the bird crosses the landscape, "rais[ing] // its emblem," scanning by its own wingbeats, and manipulating the V of its body. Thus, the poet and the frigate bird both engage in forms of writing. At the same time, the distance between Latin and St. Lucian lessens as it becomes obvious that all the frigate bird's names are, in the Borgesian sense, "poems": "sea scissors, / *Fregata magnificens, // ciseau-la-mer.*" For Walcott Caribbean languages differ from their European counterparts only in that because they are newer, their "naturalness" is more often visible. They are therefore *more* rather than less literary for being new. The word *ciseau-la-mer*, precisely, is Walcott's example of this phenomenon:

The word "beetle" must have some metaphoric root, but who knows what it is now? Let's say you're looking up at a bird in the sky over St. Lucia and somebody says "ciseau la mer." Now "ciseau la mer" means "scissor of the sea," and that's much more startling, much more exciting than saying "martin" or "tern." The metaphor is almost calligraphic: when it's pronounced you can almost see it. (Hirsch 1979, 287)

Finally, the ideographic figure of the bird, "that slowly levelling V," already shows nature's poetry, "ma[kes] one with [his] horizon." When the V's wings straighten into a line in a gesture of union with the horizon, the last vestige of language merges with the world and the last vestige of the world disappears into language as well. In the moment of epiphanic victory over conflict the symbol for victory levels itself, an antivictory immersed in the external world rather than triumphant over it. Walcott's possessive, "my horizon," indicates that the horizon is also the boundary of his own self, the limit of what he can conceptualize. The Latin instructor's epiphanic experience enlarges his "horizon" and confirms him as a poet, empowered now, like the frigate bird, to sail beyond "the roofless pillars once / sacred to Hercules."[10]

Recall once again Benjamin's remark that translation from one language to another implies a common ground between the two, so that "both the original and the translation [are] recognizable as fragments of a greater language, just as fragments are part of a vessel" (78). By this logic "the original," itself a "fragment," is on a par with its "translation," and as a "fragment" is obviously *not original*. There is only a *mise en abîme* of fragments—a reverse *mise en abîme*, in which the fragments grow larger and larger until too large to perceive. When Walcott considers the world a text the same principle applies to "translation" between it and any other text. One cannot, therefore, fix the meeting place, the ground on which both writing and the object world rest, which seems at once inside both and larger than both, and which objects "[labour] . . . to become" and signifiers "resemble." Walcott's poems nevertheless imply such a site, and often graph it as a V. This letter (or figure) resembles a tree, the emblem of the continuity between leaves and paper, nature and culture. According to Irwin,

DEREK WALCOTT'S POETRY

the cosmic tree ... with its roots in the underworld, its trunk in this world, and its leafy branches extending up into the heavens—is an image of language as mediating link between the human and the divine. Foucault points out that the seventeenth-century writer Christophe de Savigny in his *Tableau de tous les arts libéraux* "contrives to spatialize acquired knowledge both in accordance with the cosmic, unchanging, and perfect form of the circle and in accordance with the sublunary, perishable, multiple and divided form of the tree." ... But the cosmic tree combines the images of both the circle and the tree: it is the fixed, unchanging point that binds together the horizontal and the vertical. (32)

Walcott first uses the figure of the universe-tree in *Another Life* ("dusk, the tree of heaven, broke in gold leaf" [10.i.30]).[11] The universe-tree recurs in "The Schooner *Flight*" as "that branched tree from which meteors are shaken" ("*SAK*," 19). In *Omeros* "the branched sky / grew downward like mangroves, or an immense banyan" (55), "Plunkett's ances-tree fountained in blossoms" (87), and St. Lucia is a "branched island" (89). In his interview with Dennis Scott, Walcott explains the "mass sensibility" of West Indian poetry by yet another tree metaphor: "People look at the flowers and not at the trunk of tree in West Indian poetry. You know, this sort of poinsettia and that sort of croton; but they don't know, they don't look at the ugliness of the bark. The strength that went down into the thing" (80). The linguistic vigor of the Caribbean is so ordinary, functional, and "ugly," like the bark rather than the flower of a tree, that everyone overlooks it. Walcott stresses the imperceptibility of this vigor: people "*don't know, they don't look*" at it. The urgency of the remark betrays not a little concern. Indeed, Walcott accents these unappreciated, barklike linguistic properties as though correcting injustices.

In "Cul de Sac Valley" (*AT*, 9–15) representation on one side and the object world on the other appear separate at the top of the language tree. Tracing either down to ground level exposes consanguinities, however, and at just the moment both disappear from sight, one glimpses their nexus. What happens beyond that point remains beyond divination. To judge by the infinite branchings Shabine glimpses at the top of the universe-tree, they probably separate again into a puzzling system of roots. Still, the poet should remain prescient of the momentary intersection at the bottom of the V.

The poem begins by comparing the poet's craft to a carpenter's:

> A panel of sunrise
> on a hillside shop
> gave these stanzas
> their stilted shape.
>
> If my craft is blest;
> if this hand is as
> accurate, as honest
> as their carpenter's,
>
> every frame, intent
> on its angles, would
> echo this settlement
> of unpainted wood.

In his *Paris Review* interview, which took place while he was working on *The Arkansas Testament*, Walcott explains his attraction at the time to quatrains:

> At this period of my life and work, I think of myself in a way as a carpenter, as one making frames, simply and well. I'm working a lot in quatrains, or I have been, and I feel that there is something in that that is very ordinary, you know, without any mystique. I'm trying to get rid of the mystique as much as possible. And so I find myself wanting to write very simply cut, very contracted, very speakable and very challenging quatrains in rhymes. Any other shape seems ornate, an elaboration on that essential cube that really is the poem. (206)[12]

Walcott doesn't question the accuracy of his comparison between two crafts, although it is hard to tell which echoes which. Still, individual poets (or carpenters) may or may not honor it, depending on whether or not their "craft[s] [are] blest." The poet could shave "C's, R's, with a French / or West African root" from the tree of Creole only if "blest" by Creole itself. In the first part of this four-part poem, he envisions Creole refusing that blessing: *"What you wish / from us will never be, /*

your words is English, / is a different tree." The poet's success does not depend at this point upon the relation between nature and culture— rather, between his two languages, English and Creole.

Walcott's route out of this situation is circuitous. The second part of the poem, still in narrow dimeter quatrains, takes us both backward and forward in its search for language's inception without leaving the poem's immediate situation. Outside the poet hears "gutturals" and "vowels" "begin[ning]" in animal and mechanical, then human, sounds:

> In the rivulet's gravel
> light gutturals begin,
> in the valley, a mongrel,
> a black vowel barking,
>
> sends up fading ovals;
> by a red iron bridge,
> menders with shovels
> scrape bubbling pitch,
>
> every grating squeak
> reaching this height
> a tongue they speak
> in, but cannot write.

A river, a dog, shovels, and human beings contribute their voices equally to this tongue. Walcott conveys this universal linguistic "history" entirely through description and without a tense change, superimposing the different stages of what we ordinarily call linguistic development. Here, writing does not develop *from* natural or human voice, but reveals its simultaneity with voice; the "mongrel" who barks *is* "a black vowel barking," and his barks are synaesthetically visible as "fading ovals." The "mongrel" language of Creole is not distinct from the creature who produces it and, as in "Forest of Europe," is at once spoken and written, audible and visible. "Dialect," with its connotation of provinciality, is a paradoxical term to apply to this language, made up of all the noises of the world. It is Earth's "dialect." And if its speakers "cannot write" in it, it writes itself, "Like the lost idea / of the visible soul / still kindled here / on illiterate soil."

Walcott personifies this language as a schoolgirl and, in a secondary metaphor, "a lime tree's daughter," a "sapling"'s youthful branching of Creole's tree who in an Ovidian metamorphosis "forks into / a girl." "Literally," the poet could (from a window?) see a girl appear through a tree's fork as she "rac[es] upstairs":

> The sapling forks into
> a girl racing upstairs
> from the yard, to enter
> this stanza. Now tears
>
> fill her eyes, a mirror's
> tears, as her nape knot is
> pulled by her mother's
> comb. . . .

Contemporary Creole is a schoolgirl because she meets the poet half-way by studying English, "reciting this language." In part two English "blinds" her so that "she ambles towards / an inner silence," but by part four, she has made headway: "trees repeat her / darkening English." His native hills school the poet at the same time, testing his fitness for the blessing he desires by trying him like "Sphinxes" (in the last line of the poem, Pigeon Island is "Cat-like") with a riddle:

> "Can you call each range
> by its right name, aloud,
> while our features change
> between light and cloud?"[13]

The riddle poses a fit challenge for a poet because, as the personification of Creole as a schoolgirl suggests, linguistic "features" do grow and change as young languages grow older, just as the landscape's features "change / between light and cloud"; these natural-cultural features fluctuate in time. The hills' riddle is not an exam in Creole competency, asking for lexical entries. Rather, the "right name[s]" would have to account for transitory natural-cultural topographies. The poet accordingly responds not with a list of words but with "lines" of topographical "poetry":

what I vaguely recall
is a line of white sand

and lines in the mahogany
of cured faces and stones
muttering under a stony
river. . . .

As "stones / [mutter] under a stony / river," Walcott's poet—like
Baudelaire's, who crosses a "forest of symbols / which eye [him] with
a familiar regard"—mutters amid a muttering world. The poet needs
to recognize the object world's language in order to produce his own,
for poetry in either Creole or English would drift helplessly in a misguided attempt to either capture or rival the world if it did not realize
its pre-existing consubstantiality with it. The poet's answer is correct
because it communicates this reciprocity. It loosens the "nape knot"
question mark of the schoolgirl/Creole's hair: "the questions // dissolving will unravel / their knots." Polysemy and wordplay reward the poet
at least twice: "the mongrel / yelping happily, repeats / vowel after
vowel, // the boughs bow to me." Not only do the "boughs bow," but
the vowels within this description of vowels ("*vowel* after *vowel*, / the
boughs bow") themselves "[yelp] happily," bow-wowing like mongrels.

In Walcott's convolved mimesis "names fit / their echo" as well as
vice versa; this turns out to have been prophetically enacted by the
poem's third stanza. The third stanza claims that the poem's structure
will follow and "echo" nature's, so that nature seems normative, the
model by which we should evaluate the poem. In this stanza's syntac-
tical ordering, however, the word "wood" follows and echoes its hom-
ophone "would." The verb denoting the poet's action precedes and
makes more significant the noun denoting a part of nature. If the hills
ask in their riddle for the names of "each range"—that is, their own
names—and, when the poet's words supply these names, the names
fit only "their echo," what has happened to the signifieds in this
scheme, to the hills themselves? And if "their echo" is some kind of
figure for "hills," then objects echo names, rather than names, objects—a construction familiar from *Another Life*, where "the *bois-canot*
respond[s] to its echo" (8.iii.4).

Finally, the poet enacts the reciprocity between nature and culture by emphasizing the substantiality of his own text. This enables him to stress the nexus of those various branches of one tree, those "concepts that permitted the exclusion of writing: image or representation, sensible and intelligible, nature and culture, nature and technics, etc." (Derrida, *Of Grammatology*, 71). The poem achieves this reintegration in at least three ways. First, by Walcott's familiar correlation of books' and trees' leaves. Here Walcott reworks an idea from *Another Life*, the poet of which "watched the vowels curl from the tongue of the carpenter's plane, / resinous, fragrant / labials of our forests." Second, Walcott revives the etymology that links stanzas and rooms when the schoolgirl "rac[es] upstairs / . . . to enter / this stanza" (*AT*, 11). When the girl again climbs, in the fourth part, "straight / up the steps of this verse," she personifies "the sap of memory / rac[ing] upward" through the poet as he "remembers" the landscape's line. The girl's figure racing upstairs, the sap "racing" to the top of the tree, and the poet's surge of "racial" memory all underscore the tree metaphor that recalls both the text's paperiness and the common "roots" of nature and culture. Last, "Cul de Sac Valley" emphasizes substance through its form, for this tall poem in narrow quatrains adopts, like Valéry's "Palme," the shape of the trees of which it writes. Since the poem can be seen as a visual double of its subject and vice versa, it keeps its promise to "echo" the setting that echoes it.

ALTHOUGH "The Sea Is History," "A Latin Primer," and "Cul de Sac Valley" emerge from cultural insecurity and self-doubt to reassert the continuity of nature with culture, it becomes increasingly obvious that in Walcott's work no doubt is ever banished for good. Walcott's temporary resolutions always bear the scars of struggle. Ideas tend to interrelate in contorted ways; even Walcott's syntax is, to use his own metaphor, liana-like ("Guyana," *G*, 71). Even against a familiar background of difficulty, however, Walcott's treatment of the nature/culture opposition stands out as at once remarkably relentless and shot through with wistfulness. The pastoral wish that poetry be simple, like carpentry or gardening, lies behind many of these poems. Although

Walcott doesn't use the word "pastoral" much—Caliban *would* view pastoral with a skeptical eye—his whole enterprise is pastoral, if we mean by that the transfer of peace to a phantasmal realm, or a verbal harmony so pure that in its hush no one can recall contention.

The ideal and its impossibility appear with startling lucidity in an image from *Omeros*. In a passage mourning the death of Maud, Walcott observes, "I knew little about Maud Plunkett. . . . / What I shared with [her] we shared as gardeners" (266). Walcott confesses a poverty of connections here: Maud and he are female and male, white and black, colonist and colonial. Only, Maud grows flowers, and Walcott, words. Solely in metaphor, when the poet is momentarily "a gardener," is the gulf between him and Maud bridged. Furthermore, Walcott compares Maud's gardening *to his own capacity to be metaphoric*. Not only are poets gardeners; every metaphor is a dream-garden, a miniature pastoral. And in this case, since this is a metaphor about metaphor, the dream-garden produces no less than a phantasmal *bridge*:

> I had wanted large green words to lie waxen on
> the page's skin, floating but rooted in its lymph as
> her lilies in the pond's cool mud, every ivory prong
>
> spreading the Japanese peace of *Les Nympheas*
> in the tongue-still noon, the heat, where a wooden bridge
> with narrow planks arched over the calligraphic
>
> bamboo, their reflections rewritten when a midge
> wrinkled the smoothness, and from them, the clear concentric
> rings from a pebble, from the right noun on a page. (266)

As Derrida writes of a bridge metaphor in Hegel, "The bridge is not *an* analogy. The recourse to analogy, the concept and effect of analogy are or make *the bridge* itself. . . . The analogy of the abyss and of the bridge over the abyss is an analogy which says that there must surely be an analogy" (*The Truth in Painting*, 36).

The appearance of Walcott's analogic bridge crowns a piece of "natural description" as rhetorical as it is radiant. The water lilies, pond, and bridge, complete with their own "reflections" and ripple effects, are not "there," but only hang, like thoughts in cloud-balloons, above

Walcott's "large green words." Moreover, the green words are not "there," either. They exist only in the past perfect (Walcott *"had* wanted" them), among once-desired things that never came to pass and are no longer hoped for. Thus, the garden bridge between Maud and Walcott is not simply a pastoral construct; it is a pastoral *manqué* that Walcott claims was never constructed. Pastoral is in the first place a compromise formation; because we can't escape social norms "in reality," we suspend them in pastoral. This is what happens in Walcott's most classically pastoral poem, "The Season of Phantasmal Peace." Here, however, Walcott's representation of a nonexistent representation of water lilies suspends the pastoral ideal of suspension. Whether this undoes pastoral or outdoes it, it is clear that by *Omeros* Walcott is searching along the seam between nature and culture for a relief whose arrival he no longer awaits.

HOMERIC MIMICRY

If ever the naval exploits of this country are done into an epic poem—and since the Iliad there has been no subject better fitted for such treatment or better deserving it—the West Indies will be the scene of the most brilliant cantos.

—James Anthony Froude, *The British in the West Indies;*
or, The Bow of Ulysses[1]

ALTHOUGH *Omeros* cannot have been the epic Froude imagined—not least because Froude couldn't have guessed his West Indian *Iliad* would be written by a St. Lucian—it is far from anti-Homeric or anti-epic. Walcott's mimicry never consists of mere mockery. Walcott aims for a Homeric scope of human conflict and visionary experience and, obviously, raises expectations for his language and characterization by comparing himself to such an illustrious predecessor. But *Omeros* is also ambitious in a second sense; for by raising the question of his relationship to Homer, Walcott defines himself against a primary Western paradigm of originality and mimetic power, and re-evaluates that paradigm as well as his own poetry.[2] The "basic impulse of the Homeric style," as Auerbach observes, is "to represent phenomena in a fully externalized form, visible and palpable in all their parts, and completely fixed in their spatial and temporal relations."[3] Walcott's mimicry of Homer thus confronts mimesis at what we usually think of as both its root and its apex. Further, the series of parallels upon which *Omeros*, like Joyce's *Ulysses*, stands presses us toward our own confrontations with mimesis. Our first impulse may be to compare Walcott's

Helen to Homer's, Achille to Achilles, Philoctete to Philoctetes, and so on. But the continuous process of doing so will likely also cause us to question our impulse to perceive, and hence to create, likenesses— especially when such questioning becomes an overt theme of the poem itself. When, for example, both Major Plunkett (a British veteran and colonist) and the persona of the poet struggle to grasp the St. Lucian Helen and then fail to determine her relation (if any) to her Greek counterpart, the validity of similitude falls into doubt.

Likewise, because Homer stands at or slightly before the beginning of Western poetic genealogy—at a distance at which genealogy evades the grasp—Walcott's rapprochement with Homer means a rapprochement with not just *a* poetic ancestor but with poetic ancestry. Walcott highlights this, too, first by making Omeros a character in the drama and casting his own persona as Omeros's poetic heir, and second by several times retelling the Odysseus-Telemachos story—a story that can be read as a parable of paternal, hence genealogical, mystery.

Omeros's two tiers of reference—Walcottian and Homeric— also complicate mimicry in new ways. I suggested at the outset that mimicry points to its own nonoriginality as well as to that of its model. *Omeros* does do this, in that "life" mimics "art" within the fiction of the poem. That is, the St. Lucian characters are ostensibly "real people" who yet appear to recall Homeric or other literary models. The character of Warwick Walcott, for example, the poet's father—who died of an ear infection at an early age—notices that his past echoes parts of Shakespeare's plays:

> ["]I died on his birthday, one April. Your mother
> sewed her own costume as Portia, then that disease
> like Hamlet's old man's spread from an infected ear,
>
> I believe the parallel has brought you some peace.
> Death imitating Art, eh?" (68–69)

Walcott once again places literary models, representations—albeit tentatively—in positions usually reserved for originals. But given two fictional tiers, one will likely shine at the expense of the other. Odds are that figures in a painting gazing at another painting gain the appearance of verisimilitude in comparison to other figures inside the painting at which they gaze. Similarly, the rhetorical effect of Walcott's references to Homer's more distant poems is to vivify his own poem. By appearing to model "real" St. Lucians upon fictional Greeks, Walcott suggests that "life" imitates "art"—and thereby distracts the reader from the fact that what he calls "life" is already "art." In this sense *Omeros* actually *disguises* its own status as representation. If elsewhere in Walcott's work we learn that mimicry haunts mimesis, in *Omeros* a trompe-l'oeil mimesis returns to haunt mimicry.

The progress of the poem complicates things still further, however, for *Omeros* gradually frustrates one's hope of defining the connections between St. Lucian and Greek characters. The persona of the poet strives to release the poem's Homeric tier—to shed "art" and henceforward to perceive "life" in relation only to "life." Although liberation from reference to "art" would spell the end of mimicry, this liberation is a goal only within the "art" of the poem. As soon as we step back from mimetic illusion and recover our suspended disbelief in the reality of *Omeros*'s St. Lucian tier, we see that Walcott's bespoken loyalty to a "life" itself fictive draws its rhetorical persuasiveness from comparisons to the prior, avowedly discarded Homeric tier. And even if we capitulate to mimesis, suspend disbelief, and accept the lessons of the poem's fiction as truth, what we learn from the plot is precisely that it is as impossible to release "life" from "art" as to make "life" and "art" correspond. In other words, "life" turns out to depend upon "art" whether we do or do not accept *Omeros*'s mimetic pretentions. Mimicry returns, in either case, to pursue the mimesis that pursues it.

A good summary of the poem—a lengthy, intricate network of plots, images, and linguistic play—would pose a challenge, and a comprehensive explication would require its own book. I won't be able to render an account of the whole poem here, nor even to negotiate all of its implications for mimicry. I can consider only a handful of related issues: questions of likeness and of the interpretation of likenesses, which occur throughout the poem but revolve with particular intensity around the figure of Helen; the related question of disfigurement, likeness's negative, which similarly afflicts most of the characters but is focused especially upon the figure of Philoctete; and third, questions of genealogy and originality, in which most of the characters in the poem become involved. These three topics often intertwine: family likeness is held to be the proof of genealogy, for example, whereas disfigurement disrupts genealogy by blurring similitude. Finally, these issues recall discussions of representation, originality, and influence in earlier chapters. *Omeros* provides several points of comparison, therefore, that help us to measure the late development of Walcott's poetic — or, as the case may be, to rethink the desire to compare early and late parts of a poet's career.

IT SEEMS NECESSARY to define *Omeros*'s relation to the Homeric poems before launching into a discussion of particulars. Exactly this relation, however, remains indefinite throughout the poem; Walcott's references to Homer inspire conflict and instability within *Omeros*. This instability ought to direct one's attention to the problem of a work's relation to its model, for Walcott's references to Homer question mimetic notions of reference to models to the same degree that they disrupt the poem's coherence.

Walcott counters Homeric expectations by fluctuating between reversal and continuity — which is certainly not to say that *Omeros* contains no important reversals. Walcott does, first of all, pastoralize the Homeric poems in *Omeros*, as though expanding upon "The Season of Phantasmal Peace." Major Plunkett, observing "an old freighter welded to the wharf by rust / and sunsets . . . felt a deep tenderness for it, / that it went nowhere at all" (258); Walcott, too, reserves his deepest praise for the pacifistic and the humble. Walcott's postcolonial American status, parallel to Joyce's as an Irish writer in English, accounts for this conspicuous modification of epic protocol. *Omeros*'s heroes are not explorers, conquerors, or imperialists, but St. Lucian fishermen, waitresses, transport drivers, and the like. Walcott distinguishes Achille from Achilles by his gentleness and modesty:

> I sang of quiet Achille, Afolabe's son,
> who never ascended in an elevator,
> who had no passport, since the horizon needs none,

186   DEREK WALCOTT'S POETRY

never begged nor borrowed, was nobody's waiter. . . .

. . . .

Who hated shoes, whose soles were as cracked as a stone,
who was gentle with ropes, who had one suit alone. (320)

It would be a mistake to conclude that Walcott always and merely pastoralizes epic, however. *Omeros*'s pastoral inclination does not, for several reasons, decode the workings of all its Homeric allusions. First, characters and events in *Omeros* both parallel and contradict their Homeric counterparts. We cannot maintain that Achille, to continue with the same example, does not at all resemble Achilles. Although he is peaceable, his "frown / [is] a growing thunderhead" (320); although (and because) he uses his fists only for sailing, rowing, or fishing, he does have "fist[s] of iron" (320); Hector and Achille do quarrel over Helen, "Like Hector. Like Achilles" (47); and in Achille's African dream of battle, "He . . . felt the same / mania that, in the arrows of drizzle, he felt for Hector" (147). Second, Homeric models are not Walcott's only models, as Warwick Walcott's allusions to Shakespeare show. These multiple models combine to corrupt the purity of any originality. As soon as we begin to claim originality for Achille by describing him as distinct from or opposite to Homer's Achilles, we remember that the same pacifism, the same humility, attaches him to Joyce's Bloom. Difference from one predecessor simultaneously suggests mimicry of another (as we saw in another context in Chapter 2), so that originality enters through the front door only to fly out the back. Connections tend to be confusingly overdetermined. Walcott's Hector "is" Hector, but when he crashes his transport, the Comet, he is Phaeton as well. The poet's wife and the narrator resemble Circe and one of her swine, yet "If History saw [Caribbeans] as pigs, History was Circe" too (64). The Homeric Polyphemos has at least three Omeric counterparts: the lighthouse at La Toc (13), Joyce with his eye patch (201), and a tourist with a camera (299).[4] Walcott, combining Homeric and non-Homeric analogies, identifies Helen with St. Lucia, with the wreck of the *Ville de Paris* (which "vanishe[s] with all hope of Helen" from

Achille's sight [46]), and with the North American pioneer Catherine Weldon (216); Helen when pregnant at Christmastime recalls Mary (275–76). Any character so laden with variegated counterparts cannot really resemble any single counterpart. And finally, the whole idea of defining Achille as different *from* Achilles only perpetuates his dependence upon Achilles. It isn't possible to eliminate resemblance by means of contrast; likeness and unlikeness shimmer like mirages, dissipating when we attempt to grasp them.

Walcott dramatizes this evasiveness most clearly in Book VII, when Omeros and his St. Lucian analogue, the blind seer Seven Seas, "ke[ep] shifting shapes" (280) in the distant surf as Walcott squints at them. Seven Seas is supposedly "natural," a real citizen of present-day Gros-Ilet, while Omeros is a mixture of traditional ideas about Homer transmuted by Walcott's imagination to somewhat resemble Walcott himself (more on this later). The figure of Seven Seas is thus "real" and Omeros "fictive," Seven Seas "objective" and Omeros "subjective." But as Walcott stands looking, the two images alternate so quickly that both lose stability:

> They kept shifting shapes, or the shapes metamorphosed
> in the worried water; no sooner was the head
> of the blind plaster-bust clear than its brow was crossed
>
> by a mantling cloud and its visage reappeared
> with ebony hardness, skull and beard like cotton,
> its nose like a wedge; no sooner I saw the one
>
> than the other changed and the first was forgotten
> as the sand forgets a shadow in widening sun. (280–81)

Walcott's sonnet on Rembrandt's "The Polish Rider" illustrated a figure and ground dilemma between art's formal and empathetic properties. Here Walcott struggles with another figure and ground tension: if the poet focuses on either "life" or "art" the other is occluded, yet focusing on one also summons the other and perpetuates the instability of both. "Life" and "art" in *Omeros* correspond fairly well to "empathy" and "form" in "The Polish Rider." Let us therefore return for a moment to Vendler's reading of Keats. According to Vendler, "in Keats's view, one cannot experience sensory participation in the represented scene and intellectual awareness of the medium at one and the same time" (127). Still, although one cannot experience both at exactly the same moment, "attention can change focus . . . rapidly from what is being represented to the medium of representation and back again" (127). Now it seems that this phenomenon is not limited to the contemplation of formal versus empathetic properties, nor to art. A comparable oscillation of attention occurs for Walcott between "art" and "life." As during "empathetic" moments one experiences art as though it were real, one may during complementary moments experience reality as though it were art. For the instant that a blind, elderly St. Lucian man reminds Walcott of Homer, Walcott may be said to lose his empathy toward reality. The scene in which Walcott glimpses Omeros and Seven Seas is not itself this experience (since Seven Seas and "Walcott" are every bit as fictive as Omeros), but it does represent such an experience. Further, the scene on the beach depicts an oscillation between a supposed given (Seven Seas) and its imagined analogue (Omeros). If Seven Seas simply became Omeros, the scene would indicate the poet's complete belief in his own analogy between the two. He would, like Keats's empathetic viewer, discard any doubt regarding the comparison he has made. But in the beach scene, the likeness between Seven Seas and Omeros "ke[eps] shifting," as though the process of comparison—of selecting a likeness—were Protean. Walcott's rapid fluctuation between Seven Seas' image and Omeros's kinetically represents the intensity with which he questions his own analogies.

Walcott's treatment of Helen interrogates analogy even more sharply. Walcott's Helen, like Homer's, is an object of great desire. Hector and Achille vie for her sexual attentions, and Plunkett and Walcott to define her intellectually; in Plunkett's interpretation of St. Lucian history Britain and France compete for St. Lucia as for "the Helen of the West Indies." By aligning these three kinds of desire Walcott compares Plunkett's and his own wish to impose poetic orders of likenesses on the world to the male desire for the female body and to colonial domination. Walcott knows, in other words, that the Helen/Helen parallel is too keenly sought, and therefore suspect. Because this supposed likeness falls prey so easily to wishful thinking, it ought to be questioned: Helen's "beauty is what no man can claim / any more than this bay" (288). Notice that Walcott challenges the motive for analogy, however, by aligning three kinds of desire—that is, by yet another process of analogy. After comparing several perspectives on Helen and her Homeric counterpart Walcott neither chooses among them nor rejects the desire for similitude. The mind can function only by seeking parallels. Although the poet cannot find a true parallel between Helens, he comes by the process of sorting possible parallels to an understanding, rather than a possession, of Helen and of similitude itself.

The plot line involving Helen runs as follows: Helen is indeed a very attractive woman, formerly a housemaid for Dennis and Maud Plunkett. When she first appears in the poem she is out of work; although she lives with Achille, she is not sure whether she is pregnant by him or by Hector, the transport driver. "Shortly after, she move[s] in with Hector" (116). In Chapter XXIII Helen admits, "I am vexed with both of them, *oui*" (124). After Hector dies in the crash of his transport, Helen reunites with Achille. Achille plans to give the baby an African name, and to have Philoctete "[stand] godfather" (318). When we last see Helen, she is still pregnant, waiting tables at the Halcyon Inn.

This outline of events shows that *Omeros* covers a period of considerable turmoil in Helen's life. Yet the poem rarely articulates her thoughts or emotions, and seems to question whether in the ordinary sense of those words she has any. Because Helen's motivations remain enigmatic the ultimate resolution of the plot questions that involve her seems formal rather than psychological. She returns to Achille, for example, possibly only because Hector is dead. Even Helen's child is all her own, since it's impossible to identify its father (it is in this sense that Helen resembles Mary). In the course of the poem she only becomes more mysterious: "Grief heightened her. When she smiled // it was with such distance that it was hard to tell / if she had heard your condolence" (233–34). Helen is in fact characterized principally by her opacity, although she is also notable by default for her autonomy and apparent disdain for the regard of others (it is typically ironic that although Helen is such an object of male desire, the only "love scene" in which she appears depicts an autoerotic act [153]). Helen is therefore someone whom others, including the persona of the poet, strive intensely to read; Plunkett and Walcott in particular find her attitude intriguing, and "[seek] grounds for her arrogance" (270).[5] To exactly the same degree, however, Helen is quintessentially what they cannot objectively see.

Walcott's presentation of Major Plunkett's method of representing Helen and that of the persona of the poet brings to mind "The Muse of History"'s contrast between linear/historical and antilinear/poetic styles. Plunkett, an amateur historian aware that "the island was once / named Helen" (31), tries to maintain a one-to-one correspondence between Helen and St. Lucia. Plunkett feels impelled, as a white colonial and Helen's former employer, by both guilt and genuine sympathy to "duty // towards her hopelessness," and wishes "to redress / (he punned relentlessly) that desolate beauty / so like her island's" (29–30).[6] He decides that he can best redress Helen's/St. Lucia's sorrow by researching a history of the British-French conflict over St. Lucia centered around his sympathy for Helen: "Helen needed a history, / that was the pity that Plunkett felt towards her. / Not his, but her story. Not theirs, but Helen's war" (30). Plunkett constructs a sort of historical allegory, collecting analogies between the British-French war and the Trojan one, and as though in honor of Helen, "ma[kes] his own flock of V's, winged comments / in the margin when he f[inds] parallels" (95):

> "Look, love, for instance,
> near sunset, on April 12, hear this, the *Ville de Paris*
>
> struck her colours to Rodney. Surrendered. Is this chance
> or an echo? Paris gives the golden apple, a war is
> fought for an island called Helen?"—clapping conclusive
> hands. (100)

Plunkett exemplifies a possible reader of *Omeros*—by no means naive, but unlikely to surrender his biases or read what he does not wish to read—"clapping conclusive hands" at the many connections he finds between St. Lucian and mythical Greek history, although he admits those connections may have been caused by either "chance / or an echo" (100). Walcott's readers will likely make checkmarks in the margins when Homer comes to mind, and will want to applaud Walcott's ingenuity in building analogies, as well as their own in discovering them. Yet the poem continually invites us to do so, throws warning flags, then reinvites us; and as Plunkett's research progresses it too becomes anxiety-ridden and *in*conclusive. It turns out that the boundaries of history extend far beyond the window of knowledge: "The battle fanned north, out of sight of the island, / out of range of the claim by native historians / that Helen was its one cause" (94). Indeed, the Trojan war is traditionally a paradigm of history's slow fade into fiction, and/or of the way a rhetorical wealth of detail can seduce readers into believing a plot as history. Plunkett's uneasiness echoes that with which commentators discuss the Homeric Helen's mysterious role in the Trojan war. Christa Wolf's novel *Cassandra*, for example, argues that Helen was only an excuse invented by Paris. Such skepticism sounds Postmodern, but a version of this hypothesis appears as early as Euripides' *Helen*. It becomes clear that Plunkett, driven by doubt as well, grasps at coincidences because they seem to indicate significance. His V-marked parallels signal momentary and wishful victories of coherence over the chaos of sheer event:

> If she
> hid in their net of myths, knotted entanglements
>
> of figures and dates, she was not a fantasy
> but a webbed connection, like that stupid pretense
> that they did not fight for her face on a burning sea. (95)

A slip in Plunkett's logic (as it is represented here in indirect discourse) rends his "net of myths" in the moment that he wishes it into being. If Helen is "not a fantasy" she is a "connection," but that connection is in turn "like [a] stupid pretense"—and a "stupid pretense" *is* a "fantasy." These lines, even as they assert Helen's intense reality (Greeks and Trojans *did* "fight for her face on a burning sea"), insinuate her unreality.

The differences between Plunkett's perspective (hence, method) and Walcott's are plain. Plunkett is a white colonist and ex-military man in "khaki," Walcott a "native"; Plunkett, perhaps as a result, "had been convinced // that his course was right[,]" while Walcott "despised any design / that kept to a chart" (270). Plunkett rarely examines his impulse to connect Helens, while Walcott spends a good deal of time trying to get out from under his own desire to do so. It is hard to tell, however, whether Walcott more nearly succeeds—or even how Plunkett's and Walcott's efforts exemplify "two opposing stratagems" (271). The supposed dichotomy between historian and poet actually seems much less firm here than in "The Muse of History":

> Plunkett, in his innocence,
>
> had tried to change History to a metaphor,
> in the name of a housemaid; I, in self-defence,
> altered her opposite. Yet it was all for her.
>
> Except we had used two opposing stratagems
> in praise of her and the island; cannonballs rolled
> in the fort grass were not from Olympian games,
>
> nor the wine-bottle, crusted with its fool's gold,
> from the sunken *Ville de Paris*, legendary
> emblems; nor all their names the forced coincidence
>
> we had made them. There, in her head of ebony,
> there was no real need for the historian's
> remorse, nor for literature's. Why not see Helen
>
> as the sun saw her, with no Homeric shadow,
> swinging her plastic sandals on that beach alone,
> as fresh as the sea-wind? Why make the smoke a door?[7] (270–71)

Walcott never assumes that politics predicts aesthetics. In "The Muse of History" Walcott observes that writers on the right and left often share the same assumptions. Plunkett and Walcott, likewise, "like enemy ships of the line, / . . . [cross] on a parallel" (270) despite their obvious differences: "the Major's zeal // to make her the pride of the Battle of the Saints, / her yellow dress its flagship, was an ideal / no different from mine" (270). Now it is the *historian* who "trie[s] to

change History to a metaphor" and the poet who "alter[s] her opposite"—whatever that is. Yet if the supposed dichotomy between Plunkett and Walcott, historian and poet, fails to hold, so too does their
resemblance. Rather, the contrast/comparison between historian and
poet wavers in the course of the passage as Walcott withdraws from the
comparison, falls part of the way back into it, and withdraws from it
yet another time. The grammatical signposts marking this argument's
twists and turns provide the most reliable road map of Walcott's
thought. Statements battle, break into exceptions and finally deepen
into questions: "Plunkett and I . . . He . . . I . . . we crossed on a parallel;
he . . . I . . . My impulse . . . the Major's zeal . . . was an ideal / no
different from mine. Plunkett . . . I . . . Yet . . . Except . . . Why not? . . .
Why?" When he can inquire no further, Walcott relaxes in the next
moment into pragmatism: "But it was mine to make what I wanted of
it, or / what I thought was wanted" (272).

Finally we can say only that neither Plunkett nor Walcott can see
Helen "as the sun [sees] her." This conclusion is neither surprising nor
tragic, as Walcott implies:

> When would the sails drop
>
> from my eyes, when would I not hear the Trojan War
> in two fishermen cursing in Ma Kilman's shop?
> When would my head shake off its echoes like a horse
>
> shaking off a wreath of flies? When would it stop,
> the echo in the throat, insisting, "Omeros";
> when would I enter that light beyond metaphor? (271)

The more Walcott's unanswered questions multiply, the more they
come to seem rhetorical. The "sails drop[ping]" like scales from his
eyes, the "wreath of flies," and the reference to a stopping point all
foreshadow the poet's death. Walcott's image of the poet "enter[ing]"
a "light beyond" evokes the light of God, or at least of near-death
experience; even the position of this image at the *end* of Walcott's string
of questions reinforces its association to the end of life. "When would
I enter that light beyond metaphor?" "Never," the reader answers silently. If we look back at the question in the preceding section, its an-

swer seems equally obvious now: "Why not see Helen // as the sun saw her"? Because we are not the sun.

In Chapter LXII a representative of the lizard species after whom the Arawaks named the island (" 'Iounalao,' 'Where the iguana is found' " [4]) volunteers some words of advice. This lizard seems jealous of Helen, his rival as an emblem of St. Lucia. His expert opinion is cynical, his questions sarcastic: "Were both hemispheres the split breadfruit of / her African ass?" (312). Here the lizard sounds like some indignant reader of *Ulysses* asking, "Do you expect us to believe that the Laistrygonians lunched on roast beef and cabbage? That Penelope played around?" He can accept the comparison between Homer's Greece and Walcott's St. Lucia only when it seems offhand and gratuitous, or exaggerated and therefore ironic:

Exchange a spear

for a cutlass; and when Paris tosses the apple
from his palm to Venus, make it a *pomme-Cythère*,
make all those parallels pointless. Names are not oars

that have to be laid side by side, nor are legends;
slowly the foaming clouds have forgotten ours. (312–13)

The lizard begins with what sounds like a conclusion: "These Helens are different creatures, // one marble, one ebony" (313). For the lizard, color ensures difference (this might be truer in the lizard world), so that "These Helens" seem perhaps of two species. We cut from one Helen to the other, as in the comparison between Omeros and Seven Seas, and at the end of the sequence lose their opposition: "One unknots a belt . . . one a cord of purple wool, the other one takes // a bracelet . . . one lies in a room . . . another in a beach shack . . . *but each* draws an elbow slowly over her face / and offers the gift of her sculptured nakedness" (313; italics mine). The distinction, "one marble, one ebony," also locates a common ground. *Neither* marble *nor* ebony is animate, and both are artist's materials. (Omeros and Seven Seas are likewise described as "marble" and "ebony," respectively.) Both Helens, similarly, are bound to be changed and molded in the hands of their perceivers.

Two chapters later Helen is working at the Halcyon Inn; it is the last time we see her. Now the various ways of representing her appear in primary colors, without moral judgment or uneasiness:

> you might recall that battle
> for which they named an island or the heaving wreck
> of the *Ville de Paris* in her foam-frilled bodice,
>
> or just think, "What a fine local woman!" (322)

At this point the possible ways of interpreting Helen no longer contest each other. Names don't "have to be laid side by side" or "kept to a chart," but it would be equally awkward always to store names in separate drawers. Whereas it's not reasonable to expect to "see Helen // as the sun [sees] her," it *is* reasonable to "just think, 'What a fine local woman!'"—this, too, is a subjective representation and a rhetorical strategy, if not a fancy one. But neither is it *un*reasonable if historical or literary analogues come to mind. The same applies to *Omeros*'s other analogies; Walcott therefore submits serious parallels and "pointless" ones in *Omeros*, telling contrasts and some that don't turn out to matter. Analogy is never absolute, but it is the imperfect vehicle of discernment.

In an aesthetic or linguistic context Helen's combination of autonomy and indifference and the inevitable futility with which parties attempt to grasp her would sound familiar. Helen would stand, in an allegory of representation, for the thing itself, the thing that is one with itself: "she and her shadow were the same" (97). But she cannot be apprehended as such and at the same time retain the autonomy that makes her apprehension desirable: "There is something too remote / about her stillness" (322). Helen can only be left alone or approached as a phenomenon to be transmuted in perception.

HELEN ILLUSTRATES the difficulty of locating similitude from the perspective of one of the objects to be compared, and the difficulty of grasping a thing in language from the perspective of the thing to be grasped. The figure of Philoctete illustrates similar problems of representation from the perspective of the language user. Helen discloses the evasiveness of the signified; Philoctete, the infirmity of the signifier. As Walcott draws out the enigma of similitude and of his own wish for it in the process of testing more specific allegorizations of Helen (Helen as the coveted St. Lucia, as object of male desire), through the process of more specific allegorizations of Philoctete's infirmity Walcott confronts the infirmity of his own medium. The allegorizations on which we hope to depend, in Philoctete's case as in Helen's, instruct us in the deficiencies of the process by which we've attempted to advance.

The legend of the Achaian Philoctetes varies from telling to telling but runs more or less as follows: Philoctetes is an admirable archer, a former member of Jason's expedition, and a friend of Heracles who inherits Heracles' personal weaponry. Philoctetes' life changes for good, however, after he suffers a snakebite on the island of Chryse. Odysseus and his company desert Philoctetes on or near Chryse—for obscure reasons, but perhaps because Philoctetes' grievous wound and/ or his loud and unattractive complaints demoralize and inconvenience the crew. Several years later, the Achaians learn that they cannot conquer Troy without Philoctetes and/or his bow (nor can Philoctetes recover, apparently, until he returns to Troy), and so Odysseus retrieves him. Commentators have noted[8] that abandonment embitters Philoctetes (especially in Sophocles' version of the story), so that he no longer wants anything to do with the Achaians, and least of all with Odysseus. The Homeric model for Walcott's Philoctete, then, is an anti-Greek Greek hero and an exile who lives on an out-of-the way island, all of which sounds rather familiar. Further, since Philoctetes' injury and abandonment is a tiny incident in the scheme of the Trojan war, it would be reasonable to suppose that the Achaians might not think it worth attending to Philoctetes until the war had ended, and that his wound therefore couldn't heal until then. But the legend reverses these expectations, so that the war cannot end until the individually negligible Philoctetes returns and recovers. To begin with, then, the legend founds the central upon the marginal and the memorable upon the forgettable; Philoctetes and Walcott's Philoctete alike can easily be seen as stranded postcolonials "divided to the vein" by disparate allegiances.

Walcott's Philoctete is a fisherman—Achille's mate, to be exact—who bears a scar on his ankle "made by a rusted anchor" (4). Philoctete believes that "the swelling came from the chained ankles / of his grandfathers. Or else why was there no cure?" (19). The wound continuously torments him, and has two notable additional consequences: it gives him a sort of lockjaw—Philoctete hobbles around "with locked teeth" against the pain (10)[9]—and, possibly, makes him impotent ("He felt the sore twitch / its wires up to his groin" [10]). The wound therefore impedes Philoctete verbally and bodily from expressing himself. Philoctete spends his days in Ma Kilman's No Pain Café, comforting himself with "a flask of white / acajou, and a jar of yellow Vaseline, // a small enamel basin of ice" (18). Ma Kilman (an "obeah-woman"-cum-sybil [245] as well as the proprietor of the No Pain) finally cures Philoctete by visiting a wood and calling upon "Erzulie, // Shango, and Ogun" (242). The gods send her a sign, namely a line of ants. The ants in turn lead her to a curative flower whose African seed has been planted centuries before by a swift. Ma Kilman "bathe[s] [Philoctete] in the brew of the root" (246), "The yoke of the wrong name lift[s] from his shoulders" (247), and "he st[ands] like a boy in his bath with the first clay's / innocent prick!" (248). Philoctete, as a descendant of deracinated slaves, is thus the male complement of Helen, who in Plunkett's historical allegory represents St. Lucia. As Plunkett's history depends upon his wish to "redress" Helen's losses, *Omeros*'s closure depends upon the closure of Philoctete's wound.

"[A]ffliction is one theme / of this work," as Walcott observes politely (28), and so nearly every character in the poem bears some wound. Major Plunkett has a "head-wound" from the Afrika Korps (25), and like an abandoned soldier, often "[shakes] off the old hallucination again, // . . . that they were back at war" (253). The poet is a domestic castaway, alone in his house—"I grew tired, like wounded Philoctetes, // the hermit who did not know the war was over, / or refused to believe it" (171)—and compares his own lost romantic battle to the final defeat of the Sioux ("I could not believe it was over any more / than they did" [175]). Achille suffers during Helen's affair with Hector, when "his wound was Philoctete's shin" (40; in his indignance at tourists' intrusions, too, Achille "scream[s]" with "gangrene" [299]). During Achille's absence Helen has a "hole in her heart" like "the low-fingered O of an Aruac flute" (152); Hector's transport represents the commercialization of St. Lucian society, with "its flaming wound that speed alone could not heal" (118). The founding act of *Omeros*, the fishermen's cutting down of trees, creates a "hole" (6). *Omeros's* fabric is also perforated by a series of smaller, O-shaped wounds—such as the "oval portrait[s]" of admirals (315), the "holes" of cannon mouths (312), and the "terrified 'Whoas!' " of a boy on a horse galloping out of control (247). The very opening, or surrogate mouth, of Philoctete's wound was created *by* a mouth—by "chains from the Bight [*bite*] of Benin" (273). The flower from which Ma Kilman brews Philoctete's medicine has in its turn been uprooted "centuries ago from its antipodal shore" (238); it, too, bears a wound ("its gangrene, its rage / festering for centuries" [244]) and an "antipodal odour" (245).[10] Thus Philoctete's wound is bathed in medicine distilled from a wound, in a basin that resembles a wound, by Ma Kilman, a doctor whose overly tight stockings' "vise / round her calves reminded her of Philoctete" (236). All this takes place in a Caribbean "basin" which is itself one immense wound. This proliferation does not stem merely from Walcott's love of repeated details (though partly from that), for if Philoctete's wound represents the pain of postcolonialism every resident of St. Lucia must endure it. Yet we cannot interpret Philoctete's wound finally and simply as a symbol of postcolonial desolation. Philoctete's "scraping, rusted anchor" (10) also represents the "incurable // wound of time" (319)—the gravity that pulls everyone eventually into the earth.[11]

More important, Philoctete finally resembles any language user and the wound, language itself. (The wound hampers Philoctete's ability to speak, yet speaks itself; its round chancre visually expresses an O of pain, and its opening recalls the "mouths" of conches Achille lifts from the water [41]).[12] The Achaian Philoctetes has often been seen as an archetype of the artist. For Edmund Wilson Philoctetes is "a literary man" who exemplifies "the conception of superior strength as inseparable from disability"; "The victim of a malodorous disease which renders him abhorrent to society and periodically degrades him and makes him helpless is also the master of a superhuman art which everybody has to respect and which the normal man finds he needs."[13] Walcott's Philoctete, too, exemplifies the thinking man and the poet: local children call him "'Pheeloh! Pheelosophee!'" (19). But the wound's ubiquity indicates that in *Omeros* Wilson's correlation between language and disfigurement holds true for more than poetic language. The shift from Modernism to Postmodernism has meant in part moving from seeing the poet as an afflicted man who yet masters language to seeing language *as* his affliction, that which masters *him*. Walcott parallels Philoctete's deracination as descendant of slaves to his physical disfigurement and thence to his status as language user. Hence, Walcott suggests that language itself is an enslavement and a disfigurement (which nevertheless "everybody has to respect").

When we first see Philoctete he is telling some tourists a story. Philoctete's opening tale is firmly associated with the tale of *Omeros*, since his first sentence is also the first sentence of Walcott's poem. Philoctete's story describes how he, Achille, and others made canoes out of trees. Walcott identifies sailing with writing in *Omeros*, as he so often does; *Omeros* begins with the construction of canoes and ends when Walcott's "craft slips the chain of its anchor" (323). Philoctete's opening story therefore amounts to a story about how *Omeros* itself gets started. Philoctete draws his words from the idiolect of popular epic, the genre to which Walcott's poem hopes to belong. His opening words strike a tone somewhere between those of a folk tale and of a Universal Pictures war movie:

> "This is how, one sunrise, we cut down them canoes."
> Philoctete smiles for the tourists, who try taking
> his soul with their cameras. "Once wind bring the news
>
> to the *laurier-cannelles*, their leaves start shaking
> the minute the axe of sunlight hit the cedars,
> because they could see the axes in our own eyes.
>
> Wind lift the ferns. They sound like the sea that feed us
> fishermen all our life, and the ferns nodded, 'Yes,
> the trees have to die.' So, fists jam in our jacket,

cause the heights was cold and our breath making feathers
like the mist, we pass the rum. When it came back, it
give us the spirit to turn into murderers.

I lift up the axe and pray for strength in my hands
to wound the first cedar. Dew was filling my eyes,
but I fire one more white rum. Then we advance." (3)

Philoctete heightens and heroizes his story with crowd-pleasing rhetoric: flamboyant metaphors and similes, personification, and hyperbole. Even his smile is a piece of rhetoric, since he "smiles *for* the tourists," not at them.[14] The audience pays Philoctete for his performance; one has to wonder to what extent Philoctete inflates the drama of events *because* he wishes to please the audience. It's clear, at any rate, that Philoctete misrepresents what he narrates, and that distortion is an essential rather than incidental part of his presentation. And Philoctete's exhibitionistic linguistic disfigurements specifically recall his own wound when "For some extra silver . . . he shows them a scar" (4). Philoctete's aesthetic tendencies clearly approximate Walcott's own. But there is another kind of representation going on in the same scene. As Philoctete tells his story the tourists commemorate it "with their cameras." The potential vulgarity of photography, especially of tourists' responding to colorful poverty by "flying . . . to capture the scene / like gulls fighting over a catch" (299), is a commonplace. Any framing can be seen as a misunderstanding, a "process by which men are simplified" (298). Achille apparently believes that photography is such a simplifying process, for he "howl[s] / at [the tourists'] clacking cameras" (299), enraged at "being misunderstood // by a camera for the spelling on his canoe" (298).

An implicit parallel exists here between the method of photography as Walcott sees it and that of history, which he so often opposes to poetry. Walcott argues in "The Muse of History" that the linear mentality, which he terms "historical," likewise leans toward convenient simplifications; history has too often left Afro-Caribbeans out of the picture. Walcott now repeats this accusation:

> History has simplified

[Achille]. Its elegies had blinded me with the temporal
lament for a smoky Troy, but where coral died
it feeds on its death, the bones branch into more coral,

and contradiction begins. (297)

The problem is that it never becomes clear, here or anywhere in Walcott's work, where "history" or the "historical" begins and ends. Walcott names some of history's qualities (it is elegiac, it is temporal; it is
elegiac *because* temporal, since finitude raises lament), but this is hardly
a working definition; it could as easily describe poetry as history. In
"The Muse of History" Walcott's categories are rhetorically firm but
practically vague: we learn only that Césaire, Perse, Harris, Neruda,
Borges, Whitman, Hughes, Beckett, and Walcott are not "historical"
writers, and that Brathwaite probably is. In *Omeros* Walcott further
loosens the distinction between historian and poet. He identifies himself with Plunkett, the amateur historian, and identifies too with these
"crouching photographers" (298):

> Didn't I want the poor
> to stay in the same light so that I could transfix
> them in amber, the afterglow of an empire,
>
> preferring a shed of palm-thatch with tilted sticks
> to that blue bus-stop? (227)

Moreover, who could have written these "elegies" ' "temporal / lament
for a smoky Troy"—except Homer, Virgil, or Walcott himself? The elegies of history are "blind"; wasn't Homer, too, blind, perhaps "blinded
by lament"? In Book VII Omeros confides, " 'The Aegean's chimera //
is a camera, you get my drift' " (282–83). *The Odyssey* and *The Iliad*,
then, the most powerful canonical paradigms of poetic value, are mov-
ies filmed by a blind photographer. We may infer that in *Omeros* the
disfigurement of "crouching photographers" suggests the danger
within any kind of representation.

Philoctete embodies the disfiguration within language as a whole;
Omeros illustrates the blindness of language at its poetic apex. In the

miniature *Inferno* of Book Seven, Omeros leads Walcott to a sense of his own sin—which turns out to be "Pride in [his] craft" and hence in "Elevat[ed]" language (293). Still, Omeros, who alone can show Walcott his sin and rescue him from it, is blind as well; Omeros can only lead Walcott through "veils of stinking sulphur" "till [he] [is] as blind" (293) as Omeros himself. The chain of poets, conventionally an image of genealogical progress, is here an emblem of "the blind leading the blind."

Omeros also stands at the inception of both originality and of genealogy, as prototype of the wholly original, inspired poet and patriarch of the Western tradition. As such he demonstrates both the extent to which genealogy and originality intertwine and the disfigurement that troubles both. Telemachos observes in *The Odyssey* that "Nobody really knows his own father" (32); indeed, the Odysseus-Telemachos story can be interpreted as an allegory of genealogical mystery, in which Odysseus's absence merely literalizes and underscores the distance between all children and their fathers. More to the point, doubts about genealogy readily infect representation, since sons who don't resemble their fathers, or who seem to have no fathers, provoke suspicions about the authenticity of origin and/or the significance of resemblance itself. It is not surprising that Walcott should take up this subject, since, as noted earlier, his own father, Warwick Walcott, died early of an ear infection. Walcott grew up without a father and with a twin brother—dual reasons to question "originality" in dual senses of the word.

In *Omeros* relations between parents and children both overlap (because each child is someone's parent, sometimes even its parent's parent) and prove reversible. Conventional genealogy is entirely at odds with reversibility, but the links in Walcott's familial chains face both past and future like "twin-headed January, seeing either tense" (223). The chains make as much sense read backward as forward. When Achille journeys to Africa he resembles Odysseus in search of *nostos*; but like Telemachos, he finds his father, Afolabe, in the course of the journey. For Plunkett, as for Leopold Bloom, "Only a son [is] missing" (29). But Plunkett assuages his hunger for a son by looking for fathers; this Bloomian figure becomes a Telemachos of the library, researching

his ancestry. There Plunkett discovers that one forefather, a Dutch spy,
died in the British-French naval battle for St. Lucia. Because this ancestor died as "a young Plunkett" (101) the Major thinks of him as a
son (99). Catherine Weldon performs a similar psychological maneu-
ver when she grieves for a dead son, then immediately notes, " 'More
and more we learn to do without / those we still love. With my father
it was the same' " (179). The persona of the poet also plays "both
father and son" (166) to both of his parents. One of Walcott's parental
obligations toward his aged mother is paradoxically to invest her, who
has given him *his* identity, with her own identity and with a proper
sense of maternity. She, meanwhile, belies age, gender, and familial
convention by responding to the maternal role urged upon her with a
version of Telemachos' question:

> "Who am I? Mama, I'm your son."
"My son." She nodded.
> "You have two, and a daughter.
And a lot of grandchildren," I shouted. "A lot to
remember."
> "A lot." She nodded, as she fought her
memory. "Sometimes I ask myself who I am." (166)

Warwick Walcott bears out familial apophrades—Warwick has died
at so young an age that Walcott could now be his long-dead father's
father—and serves as a bridge from literal to poetic filiation. Walcott's
relation to Warwick is explicitly poetic: the son has read his father's
verses and long since surpassed their skill. The familial and the literary
merge in the image of the poet's childhood house, now "a printery"
(67). In Chapter XII Walcott visits this house/printery, encounters Warwick's ghost, and plays Hamlet to Warwick's spectral patriarch:

> there was a figure
framed in the quiet window for whom this was home,
tracing its dust, rubbing thumb and middle finger,
then coming to me, not past, but through the machines,
clear as a film and as perfectly projected
as a wall cut by the jalousies' slanted lines.
He had done a self-portrait, it was accurate.
In his transparent hand was a book I had read.
"In this pale blue notebook where you found my verses"—
my father smiled—"I appeared to make your life's choice,
and the calling that you practise both reverses

and honours mine from the moment it blent with yours.
Now that you are twice my age, which is the boy's,
which the father's?"

> "Sir"—I swallowed—"they are one voice."
>
> (68)

Since the father and the son share a common interest in poetry, Walcott "honours" Warwick's own poetic ambitions by "reversing" him. To "reverse" means to "verse again" and therefore connotes continuity, but also means "to undo" and so connotes rebellion and discontinuity. *Omeros* "reverses" Homer respectfully in that it clothes Homeric episodes in new meters, yet also reverses Homer by casting Homeric parallels in doubt even as it evokes them.

In his meeting with Omeros Walcott employs Warwick Walcott's ambivalent notion of reversal/honor. Reversal and honor first appear in sequence when Walcott insults and compliments Omeros in succession. Walcott at first slights Omeros's work: " 'I never read it,' / I said. 'Not all the way through' " (283). The slight decreases rather than increases Walcott's sense of his own vivacity, however, for he "turn[s] cold the moment [he says] it" (283). He tempers his insult as a result, hurriedly explaining, " 'The gods and the demi-gods aren't much use to us.' " The poetic father and son then reach an agreement about the father's imperfection and merit: " 'Forget the gods,' Omeros growl[s], 'and read the rest' " (283). Once this agreement has been achieved Walcott speaks to Omeros more politely: " 'I have always heard / your voice in that sea, master. . . . / Master, I was the freshest of all your readers' " (283). In "Names" one can either repeat a name, then change it, or repeat and, *by* repeating, change it; so Walcott reverses, then honors, and/or *by* reversing honors Omeros. Although insult and compliment occur in sequence in this piece of dialogue, the two may well occur simultaneously. The phrase "I was the freshest of your readers" glints with such a double edge. "Freshest" implies that as a youth Walcott was a most innocent, most open reader of Homer—and that he was also most insolent, most "fresh."

Once Walcott has played out reversal and honor, first separately, then together in "freshness," Omeros replies, " 'Ready?' " (283) and, seeing "how deeply [Walcott] love[s] the island," announces, " 'We will both praise it now'" (286). Walcott at first feels too embarrassed to speak, but almost immediately his voice "rid[es] on [Omeros's] praise," and finally "was going / under the strength of his voice, which carried so far / that a black frigate heard it" (287). Although Walcott's and Omeros's voices become "one voice" (as do Walcott's and Warwick's), the unity Walcott asserts is not simple. The son reverses and honors his poetic father, the father smothers and encourages his son—even as the strength of Omeros's voice supports Walcott's, Walcott's "go[es] / under" or drowns in it. Further, we should not forget that "Walcott" and "Omeros" alike are characters in a poem by Walcott. Walcott therefore produces the voice that supposedly overwhelms his own. Everything seen or said within a fictive system, as in a dream, must be "projected"; characters speak only languages the dreamer knows. For this reason God speaks St. Lucian Creole to Achille, Omeros speaks like an unregenerate "old goat" to Walcott ("'Did you, you know, do it often?'" [284]), and the Charon who rows Walcott to the underworld is a familiar alcoholic St. Lucian domino-player who "spoke my own language, the one for which I had died" (287). In "The Hotel Normandie Pool" Ovid's features seem suspiciously reminiscent of the profiles on Roman coins; it makes a similar sense that Omeros resembles a marble bust of Homer which Walcott can animate ("The moment I named it, the marble head arose" [280]). Nor is the fictional character "Walcott" certain of his own reality; Omeros is Walcott's projection, yet as he accompanies Omeros he "could see through [his] own palm with every crease / and every line transparent" (282).[15]

When the poet follows Omeros up the goat track and then out to Soufrière, Walcott adopts and adapts Dante's metaphor of poets following in their predecessors' footsteps. Precisely the Homer-Virgil relation traditionally symbolizes the relation between *original* and *successor*. Yet here Omeros, the great original, plays the role of Virgil, the great refiner, in a script modeled upon that of Dante, the successor of both. Should Walcott parallel Dante more precisely, Dante himself (or perhaps Joyce) would be Walcott's guide in the poem. Instead, at the moment that he employs the image of an orderly chain Walcott belies it by leaping over Joyce, Dante, and Virgil to Homer.

Soufrière has always been a supernatural spot in Walcott's private mythology. Soufrière's volcanic sulphur pit now becomes Walcott's tourist-trap Malebolge—a "Pool of Speculation" (289) in which the St. Lucian Paradiso goes up for sale. Walcott's criticism here is not merely external, because he connects financial to poetic "speculation," and makes the pit a speculum in which he faces his own reflection. The only sufferers other than speculators are the "Selfish phantoms" of poets; the poet admits, "that was where I had come from" (293). Walcott has by now seen "the light of St. Lucia at last through her own eyes, / her blindness" atop his miniature Purgatorio, and "felt every wound pass" in that blindness "because a closing darkness brightens love" (282). Epiphany arrives at the cost of "darkness" and "blindness," however, so its elevation is not entirely desirable. The speculators flounder in their sulphur pit precisely for the sin of elevation: they "elevated into waiters / the sons of others, while their own learnt something else" (289).[16] Walcott, like the damned speculators and poets, is in danger of "Elevating [him]self" (293).

On the one hand, Omeros momentarily saves Walcott from the damned poets' fate: "Omeros gripped / my hand in enclosing marble and his strength moved // me away from that crowd, or else I might have slipped / to that backbiting circle" (293). On the other, Walcott's deliverance remains dubious:

> As I, contemptuously, turned my head away,
> a fist of ice gripped it from the soul-shaping forge,
> and it wrenched my own head bubbling its half-lies,
>
> crying out its name, but each noun stuck in its gorge
> as it begged for pardon, willing to surrender
> if another chance were given it at language. (293–94)

Walcott cannot turn away from the poets' "backbiting circle" because he himself, like Milton's Satan or Lowell's, is hell; the landscape through which he passes recurs within him. He resembles the sulphur pit, "bubbling" his "half-lies"; his throat is as a "gorge" from which nouns struggle to rise. It is hard to tell, however, whether this piece of self-criticism braces Walcott against the sulphur pit or pushes him towards it. When Omeros's fist grips him *"from* the soul-shaping forge," Omeros may stand at the forge,[17] but the forge could also *be* that self-aggrandizement from which Walcott needs saving.[18] The "half-lies" Walcott claims he utters likewise express a mixture of self-criticism and self-celebration. They may be "half" lies either because they are half true or because they are half Walcott's; and since Omeros and Walcott are as halves of a two-faced head, the other halves of these lies can belong only to Walcott's supposed savior, Omeros. Walcott claims that he is "willing to surrender," but "surrender" can mean "ecstasy" and hence, elevation again. His willingness to surrender is a *part* of the problem as well as a reaction against the problem. Walcott's repentence could merely reformulate his poetic resolution in the same way that his assertion of art's limitations in "Crusoe's Island" does. The poet may request pardon, in other words, and "another chance . . . at language," only to be able to better repeat his sin of poetic transcendence.

The poet-narrator in "Cul de Sac Valley" answers the riddle of the Sphinx; Walcott now undergoes another test. Omeros remarks,

> "You tried to render
> their lives as you could, but that is never enough;
> now in the sulphur's stench ask yourself this question,
>
> whether a love of poverty helped you
> to use other eyes, like those of sightless stone?" (294)

The poet answers with a gesture:

> My own head sank in the black mud of Soufrière,
>
> while it looked back with all the faith it could summon.
> Both heads were turned like the god of the yawning year
> on whose ridge I stood looking back where I came from.

These lines hinge upon an ambiguous pronominal referent: *"it* looked back." Omeros's is "an ice-matted head" (294) in this passage, so "it" is Omeros's head that looks back while Walcott's sinks. At the same time Walcott's reference to Janus (January, the "ridge" of "the yawning year") reminds us again that he and Omeros can be seen as two halves of a single head. In this sense Walcott as well as Omeros looks back. And in the moment that this happens Walcott finds that "The nightmare was gone" (294), that he is not only looking back at life, but also "looking back where [he] came from," as when he first departed from his father upon the wharf. The implication is that *by* looking back Walcott passes this new poetic test.

References to backward looks recall the story of Orpheus, in which Orpheus loses the chance to give Eurydice life because he succumbs to the temptation to look over his shoulder at her. Walcott's Orpheus follows rather than leads, taking a position analagous to Eurydice's even as he bears Orpheus's obligations to keep faith: "the guide // needs the trust of the wounded one to begin with; / he could feel my doubt behind him. That was no good" (293). Walcott accuses himself of depriving his subjects of life by *not* looking at them—which is to say, by looking at them with too visionary "[']eyes, like those of sightless stone' " (294). Therefore, in response to Omeros's challenge Walcott's/Orpheus's head *deliberately* "look[s] back with all the faith it could summon." Whereas Orpheus must have faith that Eurydice and Hermes follow him and must prove that faith by not looking back, Walcott proves his faith in life by keeping his gaze *upon* life.[19]

The journey through which Omeros guides Walcott instructs him, then, in his poetic deficiencies: the poet has elevated his work beyond the grasp of its subjects, and at the same time transfixed those subjects in a too-romantic poverty. Yet Omeros himself is implicated in each of the poet's failings, since the figure of Homer above all represents "high" rhetorical style and heightened mimesis. Thus, instruction here does not mean objective description but, rather, the turning inside-out of conventions used by instructor and student alike. And the roles of ancestor and descendent, poetic original and imitator, are themselves among the conventions anatomized.

WALCOTT IS a magpie-poet in at least two senses. First and foremost, like Eliot's "major poet," he steals. But we must also attend to what he does with stolen material. Like the magpie, Walcott throws nothing away. Words act as powerful magnets; if a word picks up a connotation in a poem from 1948, chances are it will continue to develop that connotation through 1968 and 1988. It is as though Walcott were *proving* the idea that each word is a poem in itself by using words with an exact memory of their etiologies within his oeuvre. At this point even very commonplace words like "branch," "swift," or "net" appear thickly encrusted with associations. It isn't possible to read more than six lines at a time of *Omeros* without coming across a fresh handful of such magnetic words, as one also finds familiar themes enacted by new characters. *Omeros* is as much a restatement as a continuation of Walcott's past concerns and motifs. It is here that Walcott elucidates the crossings to and from America he describes in "Culture or Mimicry?" and the paradoxical relations of poet to precursor he describes in "The Muse of History." These ideas are revised—usually loosened—but not radically altered by their dramatizations.

The same holds true for *Omeros*'s style, which continues Walcott's exploration of St. Lucian linguistic complexity. *Omeros*'s assortment of linguistic possibilities, like *Another Life*'s, encourages close listening. The poet spots Major Plunkett's mimicry of colonial speech, for example, by Plunkett's phrasing of a banal greeting: " 'Been travellin' a bit, what?' " As soon as Plunkett utters the words,

> he knew he'd been caught,
>
> caught out in the class-war. It stirred my contempt.
> He knew the "what?" was a farce, I knew it was not
> officer-quality, a strutting R.S.M. (269)

Plunkett stumbles again when he misspells "Iounalao" as "Iounalo" (92) and fumes, "History will be revised, // and we'll be its villians, fading from the map / (he said 'villians' for 'villains'). And when it's over / we'll be the bastards!" (92). Even as Plunkett protests that he is not a bastard, his speech, like Achille's when he misspells "trust," is bastardized; and in the moment that he objects to the revision of history, his poor memory revises language—his own as much as others'.

A complementary irony befalls Philoctete's friend, the would-be local politician, Statics, so named "for . . . the short-circuit prose / of his electrical syntax in which he mixed / Yankee and patois" during his megaphone declamations (105). Statics's harangues are even more creolized than Spoiler's Trinidadian satire:

> "*This island of St. Lucia*, quittez moin dire z'autres!
> *let me tell you is heading for unqualified*
> *disaster*, ces mamailles-là, pas blague, *I am not*
>
> *joking. . . .*
> . . . .
> *Like that man hopping there, St. Lucia look healthy*
>
> *with bananas and tourists, but her soul crying.*
> 'tends ça moin dire z'autres, *tell me if I lying.*["] (107)

Creolization guarantees neither authenticity nor popularity, for Statics's language embodies his egalitarianism without promoting it. He has, in fact, the reputation for inaudibility that his name suggests: " '*Ces mamailles-là!*' Statics shouted, meaning '*Children!*' / Then Hector would tap his knee with: 'The mike not on' " (106).

In *Omeros* poetic language, as a product of mimicry, begins in error, as in the following exchange between Ma Kilman and Philoctete:

> "*Mais qui ça qui rivait-'ous, Philoctete?*"
> "*Moin blessé.*"
> "But what is wrong wif you, Philoctete?"
> "I am blest
> wif this wound, Ma Kilman, *qui pas ka guérir pièce.*
> Which will never heal." (18–19)

Walcott's (mis)translation of *"blessé"* as "blest" is play, not a mistake, yet the inexact repetition of such play is not different in effect from Achille's or Plunkett's misrememberings, or Statics's inaudibility. The mimicry that produces creole also produces paronomasia, when children call Philoctete " '*Pheelosophee!*' " (19) or when Plunkett's accent leads him to pun on "Seashells" and "Seychelles" (30).

In *Omeros* both ordinary and poetic language are founded on the errors of mimicry, and their pretensions to permanence are limited by that foundation. The poet-figure Seven Seas is not only blind but, according to Ma Kilman, nearly unintelligible: "His words were not clear. / They were Greek to her. Or old African babble" (18). It takes a while for the irony of this judgment to sink in: the Greeks defined as barbaric all languages that were not Greek, but it is now Greek that in American slang is synonymous with "babble." To Ma Kilman's ears her ancestral African languages sound as meaningless as Greek. She associates both African and Greek with Seven Seas' visionary mutterings, thus linking both to poetic language, "the dark language of the blind" (17). The language of *Omeros* is, expressly, Greek and African babble. Seven Seas' attitude toward this position may also characterize the poet's; to judge by it, by *Omeros* Walcott does not so much celebrate as accept the inherently barbaric (or "Greek") character of poetry. Absorbed in his task of "numbering things," Seven Seas "never complained about his situation // like the rest of them" (18): "Sometimes he would sing and the scraps blew on the wind" (17).

WALCOTT AND POSTMODERNITY

MOST NORTH AMERICAN critics and reviewers have come to see Derek Walcott as a deservedly celebrated poet, "natural, worldly, and accomplished" (Vendler, 26). Yet this very appreciation of the orthodox values of Walcott's work—its learning, assurance, and metrical proficiency—has obstructed consideration of Walcott's place in the Postmodern era. Enthusiastic critics usually discuss Walcott as a "literary" poet and an imitator of the poetic past who perpetuates rather than reverses a traditional formalism. Indeed, the surface of Walcott's language does not seem overtly Postmodern. Yet Walcott is obviously also a late twentieth-century postcolonial obsessed on the thematic level with cultural and linguistic displacement—a concern sometimes held to be a hallmark of Postmodern literature. The vast majority of the small body of critical literature concerned with Walcott's poetry dwells upon this dilemma, straining to reconcile the subversive postcolonial with the relatively conventional versifier. His readers most often argue that Walcott ponders displacement on the thematic level, but on the rhetorical level nostalgically denies it. By this logic, rhetoric and content in Walcott's poetry fulfill contradictory psychological demands: either his forms speak the truth or his themes do, but not both. For other readers, meanwhile—most often fellow poets such as Brodsky and Heaney—Walcott either synthesizes perceived oppositions or adopts the space between them as his own.

The difficulty in categorizing Walcott's poetry is more interesting, however, for what it discloses of our own persistent discomfort at discrepancies between form and content. While most of Postmodernism's would-be definers do attempt to correlate formal and thematic properties, the uneasy relation between rhetoric and principle in Walcott prompts one to question the correspondences between rhetoric and principle that attempts to locate Postmodernity may assume. If Walcott's poetry dramatizes the Postmodern knowledge of displacement without enacting it, this could indicate either that Walcott's poetic contradicts itself (and thus that Walcott is only halfheartedly Postmodern), or that definitions of Postmodern language in terms of its estrangement from "ordinary" language are inadequate. Indeed, defining Postmodernity by estrangement poses problems. It usually means, in practice, identifying Postmodernity with literary language. The expectation that Postmodern poets enact difference by manifest verbal dislocution also demands an orderly mutual echoing of content and rhetoric—precisely the kind of correspondence that Postmodern literature tends to disavow.

Walcott avoids separating "poetic" from "ordinary" language, but not by trying to make poetry sound ordinary. The poems do not aspire to transparency; they are as insistently figurative and artificial as they are intelligible. Walcott acknowledges and at times even rues his dependence on allegory. He also fails, however, to find transparency in any kind of language whatsoever. Beginning with the intuition that poetry can only be allegorical, Walcott extends this knowledge to language as a whole. The poems reveal the inexorability of allegorical displacement without benefit of conspicuously Postmodern linguistic disfiguration.

In this Walcott's turns of thought regarding figuration resemble de Man's. In *Allegories of Reading* de Man locates the poetic by means of figuration and in opposition to nonpoetic language, but also "equat[es] the rhetorical, figural potentiality *of language* with literature itself" (10: italics mine), and in no time asserts that "Poetic writing . . . may differ from critical or discursive writing in the economy of its articulation, but not in kind" (17). Walcott demonstrates what Postmodern poetry might look like if it lived by these words. The overt disfigurations we associate with the poetry of an Ashbery or a Palmer would seem redundant in light of any real conviction that the disfigurations of allegory necessarily occur in all language. Walcott abstains from radically conspicuous forms of rhetoric not because he seeks transparency, but because of his conviction that any and all language depends upon rhetoric.

Although Walcott does not confuse simplicity with transparency at any point in his career, his later poetry more explicitly dramatizes the ubiquity of "poetic" rhetoric—often because revaluation of the poet's own work itself becomes a theme. "The Light of the World" (*AT*, 48–51), a wonderful example of Walcott's late style, is more nearly Walcott's *ars poetica* than any other single lyric. "The Light of the World" considers the problems I've been discussing—the poet's inevitable social and linguistic displacement and the relation of poetic to nonpoetic language—more completely than any other single lyric. The poem once again addresses Walcott's persistent fear—expressed as early as "Homecoming: Anse la Raye" (*G*, 84–86)—that poetry may be tragically removed from popular language (and indeed, from material life). But while Walcott more often deliberates this fear in terms of the poet's social separation from his culture—by virtue of linguistic choice, or of his public's literacy—"The Light of the World" assumes that poetry is based upon figuration, and inquires whether poetry's reliance upon figuration divorces it from other linguistic forms.

The poem's aim to revaluate Walcott's poetic is transparent, since *Another Life*, which first comprehensively narrates Walcott's choice of vocation, turns upon its title phrase: "Gregorias, listen, lit / we were the light of the world!" (*AL*, 23.iv.11–12; also 12.iii.21–22). Indeed, "another life" metamorphoses, in that volume, into "another light": "another light / in the unheard, creaking axle . . . / in the fire-coloured hole eating the woods" (12.iii.13–14, 17). In *Another Life* these phrases, "the light of the world," *"lux mundi,"* "another light," signify the passion, inflamed by mortality, that drives both desire and creativity. In the course of the poem Walcott's protagonist learns to sublimate passion into art which acknowledges its own origins in anxiety and ephemerality.

"The Light of the World" even more explicitly represents Walcott's art as a combination of transience and transport. Here the poet is a "transient" or tourist in his own culture, and the entire poem literally takes place in a "transport," or van, between Castries and Gros-Ilet. Although Walcott has not altered his own position regarding the value of these qualities, "The Light of the World" now asks whether reliance on figuration severs the poet from the community and the communal language with which he would most like to share transport.

The poet is first inspired to think of the title phrase when he sees a beautiful woman sitting in the "transport" with him:

> Marley was rocking on the transport's stereo
> and the beauty was humming the choruses quietly.
> I could see where the lights on the planes of her cheek
> streaked and defined them; if this were a portrait
> you'd leave the highlights for last, these lights
> silkened her black skin; I'd have put in an earring,
> something simple, in good gold, for contrast, but she
> wore no jewelry. . . .
> . . . .
> and the head was nothing else but heraldic.
> When she looked at me, then away from me politely,
> because any staring at strangers is impolite,
> it was like a statue, like a black Delacroix's
> *Liberty Leading the People*, the gently bulging
> whites of her eyes, the carved ebony mouth,
> the heft of the torso solid, and a woman's,
> but gradually even that was going in the dusk,
> except the line of her profile, and the highlit cheek,
> and I thought, O Beauty, you are the light of the world! (48)

Although the poet perceives her at first as an individual woman, "the" beauty—"the beauty was humming the choruses quietly"—in the next moment he begins trying ways of seeing her as art, manipulating her image in a series of framings and figurations: "[I]f this were a portrait . . . the head was nothing else but heraldic . . . like a statue, like a black Delacroix's / *Liberty Leading the People* . . . the carved ebony mouth." At the end of this sequence of figures, the poet finally addresses her as Beauty itself. The unnamed woman is now named "Beauty" with a capital B, and seems completely assimilated to the poet's conception of her. Indeed, Walcott's deepening aesthetic possession of the woman coincides with the gradual disappearance of her physical self in deepening darkness. In the moment before she becomes Beauty, nothing remains but a "profile" and a highlight. It is entirely possible that in the moment Walcott apotheosizes her, she completely disappears. Beauty may be "the light of the world," but the apotheosizing capacity of Walcott's own language is firmly associated with darkness.

Although in his address Walcott's comparison attains to metaphor— the woman *is* Beauty—the similes leading up to this transfiguration had been conscious of the tension between the individual woman and Beauty: "*if* this were a portrait"; "*you'd* leave the highlights"; "she looked at me, then away from me politely"; "*I'd* have put in an earring, . . . *but she* / wore no jewelry" (italics mine). Walcott's conjunction in "the heft of the torso solid, and a woman's," marks an uneasy nexus of formal strength with individual vulnerability, and of solidity with femininity (the sense of straining double consciousness, of near-paradox, is even stronger in an earlier version,[1] where Walcott writes, "solid, *but* a woman's"). Yet the woman's individual vulnerability, her mortality—"even that [solidity] was going in the dusk"—itself reminds the poet of art. *Another Life* had celebrated precisely that art which allows one to perceive its temporality, its "going in the dusk." Even though the poet apprehends the woman's apartness ("she wore no jewelry"), he still can't completely distinguish, at least on temporal grounds, between her mortal, breathing beauty and his own also fragile idea of Beauty. On the other hand, if he cannot hold on to the distinction between the two, neither can he grasp their identity. His momentary metaphorization of her slips at the very moment at which it is apparently achieved. He names her "O Beauty," but only in "thought," in darkness, and in the ambivalent rhetorical figure of (de Manian) prosopopeia. Even the triumphant moment of her naming requires its highly conventional capitalization of "Beauty" and interjection of "O" in order to ensure its recognition as poetic triumph. The presence of the beholder intrudes between the reader and the ostensible triumph, and between the reader and the object supposedly completely beheld. In the next moment it is no longer enough that the woman be Beauty. Beauty itself needs renaming by a further figure, "the light of the world," and disappears into this figurative excess. In later references the woman is once again only "the woman by the window," "her beauty."

Walcott's correlation between the poet's expanding transport and expanding darkness magnifies the connotations of "transience." The poet passes from town to a hotel "full of transients like [him]self" (51),[2] and at the same time voyages from life toward death. If this protagonist is a tourist, however, we are all tourists, since this is "the town / where [he] was born and grew up" (49). As tourist, he travels through a society itself transient: St. Lucia, since it is now so "full of transients," may not last much longer in its present form. Walcott represents St. Lucia at large by means of the female figures in "The Light of the World," just as he calls the Antillean population by a series of female names in "Sainte Lucie." *Luce*, of course, means "light," and Beauty in the poem is also tied to light. The woman in the transport therefore represents St. Lucia, which for Walcott coincides with Beauty. Walcott underscores the fragile temporal development of St. Lucia by depicting a series of women at various stages of life, moving from "the beauty" to "drunk women on pavements" and a thought of his mother, "her white hair tinted by the dyeing dusk" (49).[3] These secondary women seem even more exposed, more obviously mortal than "the beauty." These elegiac thoughts further give rise to a reminiscence of the Castries market in Walcott's childhood, in which the poet-figure of a lamplighter prominently appears: "wandering gas lanterns / hung on poles at street corners . . . / the lamplighter climbed, / hooked the lantern on its pole and moved on to another" (49). In the earlier draft, Walcott accents the fragility of the lamplighter's art—"the light . . . was poised to be lit / on the one hand, and on the next to go out," like that of the "fireflies" that act as "guides" later in the poem. Finally, the transport's forward motion gives the sensation (as in Bishop's "The Moose" or Frost's "Stopping by Woods") that everyone inside the transport is being carried toward death: "The van was slowly filling in the darkening depot. / I sat in the front seat, I had no need for time."

At the same time that the transport functions as a sort of Charon's ferry, however, "transport" is also a synonym for "metaphor," whose etymology includes the notion of "carrying." Moreover, it's clear that Walcott means "metaphor" in its larger sense, to include all figuration, and accepts figuration as a defining feature of poetry—so that "metaphor" functions, as usual, as a figure for figuration. Then too, "transport" can mean "ecstasy," which bears the connotation of sexual desire as well as of rapturous lyric inspiration. In other words, the poet's desire for "the beauty" and his aspiration toward poetic and formal Beauty simultaneously carry him—and all kinds of "beauty" with him—toward equally simultaneous would-be possession and oblivion. The poem begins with an epigraph from Bob Marley, "Kaya now, got to have kaya now. . . . / For the rain is falling"; the earlier version shows that Walcott originally misheard Marley, believing, charmingly enough, that Marley was singing "Zion-ah, / I've got to have Zion-ah"—a rendering that magnifies the apocalyptic character of the transport. "Kaya" is marijuana, as it happens, but whether the desired object be marijuana or Zion, "kaya" functions tautologically here, simply as "the desired," as whatever it is one has "got to have." "Kaya" also functions, like poetic transport, as a vehicle toward the destination of simultaneous heightened elevation and oblivion. By this point Walcott has accomplished more than a delineation of concurrent desires. He has asked whether metaphorical transport, in its ecstasy, either leaves its supposed subjects behind to unecstatic life and death, or carries them to oblivion by sweeping them up with it. The potential conflict is particularly obvious and painful when the inspired poet's subjects are St. Lucian, poor, and, in this case, mostly female.

Yet another female figure enters the scene at this point—an old woman qualified by experience to speak for "her people," whose voice alone the poet represents:

> An old woman with a straw hat over her headkerchief
> hobbled towards us with a basket; somewhere,
> some distance off, was a heavier basket
> that she couldn't carry. She was in a panic.
> She said to the driver: *"Pas quittez moi à terre,"*
> which is, in her patois: "Don't leave me stranded,"
> which is, in her history and that of her people:
> "Don't leave me on earth," or, by a shift of stress:
> "Don't leave me the earth" [for an inheritance];
> *"Pas quittez moi à terre,* Heavenly transport,
> Don't leave me on earth, I've had enough of it."
> The bus filled in the dark with heavy shadows
> that would not be left on earth; no, that would be left
> on the earth, and would have to make out.
> Abandonment was something they had grown used to.
>
> And I had abandoned them, I knew that there. . . . (49–50)

Several things are surprising about Walcott's development of this metaphor (this transport). First, a North American critical audience will probably associate "transport" with politically undesirable transcendence and forgetfulness. But the old woman believes transport is "Heavenly," a relief from her burdens, and so begs to be transported-and-not-abandoned—even though "abandon" is itself a synonym for "transport" when both mean "rapture." At the same time, "abandon[ment]" in the negative sense inevitably accompanies figuration, since writing—substituting figuration for presence—marks the site of perpetually abandoned presence. Walcott further highlights the constitutional ambivalence of these words in his self-reversing line about shadows "that would not be left on earth; no, that would be left." The line remains ambiguous in at least three ways. Walcott's reversal could indicate the passage of time: it at first seems that all the shadowy bodies of villagers (also "shades" crossing between worlds) outside the transport will fit in; after a while, it does not. In addition, the first half of this line is "literal" (the passengers will not be left behind because they will get in the transport), and the second half "figurative" (they will be "left behind" because the poet will abandon them emotionally and linguistically). But, third and finally, "would" can also suggest preference or volition: they wanted transport, they wanted to be left on the earth. And this is what everyone is likely to feel: we want the universal, we want the particular. In "The Light of the World" (as in "The Schooner *Flight*," whose protagonist Shabine is "nobody or a nation"), Walcott maintains a fierce consciousness of both poles.

Further, if one believes that figuration is a specialized form of language that abandons the object world by its abstraction, it will confound one's expectations that, as Walcott's explication demonstrates, the "poetic" multiplicity of meanings in "transport" and "abandon" also occurs in the old woman's speech. Her phrase is figurative to its core, as Walcott's translation makes clear. "*Pas quittez moi à terre*" does not "denote" "Don't leave me stranded." Besides, "Don't leave me stranded" is itself figurative, unless one's friend is sailing away from the beach (as St. Lucia's colonizers figuratively *and* literally did sail away). Translation begins by substituting supposed denotations, but can never end. Denotations, too, continually dissolve by mere "shift[s] of stress." Likewise, poets sometimes do things for purely formal reasons, but Walcott recalls that people in his childhood neighborhood also "quarrelled for bread in the shops, / or quarrelled for the formal custom of quarrelling" (49).

Walcott, rather like Wordsworth, is now moved by his own reflection that he "had abandoned them . . . / had left them on earth," to feel "a great love that could bring [him] to tears" (50). In this ecstatic experience of *agapē*, of course, we reach yet another connotation of "transport." Contrary to what one hears about *agapē*, the poet's love actually denies him oneness with the people around him. Instead, it takes the form of "a pity" that makes him feel his own isolation the more, the more hyperconscious he grows of "their neighbourliness, / their consideration." His pity, in other words, pulls him both toward and away from them, following the two directions of language—"tearing him apart," as we so Orphically say. The poet suffers further when, in accordance with the transport's mission as an engine of time, even those people who fit into it begin getting off. Each departure enacts a miniature death and too clearly foreshadows the poet's own:

> I wanted the transport
> to continue forever, for no one to descend

> and say a good night in the beams of the lamps
> and take the crooked path up to the lit door,
> guided by fireflies; I wanted her beauty
> to come into the warmth of considerate wood,
> to the relieved rattling of enamel plates
> in the kitchen, and the tree in the yard,
> but I came to my stop. Outside the Halcyon Hotel.
> The lounge would be full of transients like myself.
> Then I would walk with the surf up the beach.
> I got off the van without saying good night.
> Good night would be full of inexpressible love.
> They went on in their transport, they left me on earth. (51)

Another reversal occurs here, when, after having left his neighbors on earth through his language and his "transience" (his exile), his neighbors in turn leave the poet. One often encounters, in Walcott's poetry, the idea that home can leave you. In the structurally similar "Homecoming: Anse la Raye," the poet already feels like "a tourist." "Hop[ing] it would mean something to declare / today, I am your poet, yours," he finds no one to listen to such a declaration except throngs of children who want coins or nothing. Caught in the impasse of this "[homecoming] without home," "You give them nothing. / Their curses melt in air" (85). In contrast, fishermen cast "draughts" of nets, "texts" that help the children more ably than the poet's. The poet can give the children only words, "nothing" in the way of coins; they return to him, in kind, words that are curses.

"The Light of the World" also features a mutual abandonment, the poet's sense of pity and guilt, a confrontation between a "transient" and his people, and jealousy toward another artisan. Many critics, having cast Walcott in the role of "literary poet," oppose him to the Barbadian poet Edward Brathwaite, a more "folkish" writer. In "The Light of the World" Walcott compares himself to an apter and stronger competitor, Bob Marley. "Marley" is the poem's first word; as the poem's text stands under its epigraph from Marley's "Kaya," so Marley's song—"rocking" (48), "thud-sobbing" (51), popular, choric, mnemonic—suffuses the whole transport. The "beauty was humming" Marley's choruses, not Walcott's; when the whole transport "hum[s] between / Gros-Ilet and the Market" (48), Marley's song becomes indistinguishable from the motor that drives the transport forward. This realization, as much as his confrontation with mortality, brings the poet "down to earth" (and leaves him there). The poet leaves his people on earth—that he could bear. What's worse, he "le[aves] them to sing / Marley's songs of a sadness as real as the smell / of rain on dry earth" (51), and the thought that they so gladly sing the songs of a competitor drives him to tears. The pill Walcott swallows here is, then, at least as bitter as that in "Homecoming: Anse la Raye."

But in "The Light of the World" Walcott's greater awareness of linguistic ambivalence and of tensions between universals and particulars far more precisely and gently renders a similar experience, without assuming a wishful intimacy or erasing difference. Walcott explores his own universalizing impulse most completely here. And in the end, the poem suggests that the "poetic" language of metaphor cannot be held apart from Marley's language, from the old woman's language, from all language. The poet faces insoluble problems of representation; and in a way, it doesn't help that everyone who uses language faces these same problems and temptations. On the other hand, in the impossibility of controlling language and the inescapability of desiring to do so, as in the inescapability of death, we find a kind of community in poverty. The poem's last stanza, which takes up after the poet has been "left on earth," arrives like an extra gift, an unexpected bit of afterlife:

> Then, a few yards ahead, the van stopped. A man
> shouted my name from the transport window.
> I walked up towards him. He held out something.
> A pack of cigarettes had dropped from my pocket.
> He gave it to me. I turned, hiding my tears.
> There was nothing they wanted, nothing I could give them
> but this thing I have called "The Light of the World." (51)

Again, as in "Anse la Raye," the poet and his counterpart, representing his community, exchange virtually "nothing." The man returns the cigarettes, while the poet turns away speechless: "There was nothing they wanted, nothing I could give them." Walcott once again revises the Orpheus and Eurydice story here in a manner unflattering to the Postmodern Orpheus.[4] This Orpheus cannot take his Eurydice home because he is mortal himself, has no particular powers against death, and besides, she doesn't belong to him and never did. He is too overcome to look back and deliberately leaves without parting, having accomplished nothing. In fact he assumes the passive position, so that the mortals (who have their own transport and their own music) look back at him. Much of this diminishment already occurs in Rilke's "Orpheus. Eurydike. Hermes," in which Eurydice reacts to news of Orpheus's failure by asking, "Who?" As de Man points out,

> The genuine reversal takes place at the end of the poem, when Hermes turns away from the ascending movement that leads Orpheus back to the world of the living and instead follows Eurydice into a world of privation and nonbeing. On the level of poetic language, this renunciation corresponds to the loss of a primacy of meaning located within the referent and it allows for the new rhetoric of Rilke's "figure." (47)

In Walcott's as in Rilke's version of the story, the poet figure retains little power or tragic dignity.

Yet the two "nothings" the poet and the others in the transport exchange—unlike the "nothing" and "curses" in "Anse la Raye"—mean everything. This is how language works, conveying in spite of itself. The man's gesture embodies all the warm "neighbourliness," "consideration," and "polite partings" of his society that have moved the poet to write about it, and Walcott gives that society what he loves most, his *lux mundi*, beauty, poetry, even though he realizes that is all "but" nothing, and even a repetition of abandonment. Walcott's description of the poet's diminished powers sounds characteristically Postmodern, if we understand Postmodernism as a folding back from Modernism's totalizing ambitions. But notice that this diminishment does not free the poet from communal responsibilities, or from his aesthetic and sexual desires.

Poetic humility takes paradoxical forms. The more humbly the poet describes her or his own efforts, the greater she or he may believe poetry to be. In a way, Walcott's recognition of the poet's limitations makes his task even more ambitious, since it will be more difficult. Without the illusion of mastery over language, the poet still aims for communal relevance, beauty, and "truth"—which in "The Light of the World" means precisely recognizing the inescapability of rhetoric. Paradoxically, Walcott brings every poetic resource to bear upon the task of convincing us that "poetry makes nothing happen." The performance is convincing—so convincing that it undoes its own point. Rhetoric here struggles to dismiss itself, and, predictably, cannot. Walcott's last small "but" opens a floodgate through which poetic grandiosity and linguistic transcendence stream. Even by calling his poem "this thing," he simultaneously metaphorizes and reifies it. By further calling "this thing" (already metaphorized by being called a thing) "The Light of the World," Walcott enters the realm of undecidability. On the one hand, this last line is figurative and glorious: poems are, after all, the light of the world. On the other, it is merely literal and tautological. The title of the poem is, inarguably, "The Light of the World"; the phrase is a citation, referring us only to itself, and distances itself by its quotation marks from the notion of poetic glory. That is, since the title comprises a proper name, we cannot, as when Derrida writes of Ponge, "know with any peaceful certainty whether [it] designate[s] the name or the thing."[5] The reader cannot stand between these two interpretations to choose one. Neither can we decide whether "The Light of the World" actively produces and undoes these contradictions or whether these contradictions actively produce and undo it, for the process of disclosing the ubiquity of rhetoric also begins in self-knowledge and moves toward generalization, following the route of the universalizing impulse it queries. If Walcott's interest in this particular query is Postmodern, his Postmodernity trails behind it Modernism's tendency to universalize.

But in this, too, Walcott's example is at least instructive and at most representative. Attempts to define Postmodernism solely by its difference from Modernism themselves echo Modern self-definitions. It may be typical of Postmodernism to lose itself in the perspectivism of which it is so fond. According to Linda Hutcheon, Postmodernism asks us to see "Historical meaning . . . today," for example, "as unstable, contextual, relational, and provisional," and at the same time "argues that, in fact, it has always been so" (67). If this is true, Postmodernism can best be defined not as a noun, but as a verb; not as a set of attitudes or a grammar of rhetoric, but as inseparable from the propensity to read Postmodernly. And if Postmodern poetry characteristically inhabits and describes the circulation of these perspectives, Walcott's metaphorization of himself as the figure of the contemporary American poet will be difficult to assail.

NOTES

INTRODUCTION

1. Vera Kutzinski, who considers similar issues in *Against the American Grain: Myth and History in William Carlos Williams, Jay Wright, and Nicolas Guillén*, asserts that "As long as American Literature is used as a general denominator for all New World literatures, while at the same time being implicitly associated with the Anglo–North American literary canon, it preempts the formulation of pluralistic and comparative approaches that would collapse such a hierarchy," and that therefore "New World writing appears to be the best terminological alternative" (13). While I agree that many readers will associate "America" with North America, I am still interested in trying to recover the term, because the exertion of remembering that the United States is at once a colonizing force and an African-, Hispanic-, and Asian-inflected piece of the New World seems instructive. As Walcott puts it in "Culture or Mimicry?," "[I]t is the black who energized that [U.S.] culture, who styles it. . . . We can see this and still keep distinctions" (4). Walcott uses the term "New World" a good deal, and "New World" and "America" are often synonymous in his lexicon: "I use the word American regardless of genetic variety and origin" ("CM," 6). Yet he is not completely consistent; at other times, "America" refers to the U.S. Here, "America" will *always* refer to the entire hemisphere. By using "New World" and "America" synonymously, I am adopting that part of Walcott's thought about this issue which I find most interesting and valuable.

Complete information on all texts cited in short form in these notes can be found in the bibliography below ("Works Cited").

2. Sharon Ciccarelli, "Reflections Before and After Carnival: An Interview with Derek Walcott," in *Chant of Saints*, 302.

3. *Simulations*, 1.

4. "The Schooner *Flight*," *SAK*, 5.

5. "The World of a Cosmic Castaway," 8.

6. *Omeros*, 159.

7. Please see Chapter 3, note 2, regarding my usage of the term *creole*.

8. *Alien Tongues: Bilingual Russian Writers of the "First" Generation*, 104.

9. "Conversation with Derek Walcott" (interview with Edward Hirsch), *Contemporary Literature* 20 (1979), 287. In future references I will distinguish Walcott's two interviews with Hirsch by date.

10. Brenda Flanagan, "An Interview with Derek Walcott," *Voices of the African Diaspora (The CAAS Research Review)* VII (1991), 17.

11. I exclude Walcott's plays, on the other hand, for aesthetic rather than thematic reasons.

12. My own attitude toward this phenomenon is neutral. Although Wal-

cott's tendency to universalize is problematic, any discussion of this question must recognize that we are dealing with a problem in language, not in Walcott alone. Of course, this suggestion is itself a universalization.

13. "Cul de Sac Valley," *AT,* 14.

14. *New York Review of Books,* 4 March 1982, 23–27.

15. I refer to Walcott's revised version of the poem in *Collected Poems 1948–1984,* 17–18.

16. The fourth stanza in *In a Green Night*'s version.

17. Walcott expands upon the "gulf" metaphor, obviously, in the volume that bears that name.

18. At the close of his *Paris Review* interview, Walcott hopes that *The Arkansas Testament* will "be a compensation for all the deficiencies in the *Collected Poems*, something that will redeem the *Collected Poems*" (230).

19. "The Sound of the Tide," in *Less Than One: Selected Essays,* 173.

20. *The Politics of Postmodernism,* 37.

21. This doesn't mean, of course, that all postcolonial writers are feminists, that all feminists are Postmodernists, etc.

CHAPTER 1

1. "Caliban as Poet," 624. While I agree that "geography is not a static projection when seen from the Third World point of view," that "the redefinition of geographic space is not an end in itself" in postcolonial poetry, and that this poetry identifies "the map, itself . . . as the sign for the abstraction of cultural reality as well as topography," I do not believe it follows that "The tendency to grasp geographic relationships as mappable space is alien to this poetry" (616–17). Postcolonial poets may even be particularly quick to grasp ways of mapping space, precisely because they perceive from the beginning that maps are manipulations. Césaire's, Guillén's, and Walcott's maps are neither conventional nor repressive, but they remain recognizable maps.

2. *Allegories of Reading: Figural Language in Rousseau, Nietzsche, Rilke and Proust,* 38.

3. Mutlu Konuk Blasing discusses Eliot and especially Poe in very similar terms: "Lacking a dynastic authorization or an inherited legal status, the American writer faced an impossible choice between a provincial colonialism . . . and a provincial nationalism. . . . [Poe's] world, however, is curiously suspended between England and America, in a midatlantic Atlantis outside history. . . . Poe's distance from a dynastic tradition enabled him to question its metaphysical assumptions of central authority and to recognize the textuality of writing. . . . Poe's nostalgic yet disdainful references to the tradition he lacks reflect his American difference. . . . Such double-edged irony defines Poe's impossible position of being neither in nor out of a literary tradition" (*American Poetry: The Rhetoric of its Forms,* 17–19).

4. "Passage to India," part 4.

5. *American Hieroglyphics,* 122. I am very much indebted, generally, to Irwin's discussion of *The Narrative of Arthur Gordon Pym* as a representation of a voyage to the antipodes.

6. As the globe spins on its axis, *Omeros* begins when its fishermen, "axes in [their] own eyes," take "axes" to the trees (3), so that "the chips flew" where they might (5). *Omeros* spins on its figures of X's.

7. *Dissemination*, 44.

8. At least she does in Lattimore's translations. See *The Odyssey*, 52, for example.

9. "[T]he cross // of the man-o'-war bird" (*O*, 91) plays a similar part, because it is the swift's complement. The swift is a seamstress, and the man-o'-war, a.k.a. frigate bird, a.k.a. *ciseau-la-mer*, is a "sea scissors." As such, the man-o'-war too runs along the meridian's seam.

10. Walcott further stresses the swift's poetic function by comparing himself to the swift:

there are two journeys
in every odyssey, one on worried water,

the other crouched and motionless, without noise.
For both, the 'I' is a mast; a desk is a raft
for one, foaming with paper, and dipping the beak

of a pen in its foam. (291)

11. *The Truth in Painting*, 235.

12. *Selected Poems*, 53.

13. *An Area of Darkness*, 61.

14. See *The Light in Troy*, 98–99. G. W. Pigman classifies assimilation and transformation as parts of a "transformative" metaphor for influence dating back to Seneca and beyond: "The transformative class includes apian, digestive, filial, and simian metaphors. . . . Digestion and the resemblance of father to son represent successful transformation of a model; the ape and also the crow represent failures of transformation" ("Versions of Renaissance Imitation," 3–4).

15. *The Four Fundamental Concepts of Psychoanalysis*, 100. Also see Homi K. Bhabha, "Of Mimicry and Man: The Ambiguities of Colonial Discourse."

16. As a celebrator of error Walcott belongs in the tradition of Nietzsche, who points out that knowledge depends upon the inexactitudes of language—thus, upon a "solid, granite foundation of ignorance"—and argues that "science at its best . . . loves error, because, being alive, it loves life" (*Beyond Good and Evil*, 36).

17. *Dissemination*, 206.

18. See also *Midsummer*, LI.

19. Whatever remains fixed, in contrast, cannot survive the "process of imperialistic defoliation which . . . destroyed the original, destroyed the Aztec, and American Indian, and the Caribbean Indian. . . . We can praise them for not imitating, but . . . imitation decimated *them*" (10–11; italics mine). This need not suggest that Native Americans could have acted differently; the link between originality and "defoliation" is more tautological than that. What is always absent, what has always been destroyed, is precisely "the original" (Walcott, like Freud, places murder at the origin of civilization), while whatever speaks, gestures, or writes re-enacts mimicry. Likewise, in *Omeros* "or-

iginal" African cultures survive the Middle Passage insofar as they flexibly recombine to form African-Caribbean/African-American cultures.

20. *Écrits*, 4.

21. Carnival is thus a model for theater, calypso a model for poetry, and the steel band a model for music. Similarly, Kutzinski calls Guillén's "ability to wear different masks while at the same time calling attention to their status as masks" the "carnival link" between diverse poems (196). Derrida, too, compares the rejection of originality with the metaphysics of theater. Mallarmé's Mime "is *acting* from the moment he is ruled by no actual action and aims toward no form of verisimilitude. . . . The Mime mimes reference. He is not an imitator; he mimes imitation" (*Dissemination*, 219).

22. In "Roseau Valley," "the chapel"

> at Jacmel, whose prayers gently chain
> the joined wrists of workers (shoulders
> still bent like the murmurous cane,
> whatever the crop), stays as old as
>
> the valley. . . . (*AT*, 17)

23. See Robert Hamner, *Derek Walcott*, 140–41.

24. In *Dream on Monkey Mountain and Other Plays*, 35.

25. At the same time, Walcott's claim of isolation is not exactly accurate to begin with, especially when applied to his drama. *Ti-Jean and His Brothers*, arguably Walcott's most charming play, was first composed in 1958 and combines a "possibly European" tale with African-Caribbean trickster folklore (Patrick Taylor, *The Narrative of Liberation*, 215). Taylor argues, following Ramchand, that Walcott's plays, unlike most of his poetry, "are firmly rooted in the folk and popular traditions of the Caribbean" (208); similarly, Hirsch notes that "[his] plays lean a lot more heavily on Creole than [his] poems do" ("An Interview with Derek Walcott" [1979], 287). I agree with this, but would add that although it has taken Walcott longer to acknowledge popular traditions in his poetry, the poems finally put popular culture to better use, since they more fully admit the complexities of language.

26. Hamner, *Derek Walcott*, 119.

27. Walcott suspends the question of the actual existence of such language, since *Omeros*'s African episode takes place in a dream, and what we see, in any case, is a cultural belief in a linguistic characteristic rather than that characteristic per se. However, in that there is no such thing as linguistic significance "in the abstract," apart from its users, there is for all practical purposes no difference between a cultural consensus that the forms of language have significance and that significance itself.

28. "I Yam What I Am: the Topos of (Un)Naming in Afro-American Literature." In *Black Literature and Literary Theory*, ed. Gates, 153.

29. A name like "Pompey" may not in the end be ironic, either, regardless of the namer's intention. See the discussion of Walcott's "Names" in Chapter Three, below.

30. "Have we melted into a mirror, / leaving our souls behind?" ("Names," *SG*, 40).

31. "Night Fishing," *AT*, 56.

32. "Names," *SG*, 40.

33. This Sunday gentleman recalls Warwick Walcott, who appears in similar garb earlier in *Omeros*, and also Walcott himself. In "From this Far" he portrays himself near "wharf-piles," "eating an ice cream on a hot esplanade, in a barred blue-and-white vest" (*FT*, 31).

34. Elsewhere Walcott writes "ice cream suit"—so that Sunday may be wearing a "sundae" suit.

35. *Epitaph for the Young*, Walcott's very early long poem, prefigures *Omeros* in its parodies of *The Divine Comedy* and *Four Quartets*.

36. This description revises "Conqueror," Walcott's early and more histrionic poem about a bronze statue (*IGN*, 67–68). Both poems turn on the basic irony of the statues' simultaneous power and immobility, but *Omeros* conveys the irony by juxtaposition rather than by direct statement. These images of statuary recall Stevens's "great statue of the General Du Puy" in *Notes Toward a Supreme Fiction*, for whom "Nothing had happened because nothing had changed. / Yet the General was rubbish in the end" (*Collected Poems*, 391–92).

37. Catachresis serves similar thematic and psychological purposes for Hart Crane, a poet particularly dear to Walcott. See Lee Edelman's *Transmemberment of Song: Hart Crane's Anatomies of Rhetoric and Desire*.

38. *Imperial Meridian: The British Empire and the World, 1780–1830*.

39. *Labyrinths*, 87.

40. In *New Poems* (Book Two), trans. Edward Snow, 51.

CHAPTER 2

1. "The Language of Exile," 6.

2. An unsigned article in the Kenyan journal *Busara* exemplifies one end of the anti-Walcottian spectrum. The article charges that Walcott's frequent reference to the British canon parallels his political quietism, since on the linguistic level, Walcott "feels that he has a special obligation to the English language. . . . And he makes the attempt to produce classical Queen's English." Walcott further reveals his complicity by his "over-dependence of mood on other artists." Structurally, too, "Walcott's reason is discursive reason," the argumentative rationalism of the empirical West. As a result "the Caribbean . . . has absolutely no place for Derek Walcott" (*Busara* 6 [1974], 90–100). This article includes some astonishing interpretations of the poetry ("Walcott would not think of the islands as very lovely or beautiful"), but its "strong misreading" properly insists that, as Walcott is well aware, the echo of a phrase or the pronunciation of a vowel can mark a political allegiance.

3. "Derek Walcott: New World Mediterranean Poet," 133–47.

4. Pigman, 12. Walcott uses this figure himself and runs into the same trouble with it: "In the New World we have to ask this faceted question: (1) Whether the religion taught to the black slave has been absorbed as belief, (2) whether it has been altered by this absorption, and (3) whether wholly ab-

sorbed or absorbed and altered, it must now be rejected" ("MH," 8). If Christianity *has* been wholly absorbed and/or altered, then it is too late to reject it.

5. "Culture or Mimicry?" 6.

6. "'I Met History Once, But He Ain't Recognize Me': The Poetry of Derek Walcott" (review of *Collected Poems 1948–1984*), 175.

7. Marvell, *The Complete Poems*, 116.

8. Harold Bloom, *The Anxiety of Influence*, 141.

9. *Oeuvres Complètes*, 38.

10. *Oeuvres Complètes*, 51–52.

11. Even here Baudelaire plants the seed of this Eden's destruction, since its sun's mysterious charms resemble those of his beloved's *"traitres* yeux, / Brillant à travers leurs larmes" (traitorous eyes, / Shining through their tears; italics mine).

12. *Oeuvres Complètes*, 254–55.

13. "Poetry and Its Double: Two *Invitations au voyage*," in *The Critical Difference*, 38.

14. Francis Scarfe, note to Scarfe's edition of Baudelaire, 112.

15. In *The Complete Poems, 1927–1979*, 94.

16. "A Celebration of Charis in Ten Lyrick Peeces," 4 ("Her Triumph"), in *Poems*, 91–92.

17. Canto 74, *Cantos*, 449.

18. For this insight I am once again grateful to Stephen Yenser.

19. For example, "Who will say in what year, / fleeing what band of tritons," and "on what tennis court / near what pine trees?" (*The Cantos*, 9, 512).

20. Pound, too, being concerned with transience, often refers to fire in *The Cantos* (e.g., p. 17). Walcott's images of interpenetration also find echoes in Pound's "grass nowhere out of place" (435), "thin as Demeter's hair" (531), and "stream's edge lost in grass" (509). Walcott's line of French recalls Pound's many foreign phrasings, and in its content sounds the home key of *The Pisan Cantos* in particular.

21. "Afterthought" to *Notebook 1967–68* (New York: Farrar, Straus & Giroux, 1969), 160.

22. Walcott quotes (and slightly misquotes) Blake's "Night" at the end of the second stanza; compares the ruined house's "deciduous beauty" to "Faulkner's South" and to ancient Greece; alludes to Kipling ("I heard / What Kipling heard; the death of a great empire"); and reflects upon "men like Hawkins, Walter Raleigh, Drake, / Ancestral murderers and poets." Walcott's (mis)quotation of Blake ("Farewell, green fields, / Farewell, ye happy groves" for "Farewell green fields and happy groves") itself echoes *Paradise Lost* I.249–50: "Farewell happy Fields, / Where Joy for ever dwells."

23. Walcott again misquotes slightly: "Since our longest Sunne sets at right declensions, and makes but winter arches, therefore it cannot be long before we lie down in darknesse, and have our light in ashes" (Browne, *Selected Writings*, 151–52).

24. Epistle II.3, in *The Satires of Horace and Perseus*, 192.

25. Walcott similarly asks that African-Americans not "[skip] the part

about slavery . . . going straight to a kind of Eden-like grandeur" (Hirsch 1986, 222).

26. As a substance formed by fossils, coal, too, connotes archaeology and ancient history.

27. In *The Complete Poetry and Selected Prose of John Donne*, 441.

28. Edward Said, speaking generally of modern originality, points out that in *Dr. Faustus* Mann and Leverkühn similarly "master the art of doubling, inverting, imitating to infinity. Their originality is to play this game until they achieve a state of vacancy" ("On Originality," in *The World, the Text, and the Critic*, 136).

29. "Crusoe's Journal" and "Crusoe's Island" (*C*, 51–57).

30. Gregorias and the narrator of *Another Life* are also called "orphans of the nineteenth century" (12.i.1).

31. In even slightly later interviews with Hamner ("Conversation with Derek Walcott" [1977; conducted in 1975], 409–20) and Ciccarelli (1977), Walcott is more generous: "Every playwright who has a party or a thing that he wants done is political in a sense" (Hamner 1977, 413).

32. Walcott's structural divisions echo those of another New England poet, Bishop, who organizes by geographical principles in *North and South* and *Questions of Travel*.

33. Walcott notes that the twentieth century creates its own "credo" by crossing Voltaire with Nietzsche: "It is necessary to invent a God who is dead" ("CM," 12).

34. "The New World Poetry of Derek Walcott," 37.

35. Mandelstam, *Selected Poems*, 58.

36. *Marxism and Deconstruction*, 16.

37. Pigman explains that "'eristic'" metaphors—"the term [borrowed] from 'Longinus'' description of Plato wrestling with Homer and citation of Hesiod's *agathe eris*—often support a doctrine which contradicts the advice of effacement: an open struggle with the model for preeminence, a struggle in which the model must be recognized to assure the text's victory. Besides images of struggle, strife, and competition, the eristic class includes a large group of analogies connected with overtaking and passing people on roads and paths, in particular footsteps and leaders" (4).

38. *Dissemination*, 192.

39. Benjamin DeMott, "Poems of Caribbean Wounds," 30.

40. Sven Birkerts, "Heir Apparent" (review of *Midsummer*), 31.

41. R. W. Flint, review of *Midsummer*, 14.

CHAPTER 3

1. Lawrence D. Carrington, *St. Lucian Creole: A Descriptive Analysis of its Phonology and Morpho-Syntax*, 4. R. B. Le Page and Andrée Tabouret-Keller note that "more than one variety of St. Lucian English [is] emerging, and . . . these varieties could not be placed on any linear continuum from Standard English to some supposed basilect. The cultural links [reach] out to St. Lucia's past and to the influence also of all the other islands, Francophone and Anglophone, as

well as to that of the education system and the printed word" (*Acts of Identity*, 165).

2. Although a "creole" is often held to be a mixture of two languages, one dominant and one subordinate, actual practice may strain this precision. The English-lexicon "third strand" Carrington describes, for example, is a second-order creole, composed of French-lexicon Creole and English. Walcott has said that he translates French-lexicon Creole into his own version of Creole-inflected English (see Hirsch 1979, 289); like the English-lexicon "third strand," this language would likewise be a second-order creole involving more than two languages all together. In addition, "[T]here is no necessary historical chain or divide between pidginization, creolization, and decreolization" (Le Page and Tabouret-Keller, 200). I refer to all of these specific languages, and combinations thereof, as "Creole(s)," with explanatory adjectives where lexicon distinction is not obvious from context. The concept of creolization, however, obviously refers to something larger than mixtures of St. Lucian French Creole, French, English, or any particular languages. When I speak of "a creole," I refer to no specific combination, but to any language that is a combination of languages. To further mark these two senses, I will use Creole with a capital C when speaking of particular languages, creole with a small c when speaking of the phenomenon more generally.

3. "It is frequently supposed that we all have such a 'mother tongue' or 'native language' which represents some really fundamental properties of us as individuals who have grown up in a particular society. . . . [W]hether true or untrue, such a variety is likely to be only one of several learned in childhood, since no society is totally homogeneous. . . . [T]he concept of 'native language' or 'mother tongue' is, like all concepts, culturally conditioned" (Le Page and Tabouret-Keller, 188–89).

4. At the time of the 1946 West Indies census, 37,977 of St. Lucia's 70,113 citizens spoke both English and French Creole, but 30,357 (43.3%) spoke only or primarily Creole (Carrington, 4).

5. "Walcott and the Audience for Poetry," 21.

6. In *The Joker of Seville* and *O! Babylon*, 156.

7. "Almost all aspects of Guillén's poetry are deeply rooted in the cross-cultural imagination of the Caribbean—*mestizaje*, as Guillén himself has called it—and the resistance to any kind of dogmatism is an important part of that historical legacy" (Kutzinski, 134).

8. "A Linguistic Perspective on the Caribbean," in *Caribbean Contours*, ed. Sidney W. Mintz and Sally Price, 161.

9. "[T]he problems and processes we are discussing are in fact universal, and can be illustrated from all parts of the world (including Britain and France), and from all periods of history" (Le Page and Tabouret-Keller, 175).

10. Other nations have so far identified creolization with the Caribbean that the Singaporean Minister of Education has said he "could not countenance the 'Caribbeanization' of English there" (Le Page and Tabouret-Keller, 176). Yet in this phrase the Minister himself mints a neologism.

11. Morris has illuminated the complexities of this one phrase: "The error

in grammar may signify either that the drunk alienated writer wishes (in spite of quoting Shelley, in spite of using a fashionable German word) to identify with the West Indian dialect class; the cultured West Indian wishes to feel peasant. Or it may signify that the foreign culture is only an overgrowth. Or, least interestingly, the grammar may be the narrator's, not the writer's actual usage. And, obliquely, by placing that final anecdote next to the hedonistic scene and the writer's comment, Walcott suggests that there is indeed a West Indian *angst*, and that that may be why we fête so very much" (19).

12. "The Task of the Translator," 78.

13. "[T]he ever-present baleful influence of Yeats suddenly overshadows the patois speaker, and the song ends on an unlikely 'literary' note" (23).

14. Selden Rodman, "Derek Walcott," in *Tongues of Fallen Angels*, 234.

15. "Mary Winslow," in *Lord Weary's Castle*, 25. Both Lowell and Walcott probably derive this, in turn, from Eliot.

16. "Walcott on Walcott: Interview by Dennis Scott," 79.

17. The connotations of linguistic elegance in some of Walcott's polyglossic poems tilt toward other languages and against American English, as in "Spring Street in '58," a poem dedicated to Frank O'Hara:

> There was dirt on the peach tan
> of the girls of the gold Mid-West,
> ou sont ces vierges?
> Ah, Frank, elles sont
> aux Spring Falls, Iowa. . . . (*SG*, 57)

18. In "Sainte Lucie," *SG*, 43–55.

19. Walcott dramatizes this phenomenon rather bitterly in "What the Twilight Says": "Listen, one kind of writer, generally the entertainer, says: 'I will write in the language of the people however gross or incomprehensible'; another says: 'Nobody else go' understand this, you hear, so le' me write English' " (9). Walcott is not exaggerating. Le Page and Tabouret-Keller observe that at a Catholic school in Belize "in the early 1950s, nuns of a German teaching order were to be found teaching Maya- and Spanish-speaking children to try to pass English-language examinations" (70); in a 1971 survey in Belize "only one man claimed his family and himself to be 'Belizean'; he was of Lebanese descent and as such generally referred to as a 'Turk' " (219).

20. For Le Page and Tabouret-Keller, in a sense, each individual does speak an individual language: "Each child . . . produce[s] its own unique set of datum-points in relation to any external models—'Standard' or 'Spanish' or 'Creole' " (160). Too often "[t]he linguist . . . tends to construct an idealized grammar and then to see his informants, from whom he obtained his data, as imperfect or varying exponents of that grammar. It is this process which underlies the concept of the linguistic variable 'within a language' " (152).

21. Christopher L. Miller, "Theories of Africans," in *"Race," Writing, and Difference*, 295.

22. For Walcott, Brodsky is the poet who stands upright in the middle of

these conflicting winds, "giv[ing] the one work, simultaneously, two mother tongues" ("MI," 35).

23. Manoir's very name has to do with intersecting languages, of course; its English translation is again the Walcottian pun on "manor" and "manner" from "Ruins of a Great House."

24. During Walcott's youth academic and government officials did not allow Creole in St. Lucian schools and generally resisted its legitimization. While growing nationalism has changed perceptions of Creole, English still connotes economic mobility and Creole, economic disadvantage. Even in 1984 qualifications for membership in the House and Senate still required English proficiency. "The Speaker of the House has been known to rule out of order a member who sought to make a major contribution in Creole," so that "the average citizen, himself primarily a Creole speaker, is excluded from the formal political life of his nation" (Carrington, 172). See also Frantz Fanon, *Black Skin, White Masks*, 20 ff., regarding conditions in the Antilles generally.

25. Carrington phrases it well: "Between the years of 1593 and 1603 the island was visited briefly by no fewer than three British vessels, but it was not until 1605 that a settlement was recorded. The 67 passengers of the ship 'Oliph Blossom' en route to Guiana, landed in the island to seek their fortune after having grown weary of their journey. The Carib inhabitants soon assured the majority of them eternal rest and the 19 survivors set out in an open boat for their former destination" (1–2). (Incidentally, Carrington's own book contains an example of a transfiguring mistranslation; the cartographer who prepared the map of St. Lucia facing the first page of the introduction, one Herbert Söhmer of Bamberg University, provides a "Reverence Chart" for cartographical markings.)

26. "Of Mimicry and Man: The Ambivalence of Colonial Discourse," 129. See also Bhabha's "The Other Question—The Stereotype and Colonial Discourse," *Screen* 24 (November/December 1984).

27. The lack of institutional respect for creoles is most dramatically tied to their perceived belatedness when they are referred to as "bastardized" languages. The term "creole" reflects this thinking; even the word seems to have lived like a particolored thing, wandering through half the Romance languages: "French *créole*, from Spanish *criollo*, from Portuguese *crioulo*, Negro born in his master's house, from *criar*, to bring up, from Latin *creāre*, to create, beget" (*American Heritage Dictionary*). But what language wasn't born in "its master's house"? According to Alleyne, scholars seeking "languages analogous to the creole languages" are particularly interested in English (162). As Virginia Woolf has remarked, Mother English has been a very promiscuous maiden.

28. Søren Kierkegaard, *Repetition*, 149. Kierkegaard treats the story playfully, but there is truth as well in Constantius's anecdote about "Professor Ussing": "When Professor Ussing once gave a speech at the May 28 Society and a statement in the speech did not meet with approval, what did he do, this professor who at that time was always resolute and forceful—he pounded the

table and said: I repeat. What he meant at the time was that what he said gained by repetition" (150).

29. "One day I wrote her name upon the strand, / But came the waves and washed it away" (*Amoretti*, #75; I am grateful to Paul Breslin for this reminder). While Spenser contrasts the transience of the strand to the permanence of verse, Keats's similar "name . . . writ on water" forgoes permanence altogether.

30. Also remember Leopold Bloom on the beach, writing, "I. . . . AM. A.," then thinking, "No room. Let it go" (*Ulysses*, 375).

31. See also Roberto Fernandez Rétamar, *Caliban*.

32. The schoolchildren make one further appearance, in "The Sea Is History" (*SAK*, 25).

33. *DMM*, 88.

34. I will refer to Walcott's very slightly revised version of "Sainte Lucie" in *CP*, 309–23.

35. Elsa Triolet, for example, "succeeded in realizing her dream of being able to speak two languages simultaneously. She did this by integrating elements other than words into her texts, creating an interplay among several different means of communication" (77).

36. Valerie Trueblood, "On Derek Walcott," in *The American Poetry Review* 7 (1978), 10.

37. *Duino Elegies*, 69.

38. In *Figures in Black: Words, Signs and the "Racial" Self*, 178.

39. *New Republic* 197, 2 November 1987.

40. *The Parasite*, 43.

41. As one may speak of Caribbean polyglossia, Kenneth M. Bilby describes Caribbean "polymusicality": "In a musical environment in which it is possible for one to encounter virtually back to back . . . string bands and the complex drumming of possession cults, the call-and-response of field gangs and the layered harmony of a Bach chorale, it is not surprising that . . . the individual musician who specializes in a single form or style to the exclusion of all others is a rarity" ("The Caribbean as a Musical Region," in *Caribbean Contours*, 202–3).

42. Miller, 283.

43. See also "The Sea Is History," *SAK*, 25–28.

44. *Religio Medici* I.15, in *Selected Writings*, 20.

45. Shabine's antagonist and best friend (another characteristic unity/duality) similarly has only a nation's name: Vince, for St. Vincent.

46. Edward Said, *Orientalism*, 259. Inside the quotation marks, Said cites Auerbach citing Hugo.

47. "Poetry," in *Seven Nights*, 80.

48. *Black Orpheus*, 24.

CHAPTER 4

1. Walcott reflects, "Lowell would love to have been Constable or Vermeer. . . . But in [Lowell's] late work, the light comes not from one but from all directions, and it is dim and shifting" ("ORL," 29).

2. Dennis Scott observes in his interview with Walcott that "there are times [in Walcott's plays] when the verse takes over and what we get is not so much a poetic drama as a dramatic poem." Walcott simply answers, "Yes"; and when pressed further—"How do you react to this kind of accusation?"—he replies, "Well, I think that a play is a dramatic poem. . . . I think any play that works completely, is a poem" (77).

3. The classroom remarks I cite by date in this chapter are from Walcott's poetry seminars at Boston University from fall 1987 through the winter of 1988. I quote from notes, as nearly verbatim as possible, taken by Bill Keeney.

4. "Spatial Form in Literature: Toward a General Theory," in *The Language of Images*, 273.

5. See "Cul de Sac Valley" and "A Latin Primer" (*AT*, 9–15, 21–22).

6. See also "The Star-Apple Kingdom" (*SAK*, 48).

7. "'A Crystal of Ambiguities': Metaphors for Creativity and the Art of Writing in Derek Walcott's *Another Life*," 93–105. Mordecai's "prismatic" vision resembles the "stereoptic" vision Beaujour finds in bilinguals and polyglots.

8. *The Art of Describing*, 169–221.

9. "Holy," appropriately, is a celebration of unity.

10. *A Treasury of Art Masterpieces, From the Renaissance to the Present Day* (1939).

11. None of Walcott's poems entitled "A Map of —" is about a map in the ordinary sense at all. See "A Map of the Antilles" (*IGN*, 55), "A Map of the Continent" (*G*, 75), and "Map of the New World" (*FT*, 25).

12. Walcott's version of "A Map of Europe" in *Selected Poems* emphasizes (at the expense of music) this distinction, rather like Stevens's in "The Snow Man," between objects and objects beheld: "A broken loaf, a dented urn become / More than themselves, their SELVES, as in Chardin" (79).

13. Meanwhile, pieces of visual art decay like Walcott's father's "fading water-colours" (2.ii.20), and "Skin wrinkles like paint" (2.iii.40)—upon which we realize that human beings and works of art are linked by temporal experience after all.

14. Actually, Walcott is fond of this cliché from Virgil, and he interprets it to mean precisely "See 'things as they are' and you'll see tears in things." For Walcott, Edward Thomas's "Tears" fulfills Virgil exactly: "Thomas' tears do not solve or dissolve, do not go higher than [the] impulse to tears. [They] become invisible and clear (transparent). . . . Put him next to Pound, Eliot, Graves, Crane, and you will find a lack of pathos, but what Virgil meant—the tears that are in things." In "A Map of Europe" objects achieve their own pathos by showing marks of temporality—by being "cracked," "broken," "dented." Thus, Walcott revises Williams: "No tears but in things" (1/13/89).

15. Adam Zagajewski, "To Go to Lvov," in *Tremor: Selected Poems*, 3–5.

16. Walcott may have Marvell's "On a Drop of Dew" in mind:

> See how the orient dew,
> Shed from the bosom of the morn
>   Into the blowing roses,

> Yet careless of its mansion new,
> For the clear region where 'twas born
> Round in itself incloses:
> And in its little globe's extent
> Frames as it can its native element.

17. Vendler, *The Odes of John Keats*, 127.

18. *Word and Image: French Painting of the Ancien Régime*, 10–28.

19. "The Worlds of a Cosmic Castaway," 8.

20. Ovid has also been called, for very different reasons, "a poet between two worlds"; this is the title of a book by Hermann Frankel (1945).

21. *The Sister Arts*, 27.

22. As far as I know, Walcott has no precise allusion in mind here, but seems to echo Tolstoy's contrast of Natasha's ball to Prince Andrei's injury in *War and Peace*.

23. In Greek mythology Philomela is changed into a swallow and her sister Procne into a nightingale; in the Roman version it is Procne who is raped, mutilated, and turned into a swallow, and Philomela who becomes a nightingale.

24. See Robert Bensen, "The Painter as Poet: Derek Walcott's *Midsummer*," 257–68.

25. Walcott celebrates poetry precisely for its "Neanderthal" harshness, which is at best invigorating, in the "ape" metaphors I mention above.

26. Lowell, "At the Indian Killer's Grave," in *Lord Weary's Castle*, 60.

27. Walcott's father was also a watercolorist, and Walcott connects his father's medium to his fragility: "my father, who did watercolors, / entered his work. He became one of his shadows, / wavering and faint in the midsummer sunlight" (L).

28. Gauguin's *Where Do We Come From? What Are We? Where Are We Going?* (1897) is painted on sackcloth.

29. Otherwise Craven's note on Watteau displays the "compulsive rhapsodising" that Bryson finds "the characteristic form of Watteau writing," as if that writing wished to compensate for Watteau's "semantic vacuum . . . with an inrush of verbal reverie" (*Word and Image*, 64, 74).

30. Walcott did, however, produce an illustrated version of "The Schooner Flight" and a drawing of Spoiler for two numbers of *The Trinidad and Tobago Review*.

31. Veroboj Vildomec, *Multilingualism*, and François Grosjean, *Life with Two Languages*, quoted in Beaujour, 102.

CHAPTER 5

1. V. S. Naipaul, *The Mimic Men*, 91.

2. *The English in the West Indies; or, The Bow of Ulysses*, 347.

3. "The Garden," in *Poems and Letters*, 49.

4. Wordplay and image clusters involving leaves, lines, and "craft" pepper Walcott's work; each of these words marks an intersection between poetic and

worldly texts. "Leaves" refers variously to trees' or books' leaves ("these were the only epics: the leaves" [*AL*, 22.i.43]). "Lines" can refer to lines of verse, vegetation (especially vines), wrinkles and palm lines, rain, the "unbroken water-line" (*AL*, 23.i.6), sailors' or fishermen's equipment ("line, live in the sounds / that ignorant shallows use; / then throw the silvery nouns / to open-mouthed canoes" [*AT*, 56]), and to "liners," at which point this word converges with "craft." "Craft" refers to craftsmanship, to craftiness typified by Odysseus, and to ships (thus the poet figures Shabine and Achille are also sailors). And there are other polysemous words (palm, slate, root, etc.) that function in similar ways. These can form dense clusters, as when *Midsummer*'s poet declares, "My palms have been sliced by the twine / of the craft I have pulled at for more than forty years" (XXV). Walcott metaphorizes the network of intersections that results, in turn, by his fondness for webs, fishermen's nets, fabric (writing for Walcott is not only textual but textile), and the letter X. In this last he resembles Browne, another avid reader of nature's book, who considered "the Letter *X*" the "Emphaticall decussation, or fundamentall figure" (*Selected Writings*, 165).

5. "White" and "dark" also evoke the pigments of page and letter. As when Walcott identifies himself with the black "mongrel" of Creole (*AT*, 10), "racial" considerations and graphemic ones merge: "The wisdom of this choice is, again, not so much his own as the wisdom of his language—better still, the wisdom of its letter: of black on white. He is simply a pen that is aware of its movement" (Brodsky, 169). Irwin notes that "the hieroglyphic writing of natural history is suggested by . . . black/white imagery . . . for just as the crossing of vertical and horizontal lines is one bipolar opposition that grounds writing, so the differentiation of black and white is another. Differentiation involves, of course, a reciprocal act in which two entities are held apart by being held together" (72–73).

6. "The Sea Is History" resembles Robert Hayden's "The Diver," in which the poet-diver dons protective gear in order to sink down through the layers of the past and investigate the wrecked ship of history.

7. See Laurence Lieberman, "The Muse of History" (review of *Another Life*), *Yale Review* 63 (1973), 121.

8. "Either I'm Nobody, or I'm a Nation" (review of *Collected Poems 1948–1984*), 56.

9. The letter V standing alone does possess many meanings in English, standing for "Victory" in World War II and abbreviating, among other things, "velocity," "verb," "verse," "village," "voice," "volume," and "vowel" (*American Heritage Dictionary*).

10. Walcott's title may allude to an incident Naipaul recounts in *The Middle Passage*: "When I was in the fourth form, I wrote a vow on the endpaper of my 'Kennedy's Revised Latin Primer' to leave within five years" (quoted in Atlas, 34). In Walcott's poem the narrator uses his Latin to understand his native landscape, not leave it behind.

11. Considering *Another Life*'s other debts to Joyce, Walcott's "tree of

heaven" here may echo Joyce's "heaventree of stars hung with humid night-blue fruit" (*Ulysses*, 683).

12. Although Nabokov has said that beauty is round whereas common sense is square, a square has beauty, too. Eliot's *Four Quartets* (an empty pool or "box circle" waiting to be filled by radiance), Blake's "fourfold vision," and Browne's quincunx all seek the essence of the quadrilateral. Walcott obviously can't empty "mystique" from the form of the "essential cube"; the idea of its essentiality is already mystical.

13. In *Epitaph for the Young*, "The hills are humped like sphinxes / Telling the city's fortune in a valley's palm" (10).

CHAPTER 6

1. Froude's Homeric subtitle, *The Bow of Ulysses*, refers to Odysseus's ability, upon his return, to string the bow he had left in his house, a bow that during his absence no one else had had might enough to use. In Froude's allegory Britain is a weak-kneed Odysseus which can no longer live up to its imperial past, and which gives up on projects—such as the colonization of the West Indies—it once had energy to pursue. But the Grecian-Caribbean parallel lingers in Froude's language and outlasts his "bow" metaphor.

2. The intervening presence of Joyce's *Ulysses* troubles the question. After Joyce (and Kazantzakis, and others) Walcott can hardly gain admiration for being bold enough to mimic Homer. *Omeros* is explicitly parasitical—in its above-mentioned egalitarianism and pacifism, for example—on Joyce, and Joyce as well as Omeros appears as a character in the poem. Yet in a way Walcott's multiplication of predecessors merely raises the stakes. Once again, the more Walcott empties grandeur from his poetry, the higher it floats, as though freed of ballast.

3. *Mimesis*, 6.

4. In *Another Life* schoolchildren were likened to sheep; now they are Polyphemos's sheep. In addition, Caribbean whitecaps resemble "woolly crests . . . the backs of the Cyclops's flock, / with the smart man under one's belly" (323).

5. One immediate explanation for Helen's attitude can be found in her socioeconomic context. She finds work with difficulty because, as local gossips put it, "she was too rude, 'cause she dint take no shit" (33). Helen endures the hypocrisies of work in St. Lucia's tourist industry with a mixture of boredom, "chill," and rage (36–37). Helen's diffidence is in social terms a refusal, beautiful in its integrity, to dissimulate postcolonial bitterness. Thus Walcott attaches her beauty to her characteristic air of contempt: "her looks" depend upon both "splendour and arrogance" (96).

6. Plunkett's pun refers to a yellow V-backed dress, stolen from Maud, that Helen often wears. By "turning her back" Helen rejects the subservience that might go along with her profession as a servant, and instead flaunts the Victory of a dress taken from a colonist by a colonial.

7. Walcott can never utterly put to rest his desire to write like the sun, or like the ocean, which "ha[s] // no memory of the wanderings of Gilgamesh, / or whose sword severed whose head in the *Iliad*" (296). Sometimes, as in

much of *Sea Grapes,* he even claims momentarily to achieve such transparency. More often and more reasonably, he conveys its impossibility.

8. See Oscar Mandel, *Philoctetes and the Fall of Troy.*

9. Afolabe, too, while a slave, worked "locking his jaw // like the winch of the wheel until his temples hurt" (82).

10. Antibodies are created out of that which they counteract—antibodies for snakebite being a popular example of the phenomenon.

11. Similarly, in Lowell's "My Last Afternoon with Uncle Devereaux Winslow," the kindergarten-aged poet tries repeatedly to remove the anchor embroidered on his sailor suit.

12. The conches also resemble "delicate . . . vulvas," and so connect the wounding of Philoctete(s) with the rape of Helen/St. Lucia (41).

13. *The Wound and the Bow: Seven Essays on Literature,* 289, 287, 294.

14. Still, he won't sell just any story; he won't explain the cure of his wound because " 'It have some things . . . worth more than a dollar' " (4).

15. Likewise, when Achille first sees Afolabe, he recognizes his father because he recognizes himself, the son: "he knew by that walk it / was himself in his father" (136).

16. Recall that Achille, in contrast, "never ascended in an elevator" (320).

17. Walcott's "soul-shaping forge" recalls Stephen Dedalus's vow "to forge in the smithy of my soul the uncreated conscience of my race" (*A Portrait of the Artist as a Young Man,* 253). Stephen also calls upon "the spiritual-heroic refrigerating apparatus, invented and patented in all countries by Dante Alighieri" (252).

18. We find a similar ambiguity in Joyce when *A Portrait's* apotheosis is made to seem ironic in *Ulysses.*

19. The poet's faithfulness to the object world manifests itself in his concern for detail. *The Iliad* and *The Odyssey* brim with community news about who is whose grandson and who shares the same home town, and apparently assume that these details radiate significance. Thus, when Omeros hears that "A girl" provided Walcott with his Greek name, he asks,

> "From what city? Do you know?"
> "No. I forget."
> "Thebes? Athens?"
> "Yeah. Could be Athens,"

I said, stumbling. "What difference does it make now?"
That stopped the old goat in his tracks. He turned:

> "What difference?

None, maybe, to you. . . ." (284)

EPILOGUE

1. *Paris Review* 101 (1986), 192.

2. Walcott had written "tourists like myself" in place of "transients" in the earlier draft of "Light."

3. "[F]ading in the dying dusk" in the *Paris Review.*

4. Walcott explicitly reworks the Orpheus-Eurydice story in his new musical, *Steel* (produced at the American Repertory Theater, Cambridge, Massachusetts, 1991). There, it is Eurydice (a schoolgirl) who instructs Orpheus (a steel band musician) not to look at her as they revisit their childhood neighborhood.

5. *Signsponge*, 8.

WORKS CITED

I. PRIMARY SOURCES

Walcott, Derek. *Another Life*. New York: Farrar, Straus & Giroux, 1974.

——. *The Arkansas Testament*. New York: Farrar, Straus & Giroux, 1987.

——. "The Caribbean: Culture or Mimicry?" *Journal of InterAmerican Studies and World Affairs* 16 (1974), 3–13.

——. *The Castaway and Other Poems*. London: Jonathan Cape, 1965.

——. *Collected Poems 1948–1984*. New York: Farrar, Straus & Giroux, 1984.

——. "Crocodile Dandy" (review of Les Murray, *The Daylight Moon* and *The Vernacular Republic*). *New Republic* 200 (6 February 1989), 25–28.

——. *Dream on Monkey Mountain and Other Plays*. New York: Farrar, Straus & Giroux, 1970.

——. *Epitaph for the Young*. Barbados: Advocate Co., 1949.

——. *The Fortunate Traveller*. New York: Farrar, Straus & Giroux, 1981.

——. *In a Green Night: Poems, 1948–1960*. London: Jonathan Cape, 1962.

——. *The Gulf and Other Poems*. New York: Farrar, Straus & Giroux, 1970.

——. *The Joker of Seville* and *O Babylon!* New York: Farrar, Straus & Giroux, 1978.

——. "The Light of the World." In *Paris Review* 101 (1986), 192–95.

——. "Magic Industry" (review of Joseph Brodsky, *To Urania*). *New York Review of Books*, 24 November 1988, 35–39.

——. *Midsummer*. New York: Farrar, Straus & Giroux, 1984.

——. "The Muse of History." In *Is Massa Day Dead?*, ed. Orde Coombs. Garden City, N.Y.: Doubleday, 1974, 1–27.

——. *Omeros*. New York: Farrar, Straus & Giroux, 1990.

——. "On Robert Lowell." *New York Review of Books* 31 (1 March 1984), 25–31.

——. *Remembrance* and *Pantomime*. New York: Farrar, Straus & Giroux, 1980.

——. *Sea Grapes*. New York: Farrar, Straus & Giroux, 1976.

——. *Selected Poems*. New York: Farrar, Straus, 1964.

——. *The Star-Apple Kingdom*. New York: Farrar, Straus & Giroux, 1979.

——. "What the Twilight Says: An Overture." In *Dream on Monkey Mountain and Other Plays*, New York: Farrar, Straus & Giroux, 1970, 3–24.

II. INTERVIEWS

Ciccarelli, Sharon. "Reflections Before and After Carnival: An Interview with Derek Walcott." In *Chant of Saints: A Gathering of Afro-American Literature, Art, and Scholarship*, ed. Michael S. Harper and Robert B. Stepto. Urbana: University of Illinois Press (1980), 296–309.

Flanagan, Brenda. "An Interview with Derek Walcott." *Voices of the African Diaspora (The CAAS Research Review)* VII (1991), 16–20.

Hamner, Robert. "Conversation with Derek Walcott." *World Literature Written in English* 16 (1977), 409–20.

Hirsch, Edward. "The Art of Poetry XXXVII." *Paris Review* 101 (1986), 196–230.

————. "An Interview with Derek Walcott." *Contemporary Literature* 20 (1979), 279–92.

Scott, Dennis. "Walcott on Walcott: Interview by Dennis Scott." *Caribbean Quarterly* 14 (1968), 77–82.

III. BOOKS, ARTICLES, AND REVIEWS ON WALCOTT'S POETRY

Atlas, James. "Derek Walcott: Poet of Two Worlds." *New York Times Magazine*, 23 May 1982, 32, 34, 38, 40, 42, 50–51.

Baugh, Edward. "The Poem as Autobiographical Novel: Derek Walcott's *Another Life* in Relation to Wordsworth's *Prelude* and Joyce's *Portrait.*" In *Awakened Conscience: Studies in Commonwealth Literature*, ed. C. D. Narasimhaiah. New Delhi: Sterling, 1978, 226–35.

Bedient, Calvin. "Derek Walcott: Contemporary" (review of *The Fortunate Traveller*). *Parnassus* 9 (1981), 31–44.

Bensen, Robert. "The New World Poetry of Derek Walcott." *Concerning Poetry* 16 (Fall 1983), 29–42.

————. "The Painter as Poet: Derek Walcott's *Midsummer.*" *The Literary Review* 29 (1986), 257–68.

Birkerts, Sven. "Heir Apparent" (review of *Midsummer*). *New Republic* 190 (1984), 31–33.

Breslin, Paul. " 'I Met History Once, But He Ain't Recognize Me': The Poetry of Derek Walcott" (review of *Collected Poems 1948–1984*). *TriQuarterly* 68 (1987), 168–83.

Brodsky, Joseph. "The Sound of the Tide." In *Less Than One: Selected Essays.* New York: Farrar, Straus & Giroux, 1986, 164–75.

DeMott, Benjamin. "Poems of Caribbean Wounds." *New York Times Book Review*, 13 May 1979, 11, 30.

Dickey, James. "Worlds of a Cosmic Castaway" (review of *Collected Poems 1948–1984*). *New York Times Book Review*, 2 February 1986, 8.

Dove, Rita. " 'Either I'm Nobody, or I'm a Nation' " (review of *Collected Poems 1948–1984*). *Parnassus* 14 (1987), 49–76.

Enright, D. J. "Frank Incense" (review of *The Arkansas Testament*). *New Republic* 197 (1987), 16–17.

Flint, R. W. Review of *Midsummer. New York Times Book Review*, 8 April 1984, 14.

Hamner, Robert. *Derek Walcott.* Boston: Twayne (1978).

Heaney, Seamus. "The Language of Exile" (review of *The Star-Apple Kingdom*). *Parnassus* 8 (1980), 5–11.

"How Far Are Derek Walcott and Edward Brathwaite Similar? Is It Impossible for the Caribbean to Choose Between the Two, If So, Which Way Should They Choose and Why?" (Unsigned article.) *Busara* 6 (1974), 90–100.

Lieberman, Laurence. "New Poetry: The Muse of History." *Yale Review* 63 (1973), 113–36.

Mordecai, Pamela. " 'A Crystal of Ambiguities': Metaphors for Creativity and the Art of Writing in Derek Walcott's *Another Life.*" *World Literature Written in English* 27 (1987), 93-105.

Morris, Mervyn. "Walcott and the Audience for Poetry." *Caribbean Quarterly* 14 (1968), 7–24.

Ramsaran, J. A. "Derek Walcott: New World Mediterranean Poet." *World Literature Written in English* 21 (1982), 133–47.

Rodman, Selden. "Derek Walcott." In *Tongues of Fallen Angels*. New York: New Directions, 1974, 232–59.

Taylor, Patrick. *The Narrative of Liberation: Perspectives on Afro-Caribbean Literature, Popular Culture, and Politics*. Ithaca: Cornell University Press, 1989.

Trueblood, Valerie. "On Derek Walcott." *American Poetry Review* 7 (1978), 7–10.

Vendler, Helen. "Poet of Two Worlds" (review of *The Fortunate Traveller*). *New York Review of Books*, 4 March 1982, 23–27.

Willis, Susan. "Caliban as Poet: Reversing the Maps of Domination." *Massachusetts Review* 23 (1982), 615–30.

IV. OTHER SOURCES

Alleyne, Mervyn. "A Linguistic Perspective on the Caribbean." In *Caribbean Contours*, ed. Sidney W. Mintz and Sally Price. Baltimore: Johns Hopkins University Press, 1985.

Alpers, Svetlana. *The Art of Describing: Dutch Art in the Seventeenth Century*. Chicago: University of Chicago Press, 1983.

Auerbach, Erich. *Mimesis: The Representation of Reality in Western Literature*. Trans. Willard R. Trask. Princeton: Princeton University Press, 1953.

Baudelaire, Charles. *Oeuvres Complètes*, ed. Y.-G. Le Dontec and Claude Pichois. Paris: Gallimard, 1961.

Baudrillard, Jean. *Simlulations*. Trans. Paul Foss, Paul Patton, and Philip Beitchman. New York: Semiotext(e), 1983.

Beaujour, Elizabeth Klosty. *Alien Tongues: Bilingual Russian Writers of the ''First'' Generation*. Ithaca: Cornell University Press, 1989.

Benjamin, Walter. "The Task of the Translator." In *Illuminations*, ed. Hannah Arendt. Trans. Harry Zohn. New York: Schocken, 1969, 69–82.

———. "The Work of Art in the Age of Mechanical Reproduction." In *Illuminations*, ed. Hannah Arendt. Trans. Harry Zohn. New York: Schocken, 1969, 217–51.

Benston, Kimberly W. "I Yam What I Am: The Topos of (Un)Naming in Afro-American Literature." In *Black Literature and Literary Theory*, ed. Henry Louis Gates. New York: Metheun, 1984, 151–72.

Bhabha, Homi K. "Of Mimicry and Man: The Ambivalence of Colonial Discourse." *October* 28 (1984), 125–33.

————. "The Other Question—The Stereotype and Colonial Discourse." *Screen* 24 (1984), 18–36. Reprinted in *Out There: Marginalization and Contemporary Culture*, ed. Russell Ferguson, Martha Gever, Trinh Minh-ha, and Cornel West. Cambridge/New York: MIT Press/New Museum of Contemporary Art, 1990.

Bilby, Kenneth M. "The Caribbean as a Musical Region," in *Caribbean Contours*, ed. Sidney W. Mintz and Sally Price. Baltimore: Johns Hopkins University Press, 1985, 181–218.

Bishop, Elizabeth. *The Complete Poems: 1927–1979*. New York: Farrar, Straus & Giroux, 1983.

Blake, William. *The Poetry and Prose of William Blake*. Ed. David Erdman. Garden City, New York: Doubleday, 1970.

Blasing, Mutlu Konuk. *American Poetry: The Rhetoric of Its Forms*. New Haven: Yale University Press, 1987.

Bloom, Harold. *The Anxiety of Influence*. New York: Oxford University Press, 1973.

Borges, Jorge Luis. "Death and the Compass." In *Labyrinths: Selected Stories and Other Writings*, ed. Donald A. Yates and James E. Irby. New York: New Directions, 1964.

————. "Poetry." In *Seven Nights*, trans. Eliot Weinberger. New York: New Directions, 1984, 76–94.

Browne, Thomas. *Selected Writings*. Ed. Sir Geoffrey Keynes. Chicago: University of Chicago Press, 1968.

Bryson, Norman. *Word and Image: French Painting of the Ancien Régime*. Cambridge: Cambridge University Press, 1981.

Carrington, Lawrence. *St. Lucian Creole: A Descriptive Analysis of its Phonology and Morpho-Syntax*. Hamburg: Helmut Buske, 1984.

Césaire, Aimé. *Discourse on Colonialism*. Trans. Joan Pinkham. New York: Monthly Review Press, 1972.

Craven, Thomas. *A Treasury of Art Masterpieces, From the Renaissance to the Present Day*. New York: Simon and Schuster, 1939.

de Man, Paul. *Allegories of Reading: Figural Language in Rousseau, Nietzsche, Rilke, and Proust*. New Haven: Yale University Press, 1979.

Derrida, Jacques. *Dissemination*. Trans. Barbara Johnson. Chicago: University of Chicago Press, 1981.

————. *Of Grammatology*. Trans. Gayatri Chakravorty Spivak. Baltimore: Johns Hopkins University Press, 1976.

————. *Signsponge*. Trans. Richard Rand. New York: Columbia University Press, 1984.

————. *The Truth in Painting*. Trans. Geoff Bennington and Ian McLeod. Chicago: University of Chicago Press, 1987.

Donne, John. *Complete Poetry and Selected Prose*. Ed. Charles M. Coffin. New York: Modern Library, 1952.

Edelman, Lee. *Transmemberment of Song: Hart Crane's Anatomies of Rhetoric and Desire*. Stanford: Stanford University Press, 1987.

Fanon, Frantz. *Black Skin, White Masks*. Trans. Charles Lam Markmann. New York: Grove Press, 1967.

Froude, James Anthony. *The British in the West Indies; or, the Bow of Ulysses*. New York: Charles Scribner's Sons, 1888.

Gaggi, Silvio. *Modern/Postmodern: A Study in Twentieth-Century Arts and Ideas*. Philadelphia: University of Pennsylvania Press, 1989.

Gates, Henry Louis. "Dis and Dat: Dialect and the Descent." In *Figures in Black: Words, Signs and the "Racial" Self*. New York: Oxford University Press, 1987, 167–95.

Greenblatt, Stephen. *Renaissance Self-Fashioning: From More to Shakespeare*. Chicago: University of Chicago Press, 1980.

Greene, Thomas C. *The Light in Troy: Imitation and Discovery in Renaissance Poetry*. New Haven: Yale University Press, 1982.

Hagstrum, Jean. *The Sister Arts: The Tradition of Literary Pictorialism and English Poetry from Dryden to Gray*. Chicago: University of Chicago Press, 1958.

Hilton, Nelson. *The Literal Imagination: Blake's Vision of Words*. Berkeley: University of California Press, 1983.

Homer. *The Iliad*. Trans. Richmond Lattimore. Chicago: University of Chicago Press, 1961.

———. *The Odyssey*. Trans. Richmond Lattimore. Chicago: University of Chicago Press, 1967.

Horace. *Satires and Epistles*. In *The Satires of Horace and Perseus*, trans. Niall Rudd. Harmondsworth: Penguin, 1979.

Hutcheon, Linda. *The Politics of Postmodernism*. London: Routledge, 1989.

Irwin, John T. *American Hieroglyphics: The Symbol of the Egyptian Hieroglyphics in the American Renaissance*. Baltimore: Johns Hopkins University Press, 1980.

Johnson, Barbara. "Poetry and Its Double: Two *Invitations au voyage*." In *The Critical Difference: Essays in the Contemporary Rhetoric of Reading*. Baltimore: Johns Hopkins University Press, 1980, 23–51.

Jonson, Ben. *Poems*. Ed. Ian Donaldson. London: Oxford University Press, 1975.

Joyce, James. *A Portrait of the Artist as a Young Man*. Harmondsworth: Penguin, 1976.

———. *Ulysses*. New York: Random House, 1946.

Kierkegaard, Søren. *Repetition*. Ed. and trans. Howard V. Hong and Edna H. Hong. Princeton: Princeton University Press, 1983.

Kutzinski, Vera. *Against the American Grain: Myth and History in William Carlos Williams, Jay Wright, and Nicolas Guillén*. Baltimore: Johns Hopkins University Press, 1987.

Lacan, Jacques. *Écrits: A Selection*. New York: Norton, 1977.

———. *The Four Fundamental Concepts of Psychoanalysis*. Ed. Jacques-Alain Miller. Trans. Alan Sheridan. New York: Norton, 1981.

Le Page, R. B., and Tabouret-Keller, Andrée. *Acts of Identity: Creole-based Approaches to Language and Ethnicity*. Cambridge: Cambridge University Press, 1985.

Lowell, Robert. *For the Union Dead*. New York: Farrar, Straus, 1964.

————. *Lord Weary's Castle*. New York: Harcourt, Brace, 1946.

————. *Notebook 1967–1968*. New York: Farrar, Straus & Giroux, 1969.

Mallarmé, Stéphane. *Oeuvres Complètes*. Ed. Henri Mondor and G. Jean-Aubrey. Paris: Gallimard, 1951.

Mandel, Oscar. *Philoctetes and the Fall of Troy*. Lincoln: University of Nebraska Press, 1981.

Mandelstam, Osip. *Selected Poems*. Trans. Clarence Browne and W. S. Merwin. New York: Atheneum, 1973.

Marvell, Andrew. *Poems and Letters*, ed. H. M. Margoliouth. Oxford: Clarendon, 1971.

Miller, Christopher L. "Theories of Africans: The Question of Literary Anthropology." In *"Race," Writing, and Difference*, ed. Henry Louis Gates, Jr. Chicago: University of Chicago Press, 1986, 281–300.

————. *Theories of Africans: Francophone Literature and Anthropology in Africa*. Chicago: University of Chicago Press, 1990.

Milton, John. *Paradise Lost*, ed. A. W. Verity. Cambridge: The University Press, 1952.

Mitchell, W. J. T. *Iconology: Image, Text, Ideology*. Chicago: University of Chicago Press, 1987.

————. "Spatial Form in Literature: Toward a General Theory." In *The Language of Images*, ed. W. J. T. Mitchell. Chicago: University of Chicago Press, 1980.

Naipaul, V. S. *An Area of Darkness*. New York: MacMillan, 1965.

————. *The Mimic Men*. London: Deutsch, 1974.

Nietzsche, Friedrich. *Beyond Good and Evil: Prelude to A Philosophy of the Future*. Trans. Walter Kaufman. New York: Vintage, 1966.

Ovid. *Metamorphoses*. Trans. A. E. Watts. San Francisco: North Point Press, 1980.

Pascal, Blaise. *Pensées*. Trans. A. J. Krailsheimer. London: Penguin, 1966.

Pigman, G. W. III. "Versions of Renaissance Imitation." *Renaissance Quarterly* 33 (1980), 1–32.

Pound, Ezra. *The Cantos*. New York: New Directions, 1972.

Rétamar, Roberto Fernandez. *Caliban and Other Essays*. Trans. Edward Baker. Minneapolis: University of Minnesota Press, 1989.

Rilke, Rainer Maria. *The Duino Elegies*. Trans. C. F. MacIntyre. Berkeley: University of California Press, 1961.

————. *New Poems*. Trans. Edward Snow. San Francisco: North Point Press, 1984.

————. *The Selected Poetry of Rainer Maria Rilke*. Ed. and trans. Stephen Mitchell. New York: Vintage, 1984.

Ryan, Michael. *Marxism and Deconstruction*. Baltimore: Johns Hopkins University Press, 1982.

Said, Edward. "On Originality." In *The World, the Text, and the Critic*. Cambridge: Harvard University Press, 1983.

————. *Orientalism*. New York: Pantheon, 1978.

Sartre, Jean-Paul. *Black Orpheus*. Trans. S. W. Allen. Paris: Présence Africaine, 1976.

————. *Literature and Existentialism* (Qu'est ce que la littérature?). Trans. Bernard Frechtman. Seacaucus, N.J.: The Citadel Press, 1980.

Serres, Michel. *The Parasite*. Trans. Lawrence R. Schehr. Baltimore: Johns Hopkins University Press, 1982.

Shakespeare, William. *The Winter's Tale*. Ed. Harold Bloom. New York: Chelsea House, 1987.

Spenser, Edmund. *Poetical Works*. Ed. J. C. Smith and E. de Sélincourt. London: Oxford University Press, 1970.

Steiner, George. *After Babel: Aspects of Language and Translation*. London: Oxford University Press, 1975.

Stevens, Wallace. *Collected Poems*. New York: Knopf, 1954.

Strauss, Walter A. *Descent and Return: The Orphic Theme in Modern Literature*. Cambridge: Harvard University Press, 1971.

Vendler, Helen. *The Odes of John Keats*. Cambridge: Harvard University Press, 1983.

Wilson, Edmund. *The Wound and the Bow: Seven Studies in Literature*. New York: Oxford University Press, 1959.

Woolf, Virginia. *The Death of the Moth and Other Essays*. San Diego: Harcourt Brace Jovanovich, 1970.

Zagajewski, Adam. *Tremor: Selected Poems*. New York: Farrar, Straus & Giroux, 1985.

INDEX

Dove, Rita, 170, 240*n*8
dramatic monologue, 10, 85, 87, 107–8
Dürer, Albrecht, 143

Edelman, Lee, 231*n*37
Eliot, T. S., 11, 14, 44, 67, 113, 129, 209, 228*n*3, 235*n*15, 238*n*14; *Four Quartets*, 231*n*35, 241*n*12; "Little Gidding," 36
Enright, D. J., 108, 237*n*39
epic, 10, 66, 68, 116, 183, 200; vs. pastoral, 186–87
equator, 3, 13–17, 38, 40
eristic metaphor, 78–79, 233*n*37. *See also* imitation, Renaissance theories of
error, 22, 47, 211, 229*n*16
Euripides, 192
Europe, Walcott's, 2, 13–15, 17–18, 23–25, 33–37, 41–42, 148

Fanon, Frantz, 236*n*24
figure and ground, 134–35, 188–89
Flanagan, Brenda, 227*n*10
Flaubert, Gustave, 129
Flint, R. W., 233*n*41
Frankel, Hermann, 239*n*20
fresco, 119, 146–47
Freud, Sigmund, 137, 229*n*19
Frost, Robert, 219
Froude, James Anthony, 150–51, 153, 161–63, 169, 183, 239*n*2, 241*n*1
Fuentes, Carlos, 14
Fuller, Margaret, 74

Gates, Henry Louis, 107, 237*n*38
Gauguin, Paul, 143, 145–47, 239*n*28; *Noa Noa*, 95
genealogy, 2, 6, 46, 64, 68, 184, 186; representation and, 203
Graves, Robert, 238*n*14
El Greco (Dominikos Theotokopoulos), 124
Greene, Thomas C., 21, 229*n*14

Grosjean, François, 239*n*31
Guillén, Nicolas, 11, 84, 228*n*1, 230*n*21, 234*n*7

Hagstrum, Jean, 138, 239*n*21
Hamner, Robert, 230*nn*23, 26; interview with Walcott, 83, 89–90, 165, 233*n*31
Harris, Wilson, 69, 202
Hayden, Robert, 240*n*6
Heaney, Seamus, 43, 118, 214, 231*n*1
Hegel, G. F. W., 181
Hesiod, 233*n*37
Hirsch, Edward, interviews with Walcott, 6, 10, 27, 43, 74, 83, 86, 90–92, 96, 106, 112, 126, 128, 142, 152, 158, 174, 176, 227*n*9, 228*n*18, 230*n*24, 232–33*n*25, 234*n*2
Holbein, Hans, 127
Homer, 48, 116, 118, 124, 184–89, 192, 195, 202, 205–6, 233*n*37, 241*n*2; *The Iliad*, 59–60, 116, 202, 242*n*19; *The Odyssey*, 6, 16, 116, 202–3, 229*n*8, 242*n*19; as paradigm of originality, 183, 206, 209
Hopkins, Gerard Manley, 109
Horace, 63–64, 66, 232*n*24
Hughes, Ted, 69, 202
Hugo, Victor, 117, 237*n*46
Hutcheon, Linda, 11, 225–26, 228*n*20
hyphen, 15–17, 37, 40

imitation, 19, 21, 44, 47–48, 69, 72, 78, 80, 229*n*19; Renaissance theories of, 46, 78, 229*n*14. *See also* eristic metaphor; transformative metaphor
influence, 4, 6, 21, 43–81, 90, 186, 229*n*14
internationalism, 2, 4, 11, 118
intertextuality, 4, 25, 48–51, 54–66, 68–70, 72–78, 81, 94–95, 109–11